"Jan Meyers is a friend and colleague whose ...llingness to open her heart to the larger romance Christ has been telling since before the world's foundation has wooed countless men and women closer to the heart of Christ—myself included."

—the late BRENT CURTIS, coauthor of *The Sacred Romance*

"God is speaking, always. He invites us to hear, but the noise around us and in us keeps his voice tuned low enough to ignore. I know I need to listen, but I need more than merely being told to do so. Jan Meyers tenderly invites us to consider what we fear we may hear and helps us enter the sweet hope even in hard words. From her own suffering, she speaks of the light of his fierce kindness. What I promise from this book is that God's voice will not remain dim or slight but that in hearing his passion your joy will grow beyond measure. Thank you, Jan, for listening to God and speaking light and life for us."

—DAN B. ALLENDER, PH.D., president, Mars Hill Graduate
School, author of *The Wounded Heart* and *The Healing Path*

"Jan's unique voice offers us a bold invitation to imagine what our lives would look like if we trusted in a God whose greatest gift to us is Love, not answers. With patient and wise insight, Jan takes the risk of letting us into her own life and in the process helps us remove the obstacles that stand in the way of embracing the Love we've always longed for. This book is for anyone who hungers for more of God."

—KATHY TROCCOLI, speaker, singer, and coauthor of *Falling in
Love with Jesus*

"Jan Meyers has written a realistic, earthy, and, above all, practical guide on how to recognize the voice of God in the midst of all the other voices clamoring for our attention. And she has done it in plain English, free from all the pious code words that speak only to the initiate. She gently helps us discard the masks, blinders, and earplugs we commonly use to keep a loving God from entering deeply into our hearts."

—WILLIAM FREY, bishop and author of *The Dance of Hope*

To my precious sisters in our prayer group. So excited to be with you this year listening to Him together. Edith

L I S T E N I N G

to LOVE

LISTENING

to LOVE

RESPONDING
to the
STARTLING VOICE
of GOD

JAN MEYERS

WATERBROOK
PRESS

LISTENING TO LOVE
PUBLISHED BY WATERBROOK PRESS
2375 Telstar Dr., Suite 160
Colorado Springs, Colorado 80920
A division of Random House, Inc.

Details in some anecdotes and stories have been changed to protect the identities of the persons involved.

ISBN 1-57856-842-0

Library of Congress Cataloging-in-Publication Data
Meyers, Jan, 1964-
  Listening to love : responding to the startling voice of God / Jan Meyers.— 1st ed.
    p. cm.
  Includes bibliographical references.
  ISBN 1-57856-842-0
  1. God—Love. 2. Christian life. I. Title.
  BT140.M49 2004
  231'.6—dc22

                                                        2004010767

Printed in the United States of America
2004—First Edition

10 9 8 7 6 5 4 3 2 1

For Mary Louise Meyers

CONTENTS

ACKNOWLEDGMENTS

To Dick Meyers. Thank you for sharing with me your valley of the shadow. Death has no sting, my dear brother.

To Vance and Betsy Brown. Your love and friendship are a lifetime treasure. Thanks for cheerleading this thing to the finish line.

To Kathy Helmers. Thanks for believing in me and this message. Thanks for navigating the waters of publishing on my behalf. You are a wise woman, with an outstretched hand.

To Elisa Stanford, my editor. What a delight to meet you at the "Starbucks Tribunal" and to travel this rich and winding road with you. Thanks for your kind way with me and your keen eye.

To Cherie. Your passion for this message kept me going countless days. Thanks for allowing Love to win over fear. How can one heart be so trustworthy?

To Jen. Your constant, abiding encouragement and belief are a balm. Your words have brought beauty to me countless times.

To John. Your blessing of this book helped me to be myself on these pages.

To the group of people who were angelic and insistent on saving my sanity, creating and providing a sabbatical for me: Jim and Janet Eney, Vance and Betsy Brown, John and Stasi Eldredge, Jim and Leta Van Meter, Michael and Beth Royal, Mark and Peg Henjum. And for all those who participated anonymously to make those months life-giving and holy.

Beth, Gayle, Peg, Leta, Lori, Katy, Michele. You are *in* my life. Thank you.

Thanks to the thirsty hearts at the International Anglican Church in Colorado Springs.

This book had many birthplaces: written in Matthews, North Carolina; Bellingham, Washington; Pagosa Springs, Colorado; and Colorado Springs, Colorado. Thanks to those who provided me grace and space for the crafting of it: my friends at the Barnabas Center in Charlotte, BootJack Ranch in

Southwest Colorado, and my patient friends, family, and clients in Colorado Springs.

Those who interacted with the manuscript along the way: Betsy Brown, John Eldredge, Peg Henjum, Marcia Smartt, Gayle Wise, Kevin Kutcher, James and Amy Cole, Lisa Godman, and Steve Brinn.

One

THE VOICE OF LOVE

Listen to me, for the life of your soul is at stake.
—GOD

Today, if you hear my voice, do not harden your hearts.
—GOD

Sometimes it's just plain stupid to get into any kind of wind.
—BOB DYLAN

Love has a way of getting our attention. Actually, Love has a way of messing up our lives. We all know it to be true. If we desire a carefully ordered life, tranquil and serene, then when the Voice of Love calls, we had better run inside and bolt the door. Tight. We can never prepare for this most honored of all guests, who quietly enters and then asks us to follow.

We wonder whether we know the Voice of Love, so we strain to discern it amid the cacophony around and in us. Then we begin to recognize it, and we're not sure we welcome it. It doesn't take us long to remember tender times we labored to hear God and followed as best we could, only to end up befuddled and confused for a while. Maybe this still, small, disruptive guest is after something more than making the path clear to us.

This is a book about the call of Love. The call of Love is the call of the heart of God; it is the call that echoes the life and intentions of his Son, Jesus. And this is a book about responding to that Love, about responding to God's voice. Obedience is a whole-hearted and, as we will see, sensual response to the

Voice of Love—it involves our whole being, our deepest self. But what a wild ride. Open the door, and we have no idea what will step across the threshold. Let's take that back. When we've been around the heart of God for any length of time at all, we do have some idea. We have a suspicion that what comes through the door will profoundly jostle our well-ordered life. Our suspicion is well founded. Perhaps we know enough to be afraid he *will* speak, afraid he *will* enter. Perhaps we're just afraid of him.

Love has been calling to me lately, and it has been frightening. You would think that after decades of knowing God, I would find responding to Love's voice easier. Well, all the moments of hesitation and choice at the doorway of my heart have taught me that when Love calls, it is so I can know the life he's given me, so I can know how much I'm loved. This does make it a little easier as I reach for the doorknob and allow him in, with all his unknown intentions. But that's just it—his intentions are often *unknown*. These decades with God have taught me that the corridor between hearing Jesus's voice and seeing the goodness of what he's after is often like navigating the foreign sands of the desert between slavery and promise. At times it's like climbing the hill to Golgotha.

These decades of following have taught me that life and love without explanation do show up along the path. But it is not possible to talk about responding to Love, to God himself, without heading directly into the truth: God wants us—all of us. He wants everything *for* us and asks everything *of* us as he finds, restores, and leads our hearts. He asks us to leave our old ways—not just old habits but the way we view life, the way we *see*. He asks us to drop our nets, to face our stories, to be misunderstood and even shamed by others, believing that the hidden reasons must be spectacular.

Why begin here—with how unclear and hard it can be? Maybe I'm asking you to join me because I need to know I'm not alone as I hesitate to open the door. Love's call to me lately has been: "I want to show you how much your heart really does want me. I want to show you how much you really do love me." A beautiful invitation, isn't it? So why do I hesitate? I'm not afraid of missing or misunderstanding God's voice as much as I'm afraid of where his voice will lead me. As Love has called, I've started to realize that, more than lessons on listening or instructions on how to fine-tune our antennas to God's frequency, what we really need is courage—the courage to know we *can turn* the doorknob when we hear Love calling. What waits on the other side of the door is more than worth the risk. What's beckoning is joy beyond our dreams. Yes, we can turn that doorknob. Yes, we can follow the Voice of Love with confident expectation.

So much easier said than done.

THREE POSTURES OF THE HEART

If your heart is even remotely like mine, you can trace the movements it goes through on the way to this confident expectation. We begin in a posture of uncertainty—*Is it Jesus I hear, and even if it is, do I want to open the door?* Here the question of our hearts sounds like this: *Is it really you, Jesus?* When we have tentatively turned the knob to lean in to hear what he has to say, we move into the second posture. Here, we recognize that it is indeed Jesus on the other side of the door, but we also recognize that he can do whatever he wants with our life. *Oh no, it is you, Jesus.* And then, over time and tender experience, our hearts move into a posture of peaceful gratitude, knowing that something so much bigger than our understanding is unfolding, something for our good as well as for God's. Finally our hearts relax with the unexpected *Oh good, it is you, Jesus.*

The First Posture of the Heart: The Invitation to Respond

Years ago as a fledgling counselor just out of graduate school, I sat in the office of my mentor. Hands clammy and nervously shifting on the leather couch, I was trying to put words to the crossroads at which I found myself: Do I take my graduate training and board South African Airlines, back to the world I left several years before, where there is strong affirmation and African, European, and Indian friends who wait for me? Do I listen to the internal nudges that tell me it's time to head in a different direction? How do I read the conflicting signals?

I was midsentence in this vulnerable litany of confused thoughts when my mentor, Dan, got up from his chair, went over to his desk, picked up the phone, and began to dial. *Well, that's nice.* I thought. *So glad you're taking this struggle of mine seriously. What phone call could be so important that it can't wait until I'm done talking?* My thoughts continued in this offended, slightly resigned, judging-him kind of way as I heard Dan speak these words into the answering machine on the other end: "Brent, this is Dan. I'm sitting here with someone I've come to love and respect, and I think the two of you should be working together. If you don't at least consider this potential partnership, I will never drink scotch with you again." Click.

"Who was that? Who is Brent? What was that about?"

Dan simply replied, "You're going to have to trust me on this one, Jan."

I had no idea who this man was to whom Dan had just offered my career. But Dan knew me well, and I did trust him. I met Brent Curtis and his wife, Ginny, and their boys that next week, and then Brent and I had lunch together to discuss possibilities. It became immediately clear to both of us that Dan's intuition was dead-on. I canceled my plans to return to Africa. I moved instead to Colorado Springs (a city for which, at the time, I had little desire), and I embarked on years of a treasured counseling partnership in which I was believed in and championed, a partnership where I learned invaluable lessons about life and people. The Voice of Love had come to redirect my path into a good, rich land I never could have chosen for myself.

Of course, when Dan made the call that day, introducing me to the thought of a new direction, I had no clue what was ahead. All I knew was that there was a quiet nudging in my heart: "This is from me. Listen carefully. Trust this." My heart, though scared and a bit bewildered, knew Love was calling, but I had to really listen to determine who was beckoning to me in the midst of my fear. Even though I desired change, I feared it, as I'm guessing you do. My heart entered the first posture with tentativeness and hope: *Is it really you, Jesus?*

The first posture of our hearts is actually a posture of obedience. God asks for our hearts even though we're afraid to believe we're going to be led into something good as he changes our path, our mind, our ways. But our understanding of obedience has become skewed. If we're honest, we admit that upon hearing *obedience,* we sag inside and reluctantly wait to find out what is expected of us. "Obedience to God" can conjure a "pull yourself up and face what's required of you" salute, like a lineup of soldiers waiting for marching orders. That's our perception. But the reality is, obedience involves the kind of listening that children and lovers and sleuths do. It is not orderly. It is not so much a soldier marching because of duty as a person leaning in to hear a voice he's come to trust and wanting to go where it leads.

Hebrew scholars will tell you that the Old Testament offers only one meaning when using the word *obey.*[1] It is a central teaching in the pages of Jewish and Christian literature. For example, consider the stories of Adam and Eve, Cain and Abel, Abraham and Isaac, Moses and Pharaoh. Each story contains a dilemma of obedience. Would Eve listen to the serpent, and would Adam be persuaded by Eve? Would Cain really stoop to murder? Would Abraham perform the heinous act of killing his own son? Would Moses defy Pharaoh? Each of these people faced more than just a duty. They faced a God who had spoken to them. Those who obeyed pondered God's request; they listened and wrestled with his intentions and *then* said yes, despite the evidence. Those who did not obey did not listen well—they didn't wrestle with what was being asked—and they missed Love.

This is where we get off course in our understanding of obedience. Our English word *obey* comes from the Hebrew *shama.* It means "to hear intelligently, attentively, call together, consider, discern, give ear, hear, listen, perceive, understand." Can you hear how engaged—how intimate—this term is? It speaks of the posture of the heart that carries us through the other two postures—somewhere between the posture a child takes when his mother is whispering a secret in his ear and the posture a special-intelligence agent takes when she is receiving a specific, unbelievable assignment—a posture that leans in to make sure the message is heard correctly. It is an invitation for us to say, "*What* did you just ask? *What* did you just say? Could I *possibly have heard you correctly?*" It is precisely what I was invited to when I was asked to stay in

Colorado. My first response was, "Huh?" It is a woman leaning in and saying, "Did I hear you correctly?" when she is led in career directions that run counter to the other women in her neighborhood or social circles. It is the eight-year-old who hears Jesus telling him to give his prized computer game CD to a little boy who just lost his father. "What did you say?"

I don't know about you, but I am relieved to understand the pulse of this word that has taken on such flat-lined connotations. When I understand true obedience, then I can respond with who I am rather than perform as the person I think I should be. I move from fear of the doorknob to anticipation of the relationship, from controlling to surrendering to someone bigger than I am—someone unruly (according to my terms), someone I don't understand and whom I can't fully predict, someone who has good in mind even when I have trouble trusting him to give it.

The Second Posture of the Heart: Facing What We Fear

Fast-forward many years. I had just fallen asleep in the home of friends when I heard the phone upstairs. A group of us had flown to Indiana to celebrate our friend Sharon's birthday, and we had gardened and planted and sweated and laughed all day. We were bone tired and very content. After I heard the ring, I went quickly back to sleep. Then came the tap on my shoulder. "Jan. Wake up. Someone is on the phone for you. Something terrible. An accident." I grabbed the phone, and as the world began to spin in slow motion, I heard the words telling me that my friend Brent had died. I don't know how to express it, but in my mind's eye or spirit I saw Brent flying. So fast, flying. Flying into the arms of God. The Voice of Love had come with something new in mind. Something I didn't ask for or want. My heart felt betrayed and immediately took on the second posture of the heart as it said with fear and questioning, but with a deep acknowledgment of all that is not in my control: *Oh no, it is you, Jesus.*

We need to spend a bit of time unfolding the second posture of our hearts, because this is where we live most of our lives. This is where following God is most difficult: following when we feel tricked, betrayed, lost, confused, and angry. There's a whole story line of possibilities as to what has brought the confusion. Maybe evil has come with its insidious jabs; maybe the fallen world is pressing in with its dull ache; maybe death has stolen with a mocking laugh; maybe someone else's choices have caused havoc. But the fact remains: this is where following Jesus is hard. The most difficult part of following God is admitting it was Love who brought you here and finding gratitude for this. You were beckoned; you tentatively opened the door. And now you are faced with what you most feared. You are left to fight the thoughts and messages that seem most reasonable during these second-posture times: *You're alone. You're abandoned. You were a fool to get too attached or to be too passionate about life.* These thoughts, of course, are not the truest thing. The truest thing is Love. Beckoning. Waiting to embrace, teach, and instruct you. But during the days in this heart posture, the truth of loving purposes seems remote at best. As our hearts proclaim the second-posture cry, *Oh no, it really is you, Jesus,* they expose that we view Jesus as the God of our Worst Fear rather than the Voice of Love. Here is what I mean.

The Inelegant Art of Abandon

The art of abandoning ourselves to what God's love might have for us is not an elegant process. It is not a strong and steady one either. Sure, it produces elegant results. Strong results even. But the process is haphazard and unpolished, with bumps and rabbit trails and discouragement, misheard and misunderstood messages, and all-out tugs of war across the threshold of the door of our hearts. Think about it. Most of us would readily say, "Why, yes, I know that I should surrender control of my life to God." But few can say honestly and freely, "Yes. I *want* to surrender control—of my heart, my life, my internal world—to God because I have confidence in him." Let's admit up front how prone we are to Peter's fear: starting out like an undaunted mariner in our courage but sinking in the waves of the question, "Is it really you, Jesus?" Let's confess how we share the forgetfulness of the disciples. Devotees, all of them, because of the miracles they had witnessed Jesus perform, yet they didn't ask, "Who is this man?" until after their boat threatened to sink.

Our hesitancy, I'm learning, is mostly because we've been convinced that God is the God of our Worst Fear rather than the Voice of Love. You and I have evidence from our stories that cause us to feel justified in viewing God as someone to flee from rather than to follow. When I was young, I had too much responsibility placed on me in situations that were too adult for a child to navigate. So now my Worst Fear is that I'll be left alone to handle heavy burdens, and this comes directly from my story. When I see God as the God of my Worst Fear, I assume he only has requirements of me and will leave me completely alone to get the job done. Often when I hear Jesus calling, I hear only my Worst Fear asking for too much and wanting to be appeased with burdensome, lonely labor.

What is it about us that we would either dismiss him or cower before him? Why are our hearts persuaded that he is either powerless or malevolent when in fact he would choose the humiliation of spittle on his face, splinters in his skin, and steel through his bone to answer the question, "Is it really you?" Why do we listen to the mocking voice of evil or the faulty reasoning we extrapolate from our own stories and life messages rather than the truth that someone would want to die for us, defeat death for us, go back to the Father with our ransom in his hands and talk to the Father about us, pleading our case? And perhaps a more courageous question: what causes us to quake, not with the fear of the Lord—Jesus Christ of Nazareth—but before the God of our Worst Fear?

Fear or Freedom?

I'll never forget the terror in the eyes of Ate (Aunt) Zaide, a friend in a rural province of the Philippines. After nearly two decades of wondering if she had appeased her household gods (an eclectic shelf held up by chicken wire, full of icons and statues and images) by bringing them food and trinkets and money, she decided to trust Jesus instead. She was about to dismantle the altar, wanting so much to trust her newfound God to be more powerful. She was weary of living in the shackles of a constant threat—"Have I done enough to appease these gods?" She was ready to leave this life of fear and to enter a life of love.

Can you imagine what I saw in her eyes? The sheer anticipation of faith? Hardly. For all those years, Zaide was not just involved in a quirky ritual or habit. She was actually worshiping at the altar of her Worst Fear. It had been unthinkable to her that God really did love her and wasn't asking to be appeased. So now as she was realizing that she didn't have to appease any god because Jesus had completely appeased God's requirements of her, what I saw in her eyes was a fragile hope: "Can it *really* be true?" Maybe, just maybe, could she be loved without having to prove herself? Is it *really you,* Jesus?

We can spend a lifetime worshiping at the altar of our Worst Fear rather than listening to our need for God's love and his willingness to give it. Now that seems silly, doesn't it? Why would we so readily reject a good thing? Our Worst Fears take many forms: God will not remember me. God will shame me for what I've been involved in. God will get my hopes up and then dash them. God will ask too much of me. God will leave me alone.

Our household gods are more sophisticated than Zaide's, but they still provide a great escape from our fears. If we had a little wooden shelf, it would be filled with our gods: the need to secure our reputation in the marketplace, the voice telling us that the most important thing is to be liked, the pattern of isolation we fall into when we guard ourselves with a routine of work and television, the belief that we must keep up the facade of a perfect Christian family. My gods say, "You can't be wrong. You have to come through." Your gods may whisper, "You must alter yourself" or "You had better get it right" or "Make sure you fake your way; convince everyone." The gods of our fear drive us from behind with threats of abandonment, requirement, and rejection if we fail to appease them. Then they offer the way to appease them—hide. Hide in obvious ways, through pornography or materialism, and in less obvious ways, through self-condemnation or pride.

There is safety—these gods do keep us from facing what we fear about God—for a while. Appeasing this fear—playing with our self-crafted appeasement trinkets—keeps us very busy as we hide our hearts from God! As long as we have our Worst Fear to cower behind, we never have to face our unbelief in Love.

I can always tell when I am cowering behind my Worst Fear. I feel anxious and pressured and begin ruminating about all I'm not accomplishing. What am I hiding from? My true heart sounds something like this: *Jesus, I'm scared of what is being asked of me, and I'm convinced you are going to leave me alone to handle it.* What am I hiding behind? I'm afraid that this kind of honesty will be met with scorn, so I hide behind my safe god and say, *Just steel yourself and come up with what is required of you,* rather than risk the surprise of an embrace amid my fear and doubt.

Discovering the Love that doesn't want or need to be appeased but *desires all of us*—longing for us to be alive, confident, free—is a great thing. So why is the process so frightening? Let me say it this way: when we open the door to God, he comes to remove the obstacles in the way of our knowing the fullness of Love. He takes away our pride, our autonomy, our religion, sometimes our vocation, possibly our life. And as we'll see, he does this for our freedom.

Opening the Door

If we're honest, when we realize God will do anything to have our full affection, we're usually tempted to swear, "Oh no, it really is you, Jesus." Our expletives reveal that we know *God will ask anything of us in order to free us.* As you sense all too well, this is where life with God gets a bit confounding. He so often *is like* the God of our Worst Fear. After all, God asks us to walk out on the water. Never mind that we can't swim. He is not a passive, back-pocket pal. As Mark Buchanan says, "It's as though God (as we make him) were a half-daft old uncle, hair sprouting from his ears, a bit runny about the eyes, winking at our little pranks and peccadilloes. Well, that's nice. But God isn't safe. God is a consuming fire."[2] Right. This is the God who asks us out onto surfaces that cannot hold us.

This is the God who heard immediately Hannah's seemingly drunken prayer for a child and fulfilled her request through Eli's blessing. And this same God willingly accepted as she dedicated her son to God's service. He didn't say, "Hannah, shouldn't you check with Samuel first to see if this is what he wants to do for the rest of his life?" or, "Hannah, you've waited a long, long time for this dream to come true. Now just go enjoy being a mother." No, this is the God who knows what story he's telling: setting Samuel loose in the temple courts while his mother is made beautiful for her supplication and sacrifice. I wonder what comfort this brought Hannah when her house was quiet as she waited for more children?

This is the God who beamed as he thought of his servant Job and told Satan that he could test Job in whatever way necessary but he was not to kill Job. But Job's children—we're not told much about any negotiations here—evidently were fair game and were killed. Some days I read this story and am struck by God's loving care and advocacy of Job ("Hands off, Lucifer. He's my man. I know his true heart will show through even with all your testing"). Other days I read this story and am furious that God was so capricious with Job's children and their lives, not to mention the onslaught of loss and torment on Job himself. As my friend Brent wrote (ironically, just before his sudden death):

> There is something frightening about being in a play in which the director may allow the plot to descend on my character from a totally unknown direction, a direction that may cause me deep emotional or even physical harm. It is something like having the stage lights dropped from high overhead during one of my scenes without telling me, leaving me no chance to change my mark before they fall.[3]

This is the God who is willing for great prices to be paid and is content to let his followers wait in darkness and confounding circumstances for days, even years, in order for his intentions—good intentions—to be shown.

So how do we open *that* door? How do we get to the place of saying, "I'm trusting that the story you are writing is more important than my dreams, my religion, my definition of spirituality. My dreams matter to you. But *your purposes* matter more, and you are a God who seems quite willing to forgo my immediate relief and satisfaction in order to craft love in my heart. Maybe it is about letting go of control (a confession of our stubbornness) and allowing the release of our true hearts. And maybe it is the freedom that Brennan Manning describes: "to be grateful for an unanswered prayer, to give thanks in a state of interior desolation, to trust in the love of God in the face of the marvels, cruel circumstances, obscenities, and the commonplaces of life is to whisper a doxology in darkness."[4]

Fragile Control

Well. If you are like me, you don't whisper a beautiful doxology in darkness; you curse out the side of your mouth in broad daylight. Forgive the cliché, but life just doesn't work. This morning I was speaking to a friend with the portable phone perched under my chin and a just-poured glass of water in my hand. My friend said something hilarious, and when I laughed, the phone fell squarely into the glass of water and immediately died. Later in the day I was at my computer. On the one day when I broke my rules and sat down with a cup of coffee, my sweet (well, in theory) little cat, Phil, jumped up and, yes, spilled the coffee onto my keyboard. So now I need to go to Best Buy and replace my phone and keyboard (the one I'm using now is borrowed). Later in the day a simple knock of a glass on the counter made a shattering sound. It didn't break, but the sound produced chills because I was already braced due to the earlier hours of this slightly misshapen day. So what does that have to do with letting go? The crazy thing is, I am so convinced I have control over this life that it takes off-kilter moments to remind me that I'm deceived. I have to have my fingers pried from the doorway of my own sufficiency in order to see that I might as well open the door wide, because I'm not as much in control as I think I am. Scripture tells me that widows, orphans, and prisoners know this. Yes, they have lost everything. I just go out and buy some new stuff.

We must face how very little control we have in order to move from "Oh no, it really is you, Jesus" to "Oh good, it is you, Jesus." When we don't face this, we stubbornly chant, "Oh good. Oh good. Oh good," because we think we should, even though we don't really believe our chants. We sound more like an NFL cheerleader than one who has been captured by Love. Most of our "following" is divorced from our hearts.

Look around at how we try to make God more palatable or at least less threatening. Stroll through the local bookstore and find an assortment of books on spirituality—most promising fulfillment while never mentioning a God willing to die. We structure our church services to be user-friendly and not too disruptive to newcomers. Programs and curricula often teach us ways to "be obedient," to "live a life pleasing to the Lord" without talking about responsiveness from the heart. Religion can happen whether or not Love speaks, regardless of whether Love enters. Theological opinions can be held and espoused without jostling our comfort. A strictly moral life certainly can. We maneuver to create a Voice that we can predict, manage, even control. I prefer a manageable deity when I want to be safe. I think I intrinsically know that Love, the authoritative Voice from eternity past, is not a safe Voice to follow. But I also have all kinds of wrong ideas about his intentions.

If I'm honest, I am aware of the myriad ways I falsely assume God has it out for me. Oh, my truest heart knows that he is my advocate, that he wants relationship with me, that there's more life available to me. I know his love is true. But when I take a little walk to remember my gratitude, I am often aware that all I see are the things I am without. I grow convinced that God is withholding good things and playing a game to see if I will finally trust him. What does that say about what we all combat on a consistent basis? Bottom line: I contend with the belief that God isn't terribly concerned with taking care of my life, so I must do it myself. The truth: I am sought after, chosen, cleansed, restored, loved, and alive. But I live most of my life as a practical humanist. It is a progression we all go through every day. We believe false things about God, listening as he is accused in our hearts. Evil is the strongest accuser, of course, but we join the line of mockers; we grab the nails and hammer. We jeer him. He is not who he said he would be—at least not with our life and dreams, we think—and so we crucify the unmanageable, unpredictable, unexpected Voice of Love. This is so much easier than being the fool who believes in resurrections.

Listening to Love does not come easily. It occurs somewhere between our scoffing and nail pounding and the resurrection power that silences us in the midst of our complaints. If you are like me, those are three *long* days. Philip Yancey calls it the long day's journey of the Saturday. They are days of disbelief, wondering if his strong and knowing word at the well or his touch at the pool of Siloam or his smile as he bantered with the children was real. They are days when we cease to see with eyes fixed on the One who calls us out across the waves. Instead, we tell ourselves that he was the weak, abandoning, uncaring god of the storm after all. Our Worst Fear seems so justifiable in the hours between his parting and the moment of his return; it seems the only option when we can't see.

It is in this threshold of his seeming absence that our hearts are either released into freedom or indentured further into the slavery of fear.

Here we can remember Christ's self-proclaimed mission of healing the brokenhearted and setting the captives free and the admonitions of the epistles that it was for freedom that Christ set us free. This is the antidote to legalism and lifelessness. But we must define our terms. What is freedom? A simple way to say it is, we're freed from ourselves so we can be loved and offer love. We're freed from our unbelief as we pass through the "Oh no, it's you, Jesus" times of confusion. We're freed from our arrogant belief that we can chart our own course. That takes us to what freedom is not: freedom is not complete clarity, and it is not relief from pain.

The Third Posture of the Heart: What We Really Want

The years since Brent's death have been laced with loss. I have given my heart in two relationships that began with the tentative anticipation of "Is it you, Jesus?" and yet ended in disappointment. I have walked through family strain, career uncertainty, and financial stress. I've made some foolish choices in my grief. The enemy of my heart has been fiercely cruel as I've strained to find light. And I guess this is why I ask you to admit with me how difficult it is to follow Love's voice. Because in this crucible of experience and God's love, a purer, more trustworthy posture rises up in my heart as I feel it being transformed and as I see what God has been after. I really *do* love him. I must, because I keep following! Through the dark corridor, and I can't claim to tell you how, he has taken my lonely heart and brought me to a place where he is my companion.

Last night is a good example. There have been times in past years when the loneliness and vulnerability of waking in the night has been too much to bear, especially when the cruel assaults of evil are searching for a playground. You may relate to those nights when you wake up, married or single, and nothing will assuage you. The 2:00 a.m. shopping channel lost its appeal long ago; the Internet mocks with its impersonal, gray light; the refrigerator offers meager comfort. You look out the window, and the moon looks beautiful, but your heart can't drink it in, because it will hurt too much not to have someone to share it with in the deep ways you long to share your life. Sleepless hours like those have been familiar to me through the years, and of course the one who steals and destroys is waiting in the shadows of those moments and mocks, "You will always be alone." But last night I heard a different voice, a voice that has been coming more often to me in those crucible nights. In my sleep I had the literal, almost palpable sense of my Companion with me, covering me, loving me. As I awoke, it was not with dread of the empty space in my home or my heart. It was with an anticipation of how Love was beckoning me. I was led downstairs to look out the window, and the moon that shone did so with a light that rendered me breathless. I realized I *was* sharing it with someone as the entire mountain range radiated—the very One who crafted its mysterious craters. "You are so very special to me," Jesus said. "You really do love me." I let out a sigh and whispered, "That is for sure."

My desire for sharing life with someone is as strong as ever, and in the ache Jesus is there, grieving with me but also showing me the "more" that I often miss on my own. I've been brought into a rich life, full of friends, and my heart swells with gratitude. But even more central is an unexpected intimacy, a deep knowing that as long as I have Jesus, I have everything. More and more I'm tasting the goodness of the third posture that rises up after I've passed through the first two. It is an unexpected posture of worship: *Oh good, it is you, Jesus!*

As we live through these three postures of the heart, we learn to admit what we really want. We want to say, from a deep and confident place inside, "Yes, it is you, Jesus, and there is nothing more I need to know." We long to *hear* from God. We're creatures of the pendulum swing. Prescriptive and pressured religion grows wearisome, so we come back to the heart of our faith, remembering we have a pulse. But even in our imperative desire to live from the heart—from who we are, our true identity, rather than by something put on—we rarely encounter the Love that has authority over us. We forget that Christianity is a life of following. True obedience comes as we learn to listen to Love's call—the voice of God—and respond to it. And when we do, everything is asked of us.

Everything.

Just not in the ways we thought.

Could You Really Have More?

Lorrie had hit her forty-third birthday with an unexpected gnawing in her gut.

She had passed into her forties with a grace that had surprised and pleased her. But in the three years that followed, she took stock of her life and decided there was something flat and dull about it. Her husband, Jim, told her to stop being so hard on herself, and she appreciated his encouragement that she had much to be grateful for. She knew she did. Her son was doing well as a senior in high school, and although her daughter had hit some significant bumps in junior high, they were getting along. But she felt as though she lived with just a fraction of herself in her marriage, and she wasn't sure she had any truly authentic friendships. Lots of buddies, but did anyone really know her?

It wasn't the world around her that troubled Lorrie. It was her own self. She heard Love whispering to her, "It is time. There is more." Lorrie trembled a bit as she heard this. *I should just be more content,* Lorrie thought. But the whispering came at odd moments: in the quiet of night, in the aisle of the grocery store as she reached for apples. After a time Lorrie decided to be intentional in praying about what she was hearing. She started to ask God what he meant. Slowly it became clear to Lorrie that there were things about herself God wanted to show her. Would she be willing? It was a direct question, clearer than she had acknowledged. There was a quiet thrill in Lorrie's heart. *Is it really you, Jesus? Could you really have more for me? Are you really that personal and intentional?*

So Lorrie tentatively turned the knob and opened the door to whatever the personal, intentional ways of Love might be. After four months of puzzling over what it might mean, Lorrie began to have images—disturbing, sexual images—nipping at the corners of her mind. The moments in the grocery store or sitting in traffic became moments of disbelief and confusion as she felt a deep terror and dread fill her. Were the sexual images from her own life? Who was the young girl in the scenes she saw? Why did she feel so personally enraged one moment, deflated the next? *Is this what Jesus is after? Does he want me to be haunted by this thing I can't control? I'm not sure I want any part of it. I need to go back to being okay with life.*

There's more.

Oh no, it really is Jesus. Lorrie recognized that Love had brought her here, but she wasn't sure she wanted anything to do with it. Jesus's voice seemed remote. It took everything in her to trust that the craziness of this path was for her good. *I don't know where we're going…but okay, let's go.*

Lorrie embarked on a six-year journey in which she chose to honor the painful memories of sexual abuse that came to her from God's hand. This six-year corridor was dark, saturated with grief and the crashing of illusions, as her eyes were opened to the fact that the uncle she had cherished, the uncle who always took her to special days at the beach and always had sweet gifts just for her, had taken her away by herself to rape her from age seven to sixteen, when he moved on to court her little sister. Lorrie could never have anticipated the deaths she would have to die internally—not only from painful memory, but also from facing the reality that she had chosen to live with a falsely sweet outlook on life that never entered anyone's sorrow, including her own.

As Lorrie owned her story and her response to her story, a deep, true, passionate life began to rise up within her. The resurrection life of Christ began to show up in tangible moments for her, as when she found herself weeping with a new friend who had lost her baby. As she grieved with her friend, she heard Jesus whisper to her, "Thank you for being willing to follow my voice. Thank you for letting me love you in your grief. Thank you for now offering life out of your own sorrow." As she offered herself in love, she realized, *This is the more. Oh good, it really is you, Jesus.*

Maybe, just maybe, freedom shows up in the midst of our struggles, our pain, helping us to discern what Love might be saying and releasing us from the false messages we listen to. It tells us: *Trust me. I'm with you in this. I'm fighting off your enemies who would want you to believe that this struggle is all there is. And I will take you deeper and deeper into love, not fear.*

Love's Outrageous Voice

Yes, God can be like the God of our Worst Fear. And it is a good thing. If he were not the unmanageable, unpredictable, wild, and unruly God, then there would be no reason for us to even darken the threshold of the doorway, let alone turn the knob.

Think of the story of Abraham. When God told Abraham to sacrifice his son, Isaac, Abraham was being called to consider, discern, and wrestle with what he perceived to be the Voice of Love. Can we see that if this wasn't true, he was a madman for following through with the orders—the orders to murder? Abraham was being asked to consider who was asking this crazy thing of him. It was the faithful God of Abraham's earlier story, a God of covenant and promise, who was asking Abraham to do something without knowing how God would answer the problem. We are foolish if we think Abraham, in robotic devotion to his God, found his son and headed up Mount Moriah with gladness that he could serve God this way. No. He headed up the mountain feeling insane—wondering if he had heard correctly—but trusting the voice he had come to know as the Voice of Love.

This wasn't the first time Love had come to Abraham with a befuddling request. There was the vague "Go to a land I will show you" from God years earlier. *What did you say?* There was the receipt, at the age of ninety-nine, of the covenant promise that he would be a father to many nations. *What?* And of course the promise of a son—something that prompted his shriveled wife, Sarah, to laugh, *You've GOT to be kidding.* These wild seasons of sight-unseen, gut-wrenching invitations to walk without evidence had crafted in Abraham what was necessary for responsive obedience. He learned that Love was behind the call.

God wanted Abraham's heart more than he wanted to be appeased, more than he wanted to confirm Abraham as a faithful follower, and Abraham knew this. So when it was time to sacrifice his son, it wasn't blind duty. It was a dangerous, idiotic move; but it was responsive, and it was true. E. M. Forster's words in *Howards End* come to mind: "Life is indeed dangerous, but not in the way morality would have us believe. It is indeed unmanageable, but the essence of it is not a battle. It is unmanageable because it is a romance, and its essence is romantic beauty." God's heart had romanced Abraham through decades of outrageous requests. It was a demanding, ruthless romance, but Abraham was learning that God wanted his heart more than he wanted an indentured servant.

Will our lives be serene if we obey? Only in the same way that Peter was wet. But we will have heard the same Voice, which is wild enough to ask the unthinkable and loving enough to provide a hand up out of the waves and to provide the blood of a ram. The only Voice that draws us into the deeper, life-giving intentions of God. The Voice that allows us to say, when we come to recognize it as we would a trusted friend's, "Oh good, I was hoping it was you, God."

God's voice to Abraham seemed the voice of cruelty, but Abraham's history with the Love behind the wild requests told him otherwise. Abraham listened, leaned in, questioned, and responded. He responded to the Voice of Love that always shows up just in time to reveal that the seeming madness was never madness at all but deeper life and intimacy with God.

The Voice of Love, when responded to, draws us into the unthinkable. And the Voice of Love, when responded to, makes it all worth it. After all, God did not make this request of Abraham alone; he asked it of himself. The shocking difference is, of course, that Love made the choice to follow through.

He opened the door to his own request of ransoming our betraying hearts, and he did it by murdering his own Son. The thought is too much for me: God betraying God so he would never betray his desire for me. God himself walking into the unthinkable so that when he asks me to do the same, it allows me to say, "Yes, it is you, Jesus."

Two

LISTENING TO SORROW

Relinquishing Our "Control"

Through loss upon loss, I have severely gained
wisdom enough my slavery to see.
—GEORGE MACDONALD

The one who cannot suffer cannot love either.
—JURGEN MOLTMANN

I personally hate fire, and right now I smell it. The air is thick with the
smoke from the largest fires in the history of the West, some coming from
three hundred miles away, some from just over the ridge. The smell is nause-
ating. Soot coats windshields; hesitant raindrops splatter black ash on the hot
sidewalk. It is surreal, an otherworldly experience.

But I am tucked safely here in my suburban home, the only threat from
the fire being the dampening of my spirits. My thoughts turn to Vallecito Lake,
where fire has taken out the landscape around this lake that means so much to
my family. My dog Cito is named for this little jewel. Vallecito is—was—a
lovely, lazy, little reservoir surrounded by Colorado's oldest and tallest spruce
trees. With the exception of the years I was overseas, I've gone there every summer since I was a little girl. As a young woman, I wrote this about it:

The rolling thunder calls to me, crawling over the jagged granite peaks
and through the blue green canyon of spruce and pine. The noises are

steady—roaring river, silly squirrel's laughter, crow calls, the low tim-
pani of cicadas and grasshoppers as the hot high mountain sun lulls
this cradle of wildlife activity. It is fragile—the uprooted ponderosa
swept violently to the edge of the ravine, the meadow tundra "scarred"
by little mounds of groundhog communities. The peaks loom with
snow-spotted majesty that says everything is okay.

As a girl I was made breathless here. The dancing rapids were
mine, somehow. Bare feet in frigid alpine water, the wavering
reflection of my ten-year-old face as I spun around the pebbles and
boulders, catching glimpses of peak, trees, blue, lake, trees, blue,
lake—and my silent mantra was, "I will never forget this moment,
or this place." Childhood pledges—our vows to remain free—are
never easily erased.

Vows to freedom may not easily be erased, but they are, over time,
rearranged and refined. I can never forget Vallecito. But now I can never go
back. People keep reminding me that new growth will come. Believe me, I
have read every Sierra Club article and John Muir book about the process:
wild grasses and wildflowers first; oak shrubs, juniper, and aspen in the first
five years, making way for the seedlings of pine and spruce (which would not
have been released but for the fire's heat) over the next twenty years; and then
the growth of a mature, new, healthy forest after seventy-five. It is a beautiful
process, really—one that naturally maintains the balance of the forest over
generations.

But the reality is, Vallecito will never be the same for me. I have to let it
go. I have lived with the illusion all my life that there was one place that would
always be there, always welcoming my weary heart home. But now I realize I
was assuming things outside of my control.

Love, too, has a way of burning away what we once thought we could
count on. Just when we're comfortable or have a sense of "really knowing
Jesus," something comes to remind us that he is a consuming *fire*. He is not

only the burning bush of the law; he is also the flame of life that burns away all that keeps us from being loved by him intimately. Obedience is an ongoing invitation to relinquish control.

But Love wants our release, not our destruction. And we must remember that eternal things can never be destroyed, even by the hottest flame. These words from Hebrews help us to see that love, not harm, comes from the fire:

> You have not come to a physical mountain, to a place of flaming fire, darkness, gloom, and whirlwind, as the Israelites did at Mount Sinai.... Moses himself was so frightened at the sight [of the flame] that he said, "I am terrified and trembling."
>
> No, you have come to Mount Zion, to the city of the living God, the heavenly Jerusalem, and to thousands of angels in joyful assembly. You have come to the assembly of God's firstborn children, whose names are written in heaven. You have come to God himself, who is the judge of all people. And you have come to the spirits of the redeemed in heaven who have now been made perfect. You have come to Jesus, the one who mediates the new covenant between God and people, and to the sprinkled blood, which graciously forgives instead of crying out for vengeance....
>
> Since we are receiving a kingdom that cannot be destroyed, let us be thankful and please God by worshiping him with holy fear and awe. For our God is a consuming fire. (Hebrews 12:18–29)

If I don't have some kind of confidence that Jesus is after more *of* me, more *with* me, as we walk through the inferno together, I easily despair. Confidence in his love is the only way to say, "Oh good, it is you, Jesus," when these flames have either nipped at my heart or have consumed things that are precious to me.

My heart's first question, "Is it really you, Jesus?" surfaces quickly whenever my comfort, plans, or self-crafted security are singed. I must ask this question whether the match was struck by my own foolishness, by the Enemy's cruel attempts to scorch my heart, or by someone else's choices. My heart's question is the same as yours: *Could the precious things blazing around me possibly be under the watchful gaze of a loving God?*

GOLDEN PLACES

Some have called these precious places in our lives "golden places" that hold special terrain inside of us. Once the golden power is taken away (the illusion of a perfect family or perfect church, the image of children you'll never bear or a consistent spiritual strength you were determined to find), the terrain in our hearts is either hardened and distanced from God, or it is softened, given more fully to God. We harden ourselves by minimizing how difficult it is. ("It's no big deal; in eighty years it will all grow back.") Or we soften as we honestly face the devastation that has come and open ourselves to the good in the midst of it. ("Lord, it hurts, and I am sad and furious at the flames. What is it you want me to know of you, as I remember the smell of pine needles?") How do we let our hearts be deepened in God's fire rather than despairing the loss or feigning that we're fine?

Perhaps it is in the way we listen to what the fire is after. I've noticed, while tracking our local fire's progress, that our community breathes a collective sigh of relief each time the wind shifts and the fire turns back on itself. As the fire hits terrain already consumed, there is no "need" for it to go on. The flames lick up against already consumed earth and then "lie down"; the power of destruction is taken away, because the fuel has already been consumed.

When the fire of God comes and roars through our hearts, it is the golden places that blaze the brightest. The fuel there is rich and thick—dreams, hopes, aspirations, plans—precious fuel kept like secret treasure. We usually aren't even aware of how much we place our trust in these golden things. I didn't realize how deep my desire and dreams for marriage were until I came to the threshold of committing my life to someone only to have the relationship end. Any heart would grieve and hurt after this disappointment, but something in me literally died. Something I had thought would bring me life now was being frustrated, denied, burned with holy fire. Please hear me carefully: God never burns our desires; he only burns the chaff we make out of our desires, the things we cling to for life (such as the belief that I will never be fulfilled until I am married). My dreams for motherhood have been consumed too, but not in the same way. I come alive whenever I am even remotely close to a baby; the maternal desire is deep and rich in me. Over years made up of many moments—holding a friend's baby and having her grip my finger and then handing her back, shopping for clothes for another person's baby boy—I've had to loosen my hold on this desire.

I don't know what your golden places are—a relationship, a place, a position from which God seeks to loosen your grip. But as you think of them, I'm sure you would agree: the greatest miracle is that any of our hearts would call God good in the midst of letting go. It's hard. Relinquishing things that matter to us is difficult. And counting the cost of what we must relinquish in order to follow Jesus (which involves taking inventory of what we're going to lose) is *sad*. Over time we realize we're leaving behind things that were not big enough for our heart's passion anyway, but as it is happening, it hurts like crazy. Only Peter knows what it took, *in his heart,* to really walk away from his nets. As Jesus says, "Follow me," as he whispers, "Let go," I am the only one who knows the personal golden inventory he wants me to relinquish.

Now, before you start thinking of God as one big incinerator full of destruction, remember that love, marriage, children, career, and even reputation are beautiful things. It is the way we cling to them as though they were life itself that the fire is after. Jesus never invites me to eradicate the beautiful, life-giving desire for a baby. But he does invite me in each of the moments with others' children to let him love me in the midst of the unmet desire. He invites me to see that the desire itself is not life, but rather it leads me to life because it leads me to my need for him.

The fire may never actually touch your marriage, but it might come to do a deep, internal work on the jealousy in your heart and trust your wife to go off for a weekend with friends. The fire may never touch your children, but inside your heart the fire may burn away your judgment and cause you to see how you've been pressuring them to be someone they're not.

There is always something to be cleared away in our lives. For decades, forest service and land management studies have pointed to the importance of tree thinning and forest management as the best deterrent for devastating fires. It's not too much of a jump to think of my heart in the same way. I'm in a situation right now with a friend who is asking me to face the shrubbery and old growth of impatience and judgment in my heart. I'm asking for mercy and kindness to grow up in their place. God's fire—almost in a controlled-burn way—eliminates the undergrowth and dead fuel *surrounding* the golden places. This is the daily, hourly thing we call "sanctification."

The burning of the golden places themselves is a different story, one that forces me to acknowledge that the certainty I thought I had, I do not have. The control I thought I had, I do not have. The burning of tenderly held treasure takes me into the intimate posture of "What are you saying?" obedience. It is a far more ruthless process than we think would be good for our hearts, and it doesn't seem loving while it is happening. I guess that is why we need to really become acquainted with the Love inside this living flame. I don't want to live my life merely sanctified. I want to be transformed by Love.

The flame is after something. If it's after mere destruction, we might as well close this book—close all books for that matter—roll our eyes and join our anesthetized generation. Thankfully, the flame wants to remove what is in the way of our seeing, hearing, and tasting the Love of Jesus. It's a mystery to me, but in the charring of my sweetest dreams I've heard Jesus's voice the clearest, felt his touch the most. The wheat grain of those things I thought would make me happy withers in the smoke, as unexpected Life germinates in his whisper of reassurance: "I will never leave you nor forsake you. I am enough."

THE DILEMMA OF PROMISE

Think for a minute about how humanly impossible it is to follow this God. He asks us to listen to his promises, to ask and seek and knock for them to be fulfilled. And then along the way to the fulfillment of the promise, his flames come to burn golden places that hold our affections over his. Jesus gives us everything we need along the way—but it is *hard*.

Most of life is lived in the tension between knowing that God is taking me somewhere ("Is it really you, Jesus?") and not knowing where I'm going ("Oh no, it *is* you, Jesus"). It is in this tension where we find ourselves waiting, often in silence or sorrow, on the instruction and promises of God. Here we remember things he spoke when calling us into the journey; here we contend with all the seeming evidence that tells us the promises are not true. This can be a very, very confusing corridor, to say the least. How many times have you said to yourself in the past month, "I think I heard Jesus say _____ to me"? And how often have you felt more than slightly apologetic ("Who am I to think I hear God?") or fearful ("I'm not sure I want to hear God!")?

Making sense of how God fulfills his promises, either written promises or specifically heard promises, is a bit like trying to teach about absolutes in a hall of mirrors. We see hints and glimmers of what was intended, but the distortions of our own veiled eyes, this world's bent frame, or the illusionary, mocking ways of evil cause us to doubt what we see and hear at every turn. Let me take you through the recent experience of a friend to show you what I mean.

John, a man I know, walked through an experience that made his head spin, causing him to feel slightly insane for believing he heard God's voice. He and his wife had been separated for eight months, and though he longed for something to change for them, for a renewed relationship, there was no indication this would happen. He had changed the focus of his prayers from "Please restore us" to "Please give me the grace to let go of her." He had spent several months trying to come to terms with the fact that she didn't want the marriage, didn't want him.

One day when he was fishing along his favorite stretch of river, Jesus came to John with a promise: "I want restoration for you and your wife." Of course this man was simultaneously thrilled, skeptical, and put off by this. He fought it, wrestling with it in his mind and heart for several hours. Jesus kept pushing, asking him to articulate what he really wanted in the depth of his heart. "Well, Jesus, of course I want restoration. I've told you that. But I cannot hope for that anymore. Don't ask me to do this." He wasn't in the mood for more disappointment. Jesus continued with a strong and simple sense of promise; he wouldn't let up. John finally drank it in slowly, like a chilling glass of water that hurts if you drink it too fast. He accepted that Jesus was promising him something precious beyond words. It was scary to believe.

Months and months went by, and all evidence said that this promise from God should be discarded. It was not going to be fulfilled. He felt the fool— perhaps as Abraham and Sarah did around the age of ninety-five when they recalled the promise of a child. The fulfillment of this promise was clearly being blocked by something. The hardest part was hearing the mocking message from evil: "You don't know God's voice. Obviously you think you do, but you don't." It was a very conflicted and bewildering time. It is frightening to wonder if you don't genuinely know the voice of your God, the guiding hand of your Lover.

As John wrestled with all this, Jesus led him to a story that literally saved his sanity. It is a story about a very specific promise and very specific possibilities for disappointment. In some ways it is a classic picture of the mystery between God's loving and intimate desire and purpose for us and the loving and intimate freedom he grants us. The story goes like this:

Abraham wants to find a wife for his son, Isaac. He chooses a servant to find a young woman for Isaac in his homeland, but he warns the servant

> never to take my son there [among his relatives]. For the LORD, the
> God of heaven, who took me from my father's house and my native
> land, solemnly promised to give this land to my offspring. He will send
> his angel ahead of you, and he will see to it that you find a young

woman there to be my son's wife. *If she is unwilling* to come back with you, then you are free from this oath. But under no circumstances are you to take my son there. (Genesis 24:6–8, emphasis added)

If she is unwilling? The Lord, the God of heaven, the Alpha and Omega, makes a promise, and then it is up to a young woman to say yes or no? Is this not a graphic picture of how much God defers to us, how much he honors us? "I know exactly what I am after, and, yes, I am even making promises, specific promises. But I will not force anyone's hand. The girl I am after is there, and if she is not willing, then that's that."

Does this mean that God is not ultimately in control? No. It is a picture of how God, fully certain of his perfect way, allows us to make our choices so that both he and we know our hearts are really with him. It's the conundrum that theologians have tried to "crack" for centuries, but the bottom line is this: God does promise specific things. He speaks and intends. But the road to the fulfillment of these promises is often racked with our own doubt and laughter, as well as the lack of participation of other people. The fallenness of this world is much worse than we know. The opposition of our Enemy is more fierce than we recognize. A clearly heard and responded-to promise is nothing short of a miracle, let alone a promise fulfilled.

God's fire consumes so that he can love me without obstacle. And when I am longing for a certain, predictable, sovereign plan that won't ever shift or change, God reminds me that his having my heart along the way is more important than certainty. Following Jesus is not safe. It is hard to be loved by God. We miss out on so much if we choose the safety of not desiring, not following, not wanting more from Love. I am living with a specific promise unfulfilled. How do I get to a point of believing that anything good can come of this?

A HOLY GIVING UP

First I remember the disciples. They didn't understand. They couldn't conceptualize that anything good could come of losing Jesus. They had to enter fully into their loss, letting go of control, in order to be caught off guard by the power of the Holy Spirit. They wanted to hang on to his tangible, palpable love. But Jesus wanted to give himself more fully to them in ways that were out of their control, through his fiery presence. So the Spirit came as fire—to clear away the impediments, to make them more fully alive.

The life-giving fire of the Spirit has rarely made me comfortable. There have been many seasons when it blazed, consuming everything in its path that was contrary to its fruit: love, joy, peace, patience, kindness, gentleness, goodness, and self-control. In one friendship in particular, the fire of God has had much impatience, worry, hatred, harshness to burn away. What I forget is that the fire comes to make room for more of the Spirit. When I've tried to fill the charred places through my own efforts—trying to be a better friend, trying to be more loving—I've missed the point: Love wants to fill me, to take control. I've spent a lot of days trying to "come up with" gentleness, trying to discipline myself to be kind. The Spirit has had something else in mind. Instead of my trying harder, the Spirit has wanted me to rest, releasing the life of Christ in me. The fire blazed so I could no longer "try to be patient;" the Spirit just wanted to show up, releasing the patience that is already there. As Love has taken control, I have been able to look beyond my friend's irritating imperfections to her true heart, which is really quite rare in this world. When I "try" to love my friend, I continue to be irritated. I chide myself, and I miss the beauty of her life that shows itself in her inquisitiveness and her wisdom.

Blaise Pascal, known more for his intellect concerning God than for his intimate love relationship with Jesus, wrote this prayer in the midst of a lengthy, life-threatening illness:

> Everything that is not God is unable to fulfill my desires. It is you alone
> I seek, that I may have you. O Lord, open my heart…. Enter in, as into
> the strong man's house. But first bind the strong and powerful enemy,
> who is tyrant over it. Take to yourself the treasures that are there. Lord,
> take my affections which the world has robbed me of; spoil the world of
> this treasure. Rather, continue to possess it, for it belongs only to you.[1]

This man was experiencing a holy resignation, a holy giving up. He had fainted. He could do no more, offer nothing more. He could come up with no other devices to battle to try to please God, nor earn love.

Isaiah 57 paints a picture of God's broken heart as Israel continued, while on the unimaginable journey through the desert, to find every imaginable way to cater to her own needs: "You grew weary in your search, but you never gave up. You strengthened yourself and went on" (Isaiah 57:10). Another translation adds, "so you did not faint" (NIV). Can you hear what God is after? He is longing for us to admit defeat and turn to him. As our hearts realize what is being asked here, of course we say, *Oh no, Jesus, it is you.* He longs for us just to quit trying so hard so he can come in as the champion.

Here's how this gets worked out day to day. Let's say a wife is confronted with the fact that she is being caustic with her husband. She could respond with, "Oh, I see what the problem is. Yes, I need to work on that. I'll try hard not to use sarcastic words toward you anymore." Or she could say, "Oh, I see how my harsh words hurt you. Yes, I do that. I am sarcastic toward you. I'm sorry." The clear apology comes from a heart that has heard—taken in—what the spouse has said. Rather than scrambling internally and trying to come up with a way to make everything better, this person has fainted—has acknowledged her impact, the harm she is capable of. This opens the door for both the Holy Spirit of God to come with restoration and for her husband to know his plea was truly heard. We could call it "putting a period on it." When we put a period on the damage we do to ourselves and others through our selfishness, we faint and allow God to be strong in our weakness. When we put semicolons on it ("Yes, I may tend to be domineering; it would probably be important for me to come up with a plan to work on not being so dominant; I have an idea…"), we miss the chance for redemption because we are not yet, in our own eyes, truly in need. It would be like taking this beautiful verse by Bianco de Siena

> And so the yearning strong,
> with which the soul will long,

> shall far outpass the power of human telling;
> for none can guess its grace
> till Love create a place
> wherein the Holy Spirit makes a dwelling.[2]

and changing it to

> And so the yearning strong
> with which the soul will long
> shall far outpass the power of human telling
> for none shall guess its grace
> until we try really hard to figure out how to fix this mess and
>   determine never to do it again and make a list of ways to
>   not do it again, and we will succeed!

It loses something in the translation, doesn't it? That's what our resistance to fainting does—it steals the beauty found in the dwelling place of the Holy Spirit.

FRAGILE CONTROL

My first encounter with Julie in my counseling office was rough. She was a lovely woman with great taste in clothes and accessories, but after five minutes of being in her presence, I realized I'd have to work really hard to ever know her. Her manner was flat, her words metered, her whole demeanor controlled and stiff.

Months later I sat with an open, warm, and honest woman. What had transpired to make her an engaged, witty woman whose tears were close at hand? She began to listen to her God, and, as we've been considering, that was an invitation to feel a little crazy and an invitation for fire to blaze in uncomfortable ways. Listening wasn't as it had always been before—perfunctory, strained, pressured. She had begun to listen to God by listening to her heart, to her life. She had crossed the threshold everyone is called to when called to obedience—the threshold where God says, "Please listen, because I want to reveal *myself* to you. I hold the answers. And if I never reveal the answers to you, I will reveal myself to you." The fire of God was subtle, like the aroma of a fireplace a few houses down the street, but it wafted through her weary timidity and compelled her to awaken.

For Julie it came from the dishes. Somehow her home—a well-oiled machine—had become her prison as she threw herself mindlessly, heartlessly, into the flawless maintenance of form, function, and even beauty. It was a stunning home. Talked about. Admired by women who struggled to get laundry from one room to the other. Her trained smile hid her anxiety as she sent guests out the door. There was never any reprieve in her mind—always movement, chores, lists. Never did she linger on a sun-streaked couch, smiling with the rest as she considered the environment she had created. The environment consumed her.

So I told her to not do the dishes for a few days. Leave them in the sink. I'm not terribly prescriptive when I counsel, but this was a no-brainer. Easy to say—as easy as asking an alcoholic to forgo her drinking rituals. As I stated my request, I did not see a look of relief. It was terror. Julie knew that if she turned her face away from this familiar taskmaster of performance with which she had engaged her heart, she would have to listen.

And she did.

First came the irritation. We're all fairly furious when we are asked to deny our addictions, whether it's our favorite sport, television, illicit conversations, gossip. We get irritated because suddenly we're off balance. The firm foundation of our own making starts to shake, and we don't like it. The same was true for Julie when she began to give up the things she was compulsive about around the house. She couldn't get over how furious she suddenly became with everyone around her. Her bastion of control was crumbling, and it would not fall silently.

Then came the sadness. She began to think of all she had lost in recent years—dreams unfulfilled with her husband, a baby she had grieved only superficially after a miscarriage. Now her tenderness as a woman was whispering. Her mother's heart was surfacing. She didn't have to go looking for it—our stories so often come to us if we just give them a chance. She pondered what it meant to be the mediator between her mother and father in their abusive marriage. She had disconnected from this and switched into autopilot decades before running her own lovely home. Very early she had stopped listening to the damage, to her heart. You can hear how fragile it all is—the control and protection we try to put around ourselves, the ways we try to deny even the fire of God.

But now God was speaking. With the haze of the addictive cloud pierced for a moment, Julie could hear. She had opened her heart with vulnerability, replacing slavery and fear with a sense of being God's child. Not doing the dishes cracked a door that the Spirit poured through to bring light and healing and repentance to a singed and weary heart.

There Is Always More Than Fire

The fire clears the way for our dreams to be saturated and filled and drenched and redefined. The golden place is not gone; it is actually expanded, making room for the fullness of Christ. Augustine said, "My soul is too cramped for you to enter it—widen it out." And as David prayed, "Lord, enlarge the expanse of my heart." There is more to our golden places than we have any idea, more terrain to be made ready for the purest Love.

I love the freedom this brings. I know, you're thinking, *Freedom? So far, all this makes me want to run for the hills (or to get a fire extinguisher)!* I'm with you—I've done both. But the truth is, the refining seasons of our journey with God actually lessen our load, allowing us to "laugh at the days to come" (Proverbs 31:25, NIV). Simone Weil says that obedience to the force of gravity is the greatest sin.[3] Simply put, when we are weighed down by the gravity of our self-sufficiency, we are heavy laden, and Jesus tells us to come to him to find the freedom of an expanded heart and lightened load.

If we walk through times of fiery trials only to be drawn down, more heavy hearted, then something has gone terribly wrong. My friend Joel says that nothing has asked him to be more deeply Christian than the way he's had to respond to suffering. He says it is in the midst of fire that the resurrection life of Christ is real—carrying him through, keeping him from the force of gravity. Moses told the people that the Lord promised to deliver them, but they wouldn't listen; they had become too accustomed to the burden of their slavery. I know a man who says he recognizes when his idols show up, because he suddenly takes himself too seriously. I relate to that. I want to make a big dramatic show of it when my comfortable world is disrupted. But the fire does not exist to make things more complicated or heavy. It exists to purify, to cleanse—to lighten.

The fire invites us into the freedom to laugh, to flow with the most unthinkable situations and unmet desires. It opens our hands, prying our fingers from all we thought was necessary. Once our hands are open, we can sit back and laugh at how tight we have been holding on. That kind of laughter knows the remarkable truth: The flames of God have not burned us. Instead we are called Beloved.

THE LAUGHTER OF SURRENDER

What would it be like to get to the point where the intensity of the flames doesn't matter, living from a holy surrender that comes when there isn't anything else to lose? As the fire burned through my dreams the past few years, I noticed a strange abandon creeping in. It's been fragile, but it sounds like this: "Go ahead and take it all if you must, because I've got your love, and that is enough." No one has been more surprised than I have, because at times in the past I thought I would die if I didn't see the fulfillment of my dreams. Now I know I won't die. The dross has been burned away, and the flames lie down as they lick up against the holy terrain of my heart. There is no more kindling here, no more fuel. God's relentless heat has taken the most preciously held affections, so there is nothing more.

Recently I was taking a walk along a high trail that sits above the Garden of the Gods, a beautiful park in Colorado Springs. It was one of those days that makes a soul glad to be in Colorado—light snow covering the red earth and dusting the pungent piñon, and the sun warming my face. I was enjoying the moment when I heard Jesus say to me, "You mean so very much to me." It was one of those rare moments of crystal-clear hearing. It took my breath. I blushed. "Well…thank you," I said. I kept walking, drinking in what he had just given me. What came out of my mouth next surprised even me. "Thank you. So, are you ever going to share me?" I laughed at the statement but knew the depth from which it came. I heard him laugh too. "Will anyone compare with me?" the voice shot back. Now I *really* knew it was Jesus. I thought about it for a moment and then was so pleased at the ease with which this long-awaited, through-the-fiery-corridor answer surfaced. "No, Jesus. No one will compare with you." Again I was stunned by the moment; it revealed much about the fire's freeing work in my heart. Then Jesus came to me with something so tender, so full of promise and understanding of my desires: "You are now free to love."

The eternal is released as all that shrouds it is destroyed. As this happens, I realize that my heart and its place in the kingdom cannot be destroyed. This fragile, indestructible treasure made it through, like Bambi narrowly escaping the blaze. Now my heart holds treasure deeper, makes dreams more vibrant than I knew possible. I realize that I walk out of the burning embers with all that matters—being loved by God.

AN UNCOMFORTABLE UNVEILING

It is hard enough for us to accept that God has given us a holy, new heart. Harder still is the fact that God will do *anything* to release, to unveil, this new heart. Again, as the writer of Hebrews says: "This means that the things on

earth will be shaken, *so that only eternal things will be left.* Since we are receiving a kingdom that cannot be destroyed, let us be thankful and please God by
worshiping him with holy fear and awe. For our God is a consuming fire"
(Hebrews 12:27–29, emphasis added).

The cry of the young Muslim servant in Isak Dinesen's *Out of Africa* is like
this. He discovers a fire destroying the coffee plantation that Dinesen's character has established in the later years of her life. He runs to wake up his mis-
tress and cries, "Wake up, Mamsup—God is coming." Upon seeing the
charred remains of her dream, this persevering woman realizes all that is left to
do is throw up her hands and laugh. "Well, it is all gone anyway," she jokes
with her friend. "We're just out of coffee.... Can I offer you some tea?" The
cruel flames have left her with nothing but lightness of soul and laughter. Only
eternal things are left.

My favorite Celtic artist Loreena McKennitt says in her song "Dante's
Prayer":

> When the dark wood fell before me
> And all the paths were overgrown…
> I tilled the sorrows of stone.[4]

Sometimes it is hard to know which to grieve more—the fact that we've
allowed our overgrown affections to intrude on our relationship with Jesus, or
the fact that we have to let go of those affections for love of our jealous God.
Can we say, with George MacDonald, "What we would here and now call our
'happiness' is not the end God chiefly has in view: but when we are such as he
can love without impediment, we shall in fact be happy"?[5] With the impediments gone, the overgrown paths clear as we weep the tears of God, with God.

Jesus alone lived in this tension perfectly, as a man of sorrows acquainted
with grief. He invited his disciples into this tension in John 16:

> "In just a little while I will be gone, and you won't see me anymore.
> Then, just a little while after that, you will see me again."

The disciples asked each other, "What does he mean when he says, 'You won't see me, and then you will see me'? And what does he mean when he says, 'I am going to the Father?' And what does he mean by 'a little while'? *We don't understand.*" (John 16:16–18, emphasis added)

I'm so grateful for these words. The disciples couldn't see. The story they were thrust into was too much for their limited understanding, for their human reasoning. It didn't make sense to them, all that they had to leave behind. And the eternal promises felt hazy and unsure, even as Jesus tried to explain his plan. The same is true for me. I've been adopted into a story line that makes me weep for its beauty, but on many days it seems too vast for my small heart. It asks too much of me, and the eternal things seem far away.

I am comforted that the characters I love in most good stories are faced with the same dilemma as they struggle with the promise of the path and the cost of the path. Which will you choose, Frodo—to walk away or to continue to Mordor with all its pitfalls? Dorothy, will you choose the yellow brick road with all its scary moments? Lucy, Peter, and Edmund, will you enter Narnia with all its magic and also accept the hard lessons found there? Alice, will you go into the pull of the rabbit hole, and will you let your fearful tears flow?

The only way the disciples made it through to the end of the story was by the outpouring of the Holy Spirit. Jesus had given them a promise of a good ending, but they could not bear the path without power outside themselves. It is the same for us. The ending we believe by faith, but the overgrown path we know by heart. Some days all I can see are the old lies that I am alone and the whole thing is up to me. The way through this is the work of the Spirit.

As we walk in the soil of the tension between the promises and the cost, we will cry along the way. But we are tilling the step-by-step sorrows that lead to life. And along the way, the Spirit of Christ comes as the Paraclete to cover our backs, to walk alongside, to comfort and cheer and whisper, over and over, that we are not alone.

THE GOODNESS OF NOT KNOWING EVERYTHING

Isn't it amazing that a God who gives the gift of his Spirit still gives us only enough light to take one more step into the land behind the wardrobe, walk one more day toward the ring's destruction? His Spirit leads us into all truth; he does not clear up all mysteries. I do not understand why I've loved two absolutely wonderful men and yet walk into the future alone. I do not understand why our friend David had to undergo the rigor of a stem-cell replacement procedure to prolong his life with his dear wife and sweet boys for only a short while. I do not understand why a group of people I respect poured their efforts into a beautifully intended ministry for three years only to see it fold. I don't understand why one person struggling with sexual addiction finds some release through warfare prayers while another person knows no relief and only feels condemned for not being set free by such prayers. I have some suspicions, some revelations, some data, but the truth is, ultimately I don't understand. And this is a *good* thing.

Remember the corridor between Jesus's absence and his resurrection? The place of trust and waiting? This is what he has to say about it:

> Jesus realized they wanted to ask him, so he said, "Are you asking yourselves what I meant? I said in just a little while I will be gone, and you won't see me anymore. Then, just a little while after that, you will see me again. Truly, you will weep and mourn over what is going to happen to me, but the world will rejoice. You will grieve, but your grief will suddenly turn to wonderful joy when you see me again. It will be like a woman experiencing the pains of labor. When her child is born, her anguish gives place to joy because she has brought a new person into the world. You have sorrow now, but I will see you again; then you will rejoice, and no one can rob you of that joy. At that time you won't need to ask me for anything. The truth is, you can go directly to the Father and ask him, and he will grant your request

because you use my name. You haven't done this before. Ask, using my name, and you will receive, and you will have abundant joy. (John 16:19–24)

There is a tension in Jesus's words. A birth is coming, but for now we are in labor. There is the sorrow of his absence, but his coming is sure. For now, there is a season where sorrow *just is.* We must wait, living by faith. And at the same time Jesus is telling us there is much more for us in this waiting than we know—*you haven't asked me the way you could.* The waiting itself, the sorrowing itself, is meant to grow our thirst and expand our hearts to make more room for the Spirit.

This paradox cannot be nailed down, but it is captured in the final scene of the movie *Gladiator,* where we're given a glimpse of the eternal. Maximus, the "general who became a slave, the slave who became a gladiator, the gladiator who defied an evil emperor," has accomplished his mission in defeating Comidus (the evil emperor) and freeing Rome and its citizens. As we watch Maximus slip into eternity beyond a blood-stained door, the slave who devoted himself to Maximus is mourning him and burying the icons that were so dear to Maximus's heart. "I will see you again. But not yet. *Not yet.*" The twinkle in this man's eyes betrays any slavery; he knows the freedom Maximus died for is his own. The wait, the sorrow, is not a heavy endeavor. No, his sorrow is taking him somewhere—further into the world he's left in and further into the coming world of freedom.

Waiting for Change

Last weekend I had the privilege of being on one of Colorado's most glorious ranches. Some friends have made their home in a beautiful valley with sprawling waves of field grasses and wildflowers surrounded by granite peaks and fields of aspen. They also have a little hobby: Arabians. They own the national champion show horse from a few years back, as well as six other creatures that border on equine divinity. These horses don't run; they *flow* across the valley floor, and when they do, all who see them are rendered speechless.

On this visit I meandered down to the fence bordering the current grazing field. Sweat beaded under my hat as the afternoon sun shone and the sound of lazy cicadas hummed through the valley. The horses were under a tree in the middle of the valley, clustered together to maximize the shade. As I approached the fence, I found myself calling to them, "Here beautiful ones!"—clicking my teeth and attempting to rouse them. Nothing. The horses weren't about to budge. Now, you can imagine my first inclination. Of course I simply started to call to them *louder*—making my pleas more impassioned, my noises more pronounced. Nothing. The horses weren't about to budge. Just as I was on the verge of trying to refine my coaxing power one more time, God intervened by saying, "Shh." I stopped. Quiet. He said, "Just be still. Wait. Don't work so hard." *Of course,* I thought, *I'll just wait.* As we've well established by now, waiting doesn't come naturally. I must have waited in that hot sun for fifteen minutes, feeling a bit idiotic and saying to myself, *They will never come.* After a time (there's that phrase), one horse began to turn. One by one they turned. One by one they walked across the valley—having a whole valley to choose from for their destination away from that tree—and came straight toward me. One by one I stroked their manes, whispered hello, and nuzzled with these glorious creatures. And one by one I wept. I knew what God was saying to me. Let go, give up, let it die. This thing that you so desire will never come as long as you are trying to maneuver your way to it. Let me bring it to you.

Maybe this takes us a bit closer to what confident, relinquished obedience is: Having a spirit that is open to losing everything, actually anticipating loss. Maybe it is having a heart that seeks after—but is also willing to wait for—good things from God's hand. Maybe it is a heart that is letting go of control.

I know what you are thinking: *This sounds like a group of people watching a forest fire and not calling for help or grabbing a shovel. It sounds an awful lot like resignation ("Why bother if I'm going to lose it anyway?").* But it isn't. What we're talking about is the belief that no matter what might be taken away—whether through the fallen world, the thievery of Satan, or our own foolishness—the heart still has everything, because it has the Water of Life.

Why does a God of resurrection and power ask us to suffer loss? Shouldn't we be shaking off sorrow, as ones who have seen an empty tomb? I wonder if we look at this through the wrong lens. I wonder if the sorrow we are invited into is more reminiscent of a lover who sees that his beloved is overburdened with a garment that is just too thick, too heavy to show off her beauty. She is weary from the weight of it and the way it makes her feel cumbersome and ugly. The old self is a hideous garment that simply doesn't belong to us anymore. In Ephesians 4, we are called to put it off, to strip it away, acknowledging the corrupt nature of it, admitting it doesn't fit the new heart that has been literally circumcised, or grafted to Christ. When we recognize the ugliness of this garment, there is reason to grieve, for a time, just how much of God's glory has been stolen during the days, months, years we have worn it. C. S. Lewis says, "I do not think I should value much the love of a friend who cared only for my happiness and did not object to my becoming dishonest."[6] We have a Friend whose unwavering task is to expose the false garment. He is willing to burn it. He does not do this to shame us or harm us. He does it to release our hearts from their captivity into the unencumbered lightness of freedom.

Our buried life is sometimes nudged to the surface through the smoke gently wafting in, and sometimes it is roused with the ferocity of fire. Sometimes the water of the Spirit trickles in; sometimes it rages like a river. Sometimes the wind of the Spirit whispers through the shrubbery, and sometimes it howls and rips at the branches in the way of a clear view. Yes, God is coming. The fire is Jesus's passionate jealousy over the things that shroud our hearts. John the Baptist said of Jesus's coming: "I baptize with water.... He will baptize you with the Holy Spirit and with fire. He is ready to separate the chaff from the grain with his winnowing fork. Then he will clean up the threshing area storing the grain in his barn but burning the chaff with never-ending fire" (Matthew 3:11–12). Handel's masterpiece shouts, "For He is like a Refiner's fire" as it echoes Malachi's message that freedom is coming—in the form of a God willing to scorch in order to release our captive hearts. When we really face Malachi's question, "Who can stand in the face of such a fire?"[7] then we can be stunned that the cleansing of the grain is truly intended so we can laugh at, instead of fear, judgment.

Sometimes the fire smolders. Sometimes it rages hot and white. "Oh good, you are after something, Jesus"—the release of our shrouded hearts.

Three

LISTENING TO OUR NEED

Relinquishing Our Pride

We don't know how to be alone
So we wander 'round this desert,
wind up following the wrong gods home.
—THE EAGLES

Darkness is as nothing to God, who can look right through
whatever evil we've done in our lives
to the creature made in the divine image.
I suspect that only God, and well-loved infants, can see this way.
—KATHLEEN NORRIS

A t this point I think you can see the paradox I'm talking about: though the very life of Christ pulses in our hearts, the refining work of God and the unveiling of our true selves continues. In the midst of this process, we are needy people. One of our greatest needs is rediscovering a childlike response to God's heart—we need to rediscover the ability to ask. And children are the best examples, after all, of letting others know what they want and need.

My nephew was a four-year-old passenger with me on our annual family trek to the San Juan Mountains when his childlike eyes invited me into the wonder of God. Daniel had never seen this place. He had heard much about it but didn't have a category in which to anticipate it. He was sleepy from the long car ride along a southern Colorado highway, and rousing him was a slow process. "Daniel, we are almost there. Pretty soon we will see the lake." Daniel slowly sat up, sat cross-legged, and watched out the window as the terrain started to change. As my car wound its way past the last bend in the road, there it was—blue lake, snow-capped peaks, wildflowers. I heard Daniel catch his breath. He *held* his breath. His eyes searched and drank in what he saw. He quietly cupped his hands together, the way you do when you are earnest. After a long, silent while, he breathlessly whispered, "Beauty. And loveliness." Daniel didn't know how much he needed beauty and loveliness until he was caught off guard by them. I didn't know how much I needed them until I heard Daniel's breathless response.

The Christian life is a conspiracy of need. Life with God conspires to bring us back, over and over again, to a childlike place where we are breathlessly caught off guard by Love and reminded of all that we were created for and desire. And then we are brought back to a place where we must lean in and ask for those things the way a child does, depending fully on someone bigger than ourselves. We resist this at every turn. We don't like to think about how *costly* it is to be childlike in this world that tells us to *handle* or *hide* our need and not to be too enthralled about anything unless it is *planned.* Isn't it sad how we resist being childlike, and yet it is the very thing that reminds us of our dependence and the very thing that provides our sense of wonder, making Christianity a breathtaking experience.

Is It Really You?

The fact that Jesus conspires to bring me back, over and over, into childlikeness is really good news for me. I love to laugh and to be startled by unexpected beauty, but I so easily find myself ruminating and worrying, assuming that the weight of the world is mine to tackle, handle, and navigate. Being caught off guard means I need to let go of this illusion that I am the master of the universe, and it means I must eventually ask for something from God's heart in order to have the courage to let go.

This happened recently when my friend Stan, one of those unfortunate souls who has lived in Hawaii, shared with me something about having a childlike spirit. Evidently, some scholars have worked on a version of the Scriptures in pidgin English, a fairly isolated language used in many colonized Pacific and African areas. Hearing this uncomplicated and—forgive the term—"simple" dialect was delightful but humbling. Listen to the familiar "love passage" from 1 Corinthians 13. All you need to know is that "love an aloha" means "have the kind of love that God has—all embracing and all embraced." And no, there are no typos.

> If I wen talk all da diffren kine languages, da peopo kine language an
> even da angel kine languages, but I no mo love an aloha, wat den? I
> only talking rubbish kine, jalike one junk kine bell o one kalangalang
> cymbal. And if I was one talka for God, an I wen know all kine secret
> stuffs an all da kine stuffs dat da smart guys know, an if I wen trus God
> all da way so I can eve make da mountains move, but I no mo love an
> aloha, wat den? I worth notting, dass wat. (Numba 1 fo da Corint
> Peopo 13)

These familiar words, transformed by simple, innocent delivery, made my heart lean in immediately with the words of the first posture of the heart: "Is it really you, Jesus? Is this what you are after? Could it really be that you are just not impressed with anything but love?"

These words came when I was in the midst of a promising romantic relationship. I was beginning to realize that I had been making my view of things, my opinions and worries, so important. From the beginning of the relationship, I had been quite sure—too sure—of myself with this man. Too sure of my abilities in the relational department. The truth was, I had been really hurt in a previous relationship, and internally I was terrified of being devastated again. The relationship had hit some difficult but wise detours. We were two adults with significant histories, and wisdom was telling us we needed lots of time and space to let the relationship unfold freely and enjoyably. But in my fear I was ruminating about all that could go wrong, all that wasn't "just so," all that wasn't unfolding the way I wanted at the pace I wanted. In the spirit of "I really do know what's best," I was the interrogator, double-checking every interaction, every motive, every move both of us would make. Part of the problem, of course, was the fact that I am a counselor and am trained to see too much. But the bigger problem was my assumption that I *could* see and could predict and could know "all kine secret stuffs," acting like one of "da smart guys." Bottom line: I was being asked to let go of my pride. I was being shown that I could not love until I did so. The simple pidgin words unfurrowed my brow and put a bit of a skip back into my step.

When had I become so sure of myself and my ability to see what's best? When is it that any of us fall into the trap of pridefully plundering our way through the things of the heart, the things of life, rather than, like a child, admitting we are scared and in need of love and guidance outside ourselves? I couldn't remember. But the call of Love summoned me back to a playfulness that had been there in the early days—the early days of faith and the early days of the relationship. How familiar this passage has been to me through the years: "If I could speak in any language in heaven or on earth, but didn't love others, I would only be making meaningless noise like a loud gong or a clanging cymbal." But the pidgin rendition made me listen; it made me want to obey. I told Stan, smirking but respectfully, it was like listening to the voice of God translated through Bob Marley's five-year-old son.

How We Bury Our Hearts

On a hike with dear friends, I watched Betsy's little guy Dylan balance on logs as he charged up a steep trail. I shouted, "You are really strong, Dylan!" His lungs filled with air, and after a pause he said, "Well yes, yes I am!" Dylan *knows* he impacts his world simply by being in it. He's lost in the wonder of his world and who he is. But Dylan also knows when he is tired and is not ashamed to tell Betsy, "Mom, I'm sleepy." When he skins his knee, he cries, not ashamed to need a hug to comfort him.

Picture Dylan ten years from now in a car next to you at an intersection. His music is blaring, and his bass rocks your vehicle. There's a bit of a glazed look on his face—he's been lulled to sleep. Fast-forward another ten years, and picture him racing out the door of his home with a travel mug in one hand and a pile of folders in the other. He's not convinced of his career choice, but his job seems secure. He sits, again at an intersection, picking up a cell phone and rattling off some figures. His life is busy and useful. But his face is becoming anxious. He is slowly burying his heart, and he is not all he wants to be.

The whimsy I knew as a girl twirling on mountain river rocks gave way to internal pressure the first time I saw my mom slip into the darkness and lethargy of depression. I was about nine years old the first time my mom went for a lengthy hospital stay. I was confused by her condition and behavior but more confused about how I was to respond. For some reason I thought I was supposed to take over her household duties and was supposed to handle it all with bravery. I was never told otherwise. I began to bury my heart in response to the dull ache of knowing my world would never be carefree again. I buried it further under the commitment to be strong for myself and others. I slowly became less than who I wanted to be. I slowly lost the expectation that beauty might be around the next corner, waiting to surprise me with a jolt of exhilaration.

Sometimes it takes years for us to bury our childlike hearts. So subtle is the surrender of our freedom that we call it normal, the growing-up process. We give ourselves away in little pieces, replacing who we want to be—open hearted, unrestrained, whimsical, and breathless—with who we are expected to be and who we think we should be and who we have re-created ourselves to be in order to maintain control. We, as the Eagles say, "wind up following the wrong gods home." We structure our days in the name of the God of Being Important, becoming too preoccupied to be curious about a friend's marriage or to make a phone call we want to make but that is not on our list. In the name of the God of Our Workout, we allow two squirrels to pass our peripheral vision rather than stop to watch them demonstrate the playful hormones of spring. In the name of the God of Success, we crowd out the chance to linger on a SpongeBob pillowcase and really listen to the hearts of our children. We chart our time in the name of the God of Efficiency and miss the purity of a spontaneous conversation with a good friend or a new acquaintance on a park bench. On the surface all of these things seem to be about our schedules and our busyness, our frenetic lives. But if we draw closer and consider letting go of those familiar gods, we start to realize that we have stopped listening to the Voice of Love and are obeying instead control and pride. Let me explain.

You Are Not All You Want to Be

When we lose our childlike freedom, we quickly become "notting, dass wat," quite literally like the house Jesus speaks of that is swept clean of an evil spirit only to have seven more return with it when the house hasn't been filled with anything else. Our hearts, though fully alive with the power of Christ, become temporary shells that carry pride and self-sufficiency rather than the playful, dependent, "I need him so" energy that God intended to keep the evil spirits away. We're active and organized, and we may be articulate and insightful, but we become what Jesus called "whitewashed tombs"—people whose lives look crisp and polished and productive on the outside but have a deadness, actually a *darkness,* in our internal world. The Voice of Love echoes through the macabre chambers of our self-sufficiency, but in our preoccupation with our own "maturity," "spirituality," and "effectiveness," we don't allow its echo to shake and to slough off the dark, residual walls of our old heart. Love's childlike message is drowned out by the clanging cymbal of our own knowledge, cleverness, giftedness, resources—all the things that keep us from asking from the Father.

This is not a new thing. In the late 1800s, Canon Barnett posted a message on billboards in East London that began with this phrase: "Your lives are busy, useful, honest; but your faces are anxious and you are not all that you want to be. There is within you another life, a buried life, which does not go free."[1] Another life—innocent, free, and in need of love—gets buried. It's the life that was intended for you before the foundation of the world, whispered to you in your childhood, and reclaimed by faith in Christ Jesus. We bury this life in our own self-importance. We walk around feigning contentment and purpose, but if we're honest, we feel as if we're carrying an extra hundred pounds. Children don't carry extra weight easily.

DEPENDENCE, WONDER, AND LAUGHTER AT STAKE

We all want our buried hearts to surface, right? We all want to have the presence of mind to respond to a baby's stare in the grocery-store line, to wrestle as a little boy grabs our legs. We all want to maintain the sensitivity to tear up as a friend shares a struggle. So what keeps us moving, driven, and oh-so-serious rather than holding our breath in awe or laughing out loud? Recently I watched a friend's six-month-old baby as he tried sweet potatoes for the first time. When that creamy orange stuff hit his taste buds, he was a bundle of shocked joy. He was hilarious—at first terrified, then contemplative, then overjoyed. He loved the exhilaration of this new taste. And earlier while I held him, he watched—no, studied—my hair and my earrings. They fascinated him. So how do we go from that sense of wonder—the wonder of beauty and loveliness—to bowing to the God of Being a Good Christian, being well thought of, pretending, posturing, and moralizing, and putting pressure on ourselves and others? When do we start trying to come up with our own wonder? We get lost in DVDs, theme parks, and virtual worlds. Even when we go to church, we try to rouse ourselves (as my friend Elisa says, by singing...and singing "I Could Sing of Your Love Forever"...forever, and ever...and ever), try to force the wonder to happen rather than letting it show up because it is God's delight to do so.

I can think of two times just this morning that I was given the chance to flee into the posture of "Oh no, it is you, Jesus. Being childlike, dependent, and out of control is just too scary, vulnerable, and disruptive." The first opportunity came when a friend called me and inquired about my writing process. The reality was, I was pretty disheartened and felt like throwing the whole thing in the garbage. My heart was longing for some deep, true encouragement. I wanted to hear that the message I was writing mattered, that somehow it was all worth it. But instead, I bowed to the God of My Pride and said, "Oh, you know, I've hit a few bumps, but I think it is coming together." *Sorry, Jesus. It is just too tender to hope I'll be handled well, so I won't even ask.* My friend, though he genuinely wanted to hear how I was, was never given the

opportunity to meet my deep heart need at that moment, because of my bowing to the second posture.

The other opportunity seems more mundane, but it came when I needed
a ride after I left my car at the dealership to be serviced. I knew I could call a
friend who had offered many times to be available for such things. For some
reason I didn't want to interrupt her day, so I took a dealership shuttle instead.
You may be thinking that this choice was probably courteous on my part.
Maybe. But my heart knows that if my friend had come to the dealership, I
would've given her the gift of letting my life be a burden to her. She wants that;
she's said so. And we would have had some time to visit on the drive. We all
know how precious that can be in this world. Internally I would have made a
graphically different choice: *Jesus, it is so scary to ask for even the most understandable things, but I'm going to ask and give you a chance to show up.*

Why are we so resistant to the vulnerability that Jesus surfaces in us?
Maybe because experience has taught us that to be childlike means that we will
be dependent and vulnerable to harm. I didn't have a guarantee that my friend
would encourage me about my writing. I didn't have a guarantee that my
other friend would desire to seize time with me. To be dependent and vulnerable is counterintuitive to the junior-high hallway I navigated with a pit in my
stomach, hoping that the popular girls would not give me a condescending
sneer or, even worse, that the "normal" kids would look at me vacantly. Being
dependent and in need is contrary to the university-campus mall I walked
down daily, past a sea of other disconnected faces pretending they knew
exactly where they were going and what they wanted out of life. And sadly,
being in need has been counterintuitive to many church gatherings, the hardest moment being the blank stares received after finally mustering up the
courage to talk about despairing thoughts, addictions, or struggle—shoot,
even when we express that we're just ticked off about something.

The second posture beckons with a false security, because it tells us that if
we are not vulnerable, we will not be hurt and that if we are vulnerable, we
will not be loved. Steel yourself to Dad's sarcasm by becoming sullen; figure
out a way to get through by constantly gauging and maneuvering; put on a

brave face; scoot out quickly to avoid the woman you know will have a pre-scription for your situation. We know we'd like to let down our defenses; the deepest recess of our hearts wants care, reassurance, companionship, love. But we've learned there are very few safe places to do so. To be childlike asks us to hold our vulnerable hearts before God as we give up on predicting or con-trolling how others will handle us.

Jesus's beckoning to come as vulnerable children—to stay in a posture that asks, seeks, and knocks—is not the sweet invitation we thought it was. It is in direct opposition to what the world usually asks of our hearts, and it does not fit our definition of a safe embrace. And yet this is his call. It invites us to expe-rience the same dependent humility—actually the same humiliation—that he experienced. *Oh no, it really is You, Jesus.*

Small Plates and Dignity

Asking out of our need is humbling. And it can be humiliating. These two words in the English language flow from the same Latin root. Recall the last time you felt humbled, and this is not surprising. I was reminded of this recently when I spent a few days in Aspen with two women I know. For me, Aspen conjures images of the beauty of Maroon Bells (several magenta, fourteen-thousand-feet peaks tucked in a valley full of wildflowers), Gucci, Armani, and cowboys. It is a strange blend of glitz and mud. But for all its international snobbery, Aspen is justifiably known for its fine amenities and good service. My friends and I were there in the off-season for two days of rest, especially Gwen, who had spent the past month in the hospital with her son fighting for his life. We were all fairly weary, and the thought of being "treated" sounded great to us. We hadn't made any reservations and decided to take the risk of walking around town and finding a restaurant sight unseen.

We ran across a restaurant we'd heard was wonderful, so we took a chance. We were so glad when the hostess told us there was one table left, and as we walked into the room, the table was illuminated as if to say, "I have been wait-ing for you." We were seated and were filled with anticipation. The waitress was lovely. She greeted us and stated the specials with aplomb, and we quietly perused the menu. None of us was starving, but we looked forward to a nice meal. We made that fateful choice we so often make: each to order something different and share.

The waitress returned with her expected glow. But when we decided not to order wine that night, it was clear she wasn't sure what to do. We proceeded to order our shared meal, and it was immediately obvious that this was unacceptable to the waitress, but she was going to show a reserve and cater to us anyway. She coldly walked away. We watched as she flitted from table to table around the beautifully lit room. But now when she approached us, a cold aura sent shivers down our spines.

What happened next blew my mind. All three of us started to converse about what had just happened. It was as if we were all in disbelief and wanted to confirm with each other that we hadn't imagined this shift in our waitress's demeanor. "Did you hear that? Did you sense that?" As we bantered in defense of our fragile egos, we were all geared up and ready to say something to the waitress and to ask for better treatment. But no! When the waitress returned to the table, we all sat in silence, cloth napkins on our laps, like shamed little girls.

The *pièce de résistance* came when the waitress brought our entrées and brazenly placed them in the middle of the table and then proceeded—and this is no exaggeration—to toss three plates, one for each of us. She did not place them; she tossed them as a gambler deals her cards. And what she dealt was not a dinner plate…but a small bread plate.

We were humiliated. But for all our bravado and talk, we froze. We continued through the evening, never saying a word to this woman who had stolen our delight. We went home deflated. We tried to rouse ourselves by bantering about her abusive behavior. But it was too late. We had allowed it to happen, and we were robbed.

The next night we had reservations at a place also recommended by friends. As we walked in, we had the same sensation of being welcomed. And, you guessed it, we were afraid the warmth would unravel as soon as the waiter saw that we were not "Aspen material."

But that did not happen. This evening, from beginning to end, was one of being doted on and served with great detail, and we enjoyed one of the most lavish meals of our lives (and, as a fun side note, I am certain I saw at least three famous faces). The turning point for us, though, was our waiter. He was so kind as we fumbled with the wine list. So attuned to our desires as we ordered. Every need was observed and met. That night we walked back to our room sated and silenced for the joy of being noticed and acknowledged.

Both nights spent in Aspen restaurants were nights spent at the mercy of others. We were dependent, whether we wanted to admit it or not. During our time surrounded by glamour and glitz, the treatment we received from each waiter and waitress was completely their choice. We were, in that sense, vulnerable to them.

As I think about this story, I know I had a choice. The choice was to admit my vulnerability and with childlike heart ask for something good ("Uh...do you think I could get a *big* plate for dinner?") or to allow a shadow to be cast on me. I had the choice to believe I was supposed to be or sound like or look like someone else. I had the choice to be shut down by the opinion of someone else. Sadly, I let myself be shut down. Children are rarely ashamed when asking for a Popsicle, a Band-Aid, or a bear hug. But the choice to flee from shame kept three grown women bound to the indignity of little plates.

What is this power that can shut up three normally confident, vocal women? At core, shame invites us away from asking, seeking, knocking for good things. Just hide. Don't ask. And it provides a great escape route from the foolishness, the embarrassing posture of being dependent. A friend of mine who has known much humiliation in life, brought on by his own wandering and by others' failures, said the other day, "I'm not afraid of shame anymore. It is what I do with the shame that matters." He's right. Jesus *hated* his shame; he endured the cross, despising the shame found in that most humiliating and vulnerable of places. But rather than fleeing from it, he leaned into it fully, for the joy set before him. For the joy of knowing you, he entered his shame and asked his Father to give full restoration to your heart.

The Laughter of Maturity

We like to think that as adults we have a "higher calling," a calling to be mature about the business of God and people and to be intentional and methodical in our purpose. We're to leave behind childish things, after all. Yes, we are called to maturity. But again, maybe we have our terms wrong. You can hear the difference between being childlike and being childish.

Maybe maturity is the kind of trust that prompts belly laughs for its absurdity. When the seemingly ridiculous promise of a child was made to ninety-nine-year-old Abraham and ninety-year-old Sarah, these patriarchs of the faith did not line up in front of the angel and thank him "maturely" for his proclamation. The accounts vary, but both of them laughed out loud—Abraham on his face, Sarah hiding behind the door. I have, at moments, tried to mimic the blend of mockery and disbelief in Sarah's voice as she laughed, and my friends say I do a pretty believable imitation—probably because I recognize this as the laugh inside my own heart at the thought of God's fulfillment of some of my dearest requests. Frederick Buechner says this:

> God intervened then and asked about Sarah's laughter, and Sarah was
> scared stiff and denied the whole thing. Then God said, "No, but you
> did laugh," and of course, he was right. Maybe the most interesting
> part of it all is that far from getting angry at them for laughing, God
> told them that when the baby was born he wanted them to name him
> Isaac, which in Hebrew means laughter. So you can say that God not
> only tolerated their laughter but blessed it and in a sense joined in it
> himself, which makes it a very special laughter indeed—God and man
> laughing together, sharing a glorious joke in which both of them are
> involved.[2]

Yes. This is a God who is willing to laugh with us, knowing his promises seem audacious to us. Only he can understand. It is a laughter that tells me, "I really do see how difficult it is to trust me, to follow me. But come along and do it anyway. There is something wonderful ahead." It is the cry of a Father to his child on the trail. "You really are strong." And we say, giggling, "Yes, yes I am." This laughter is the lightness and innocence of the buried life that is brought to the surface and freed into the atmosphere of childlike trust. This is the kind of maturity I want to grow into. It is just so tiring to live otherwise.

The Exhausting Process of Pushing Down Life

Think of it this way. It takes effort to be proud and self-sufficient and prideful. It takes effort to make the clatter—even noble, honest, worthless clatter—that drowns out the laughter-filled, this-is-so-absurd-but-God-is-asking-it-of-me kind of maturity. Why? Remember, whenever we shut out love, we are shutting down the truest thing going on inside of us.

Did you ever get a blister while hiking and try to ignore it? To do so you must shut out the pain. Do you ever try to keep pushing through a workweek on only a few hours of sleep? To do so you must push the blur away from your eyes. Do you ever wake up on a Saturday morning and try to ignore the smell of bacon? All of these things take energy, but they are nothing compared to the exhaustion of attempting to keep at bay the resurrection life of Christ that has raised us with him from the grave (Ephesians 2:5) and the fullness of the life and power of God that fills us who believe (3:19). It's a bit like trying to dam the Zambezi River. Good luck. We are alive in Christ, and when we expend our energy trying to deaden ourselves to this reality, we become hardened, bitter and plastic, but definitely not childlike. Love wants to care for us, to free us from our buried life. Love is the nudge that calls us to admit our need for a nap, a hug, and a snack; to receive a cup of cold water; to have our knees bandaged; to have our feet washed. And Love wants us to burst out laughing as we realize the crazy things he is saying about the path to fulfillment of his promises.

Deadened Senses and Self-Righteousness

Spiritual deadness, the buried life, looks different for all of us. "It is dullness, not doubt, that is the greatest enemy of faith," says Boston College's Peter Kreeft. The dull lull of trying to maintain the status quo of our hearts is more likely to harden us than any amount of honest questioning or contending with dark emotions toward God.

I met a man named Jim who told me how this played out for him more than two decades after he and his wife almost split up over her infidelity. Twenty years filled with days and hours of tears, confessions of failures by both of them, reaffirmation of their commitment, the extending of grace. In some ways, they were the model couple in how to weather the damage of betrayal. They faced their marriage honestly, got the help they needed, and committed to move ahead and put it all behind them.

Even in this, though, Jim nursed a deep, understandable anger toward his wife that was causing his heart to harden toward her. The problem was, he wanted so much to maintain the status quo of all the redemptive choices they had made as a couple. He didn't want to remember the betrayal. He didn't want to mess up the seemingly good future they were walking into, which even included other people privy to their story who were lauding them for their courage and godliness.

Just like any of us, Jim was able to live for a long time without realizing his heart was callous. A defining moment came when a younger couple asked Jim and his wife to share the details of their story with them, since they were facing something similar. Genuinely wanting to help, Jim listened as his wife spoke about the affair and what it had offered her. He listened as she described the failures that led up to it. These things stung again, of course, but what lanced the scab over Jim's hemorrhaging anger was watching as this young couple oohed and aahed over Jim's wife's courage to face her own life. They gushed over how courageous she was to share her mess with them; they profusely thanked her for being so honest. Jim was thrilled, in that moment, to see the sweet power of redemption for his wife. But as he walked away, he found himself seething. He went for a five-mile run, pushing harder with every mile. He found himself lashing into his wife in ways he never had.

Slowly the severity of the rage gave way long enough for Jesus to whisper, *So what is it that you need?*

"What do I need? What are you talking about God? I need to get back to a place where I don't remember all this pain. I shed blood in my relationship with this woman, and she comes off smelling like a rose. But this is ridiculous. It has been twenty years!"

What do you need?

Finally, after almost three days of hearing only this one question from God, Jim realized what it was. He needed his wife. Jim went out into the garden where she was pruning roses, and he confessed to her that all that emerged from the lancing, the remembering of their story, was too much for him to handle. He asked his wife to pray for him. They sat on a garden bench, and she prayed for the heart of her husband. Jim told me he has never felt so strong as he did in that one, vulnerable, humbling, and, yes, humiliating moment.

Drew and Trish's Story

The *kalangalang* noise inside the tomb of self-righteousness can take many forms, and it shows up in many moments. This grave is often the hardest to break out of because it looks so, well, good, moral, and honest. It is a shell of great-looking appearances, even friend to friend. But thankfully, as Canon Barnett's billboard said of our spiritual life, "It is buried, but not dead. When it really hears God's voice it *will* rise. Men will live spiritual as well as honest lives. They will rest on Some One greater than themselves and have peace."[3] A conversation with another couple comes to mind.

I can still hear the condescending tone in Trish's voice. "How can you *possibly* think of God in that way?" she wanted to know. I had, a few moments before, wondered out loud about how sad God must feel over a struggle they were having. Drew echoed her disbelief, "How can a sovereign God possibly be moved by us?" This couple sat with me, incredulous that I would suggest God might actually be impacted—stirred, moved—by *them*. Displeased, maybe, but not sad, not impacted. They were defending God and all they had come to know intellectually about his immovable attributes, and as they did so, it was clear they felt obedient. So why did they sound so smug?

Here is the dilemma of true listening: are we listening in order to respond with our hearts, or are we robotically rattling off what we "know" to be true?

Sitting with Trish and Drew, I felt a bit like George MacDonald when he wrote to his niece, "The whole mischief has come of people setting themselves to understand rather than to do, to arrange God's business for him, and tell other people what the Father meant, instead of doing what the Father tells them, and then teaching others to do the same."[4] Something dry happens when we stop listening and start to presumptuously instruct. For Drew and Trish, God had become so impersonal in his sovereign holiness that considering his heart *for them* was no longer relevant; all they had to do was salute him and defend him. Their hearts were not involved in listening to his voice, because they were preoccupied with defending a tightly held theological position about him. Always an irony, isn't it? God gets lost in the process of our trying to defend him.

It was a tough moment for me. I respected these people; our conversations had gone in some good directions. It was their pious moralizing that saddened me. In their smaller battle of defending God through upholding "right theology," they had missed the point of all their "facts on paper." The sovereignty of God opens up greater depths of freedom and intimacy than we could ever imagine. But that was just it. They were not looking for intimacy; they were looking for a God they could define and outline. The deadening of this couple did not come from their convictions about theology. If theology—the way we view God—is correct, then he will be bigger, more vast, more past finding out than we ever imagined. He will be revealed in his Son, the Lord Jesus Christ, who said he came to give life to the full. He will be the man who defeats death by a power that shouts to all darkness that it no longer can lay claim to those who follow him. He will be the God who defies all cultural, social, and political boundaries in order to seek out those who know simply that they are thirsty for forgiveness and a healing touch. I love how Craig Barnes articulates this: "Jesus, the coming Judge, chose to descend into the ambiguities of compromised, complicated and conflicted lives. Jesus called people to be righteous, but he despised those who had become professionals at it."[5]

Again, true listening obedience asks everything of us because it is responsive. *Explaining* God asks only that we be good students of facts. MacDonald goes on to say, "I say your definiteness is one that God does not care about, for he has given no such system [of explaining God] as you desire."[6] Surely this is something of what Jesus had in mind when he said to the most religious people of his day: "You search the Scriptures because you believe they give you eternal life. But the Scriptures point to me! Yet you refuse to *come to me* so that I can *give you* this eternal life" (John 5:39–40, emphasis added).

It is hard to ask with the needy heart of a child—to be loved, to be given to, to stay responsive to God's care. And it's humbling to admit all our talk and labor and work for God are worth "notting, if I no mo love." Larry Crabb reminds us that infants don't just sit around sweetly longing. No, they fill their diapers and squawk and scream until they get what they cannot provide for themselves.[7] Their middle-of-the-night bellowing is a picture of what Jesus— the Son in whom the Father was pleased, whom we are told to listen to—says must be true of us in order to receive the kingdom of heaven.

Think about it. How often in the past week have you known the freedom in your soul to pitch a fit—a screaming desperation that says, "I don't know how you are going to do it, but I cannot do anything for myself here, and I am starving, so you had better come through for me!" Isn't it easier—more dignified and predictable—to teach, inform, and defend? Thomas Kelly said,

> I am persuaded that religious people do not with sufficient seriousness count on God as an active factor in the affairs of the world. "Behold, I stand at the door and knock," but too many well-intentioned people are so preoccupied with the clatter of efforts to do something for God that they don't hear him asking that he might do something through them.[8]

I would add that we don't hear him asking if he might do something *in* us. *What do you need?*

The words of Scripture can be managed and manipulated and explained. The Word made Flesh must be encountered and responded to—with desperate, middle-of-the-night cries.

The Response of Sorrow

In the community where I received much of my training, we had a little saying: "It is much worse than you think." This may sound cynical at first, but in
actuality it's encouraging. Years ago I was just beginning to recognize how I
tried to take care of everyone; as long as I could be "helpful," I felt secure and
worth something. I was just beginning to see that most of my giving was done
for myself, not for others. Rather than simply admit this was true and go to
God with a heart desiring forgiveness, I started to focus on the failure. I was
thoroughly disgusted with myself, saying things to myself such as, *Can you
believe what a hypocrite you are, thinking you speak for God, thinking of yourself
as helpful when it's really all about you? You are pathetic.* So when a friend told
me as I was on a rampage with my soul, "It is much worse than you think," I
was silenced. He was right. My determination to take care of myself was much
worse than I realized. Not only did the way I handle relationships reflect a self-
sufficiency, but my response to realizing this was to become more determined
to chide myself, pressure myself, and demand that I do better.

What a familiar trap for us, isn't it? When we grieve over our sin, we admit
our need for the Holy Spirit's work to produce the change we cannot produce
on our own. But when we are disgusted with ourselves, we're just ticked that
we couldn't come up with a way to "do it right," to please God, to change. I'm
often disgusted with myself that I'm not more loving and more attuned to my
friends or God's work in their lives. I'm often disgusted with myself that I don't
hear clearly or see clearly or know what to say or do to encourage someone I
love. In this disgust, I join a dark, dissonant chorus, blending the noise of my
heart with the dark noise that condemns, accuses, and seeks to keep me from
God's love. Ignatius of Loyola, the founder of the Benedictine order, said it this
way: "In those who are making spiritual progress, the action of the good angel
is gentle, light, and sweet, as a drop of water entering a sponge. The action of
the evil spirit is sharp, noisy, and disturbing, like a drop of water falling upon
a rock."[9]

When the apostle Paul wrote to the Corinthian church—a church
infected with immorality, and more importantly, a callous heart about their

immorality—he told them that their sadness over their wandering would take them, as children, to the Father. Imagine a Corinthian Christian responding with, "Oh my goodness. He's discovered what we're really like. I'm so embarrassed…can't look him in the eye…had better make sure that I, we, get our act together before he comes around again, checking on us." You can imagine that Paul would feel a bit like a camp counselor walking in on a cabin full of boys who quickly shove a *Playboy* under the sheet of the bunk. There's not much of a distinction, really, between Adam's "I was afraid because I was naked; so I hid" (Genesis 3:10, NIV) and "I'm determined to get it right the next time—or at least not to be seen while I'm failing."

No, it was godly sorrow—sadness over their flight from Love—that would bring change to the Corinthians. They did not allow a downcast gaze to keep them from the warm embrace of their friend Paul, who loved them, so they admitted their need. Can you hear how rare that response is? Our first inclination when caught in sin is to feel ashamed and humiliated rather than sad. If there is no other proof of the reality and work of the Spirit of Christ in this world, it is seen in us when, rather than scrambling and being shamed, we are children who stop and think, *Jesus knows something I don't about how hurtful—to him and to me—this thing is that I'm doing. Maybe I'm not as grown-up and independent as I think I am. He's caught me. But look, he doesn't turn away. In fact, he is laughing. He's not mocking me; He's laughing with me. He's laughing because I don't realize there is a feast being thrown for me (with big plates!).*

Paul said to the Christians in Ephesus, "Do not bring sorrow to God's Holy Spirit by the way you live" (Ephesians 4:30). He tells them to throw off their old nature (verse 22). Notice he does not say, "Overcome your old nature." The idea is this: the things that bring sorrow to God are just there—admit it. Now take off those things like an old coat, because they don't fit you anymore.

SURPRISING DELIVERANCE

The remarkable thing about Love is that it comes to those of us who, in hardened hearts of false piety, haven't discovered our true hunger yet. Let's go back to Drew and Trish. They had given themselves over to prescribed, false obedience, so there was little need in their lives as far as they could see. So what entered their polished tomb and exposed their need and God's love?

Would you believe it was by talking honestly about sex? God used sex—or better said, their struggles with sex—to drown out the clatter of religious pride. A rich relationship with God came slowly, by listening to all that wasn't in their sexual relationship. Self-righteousness is, for all of us, such an effective shield against true desire—and against true need. When the surface was scratched just a bit, all was not well for this well-polished couple. She had been having a cyberaffair in a chat room for months. He knew about it but had remained silent. While playing the role of pillars in their church and community, she suffered silently each time they were intimate because of extreme fear; he suffered rejection and frustration. As they began to honestly face and talk about the needs they each had, something began to change. They both felt a quiet "Oh good, it is you, Jesus. Oh good, the things that matter to my heart really do matter to you. In fact, you want to surface the things that truly matter to me in order to remind me how much I need you."

The Fight for Our Hearts

The good news for all of us is that our hearts, and therefore our *desire and need* for God, will find us. We were made for intimacy. When we suppress godly sensuality through self-righteousness, dark passions will rise up to take its place. The data in mental-health circles is pretty solid that abuse and addictions are rampant in home and church environs that are legalistic or overly prohibitive. It is a clear picture that our hearts were made for him, and as the beloved children of God, we will not be able to rest in the prison of stale passion. Howard Macy says, "Religion without passion is a deadly fraud. Without urgency or desire, faith neither lives nor gives life."[10]

But this does not come without a fight. This fight is usually between something that Jesus says and a commitment we make not to respond to what he is saying (sometimes referred to as vows or agreements). What Jesus says about us through the whole story line of Scripture is that we are completely dependent upon his care, provision, forgiveness, protection, and guidance. We began in a place of dependent trust: "You may freely eat of any fruit in the garden except the fruit from the tree of the knowledge of good and evil. If you eat of its fruit, you will surely die" (Genesis 2:16–17), and everything God tells us this side of the garden echoes the loving intentions of keeping us dependent.

Responding to this is always risky and vulnerable. The commitments we make to ignore Love's voice can be manipulated, making us feel in control and making God seem unnecessary. Trish had shut down her legitimate, vulnerable desire ("I long to be known by my husband") and had exchanged it for a more manageable demand ("I will connect *somehow*"). The demand was easy to fulfill through her own maneuvering; it didn't take much to track down a willing soul in the unengaged world of the Internet.

Drew had made an equally destructive choice. He had replaced what he really wanted ("I want so much to know that I am making a difference in your life, that you are impacted by me"—the vulnerable choice) with a destructive internal vow ("I will hide my strength and *will not be shamed* again, therefore I will not fight for relationship").

Paul tells us that godlessness will "suppress the truth in unrighteousness" (Romans 1:18, NKJV). Choosing to live under destructive vows had the same effect for Drew and Trish; they were suppressing the truth and choosing a lie. The truth of their vibrant, sensual desire was shut down, so obedience was suppressed. Drew and Trish were no longer obedient to God because they were no longer receptive to God or each other. And as long as they weren't receptive, they had no need at all—no need for each other, no need for God, no need for any resources except the ones they could come up with. And all they could come up with was more theology. A flimsy shell filled with noise.

Change came as they began instead to listen to their hearts, as they began to allow Love to reveal who they really are—passionate and full of desire for intimacy with each other. As they confronted what was getting in the way of this, they slowly allowed their shells to crack. Trish risked exploring past harm that made sex shameful and ambivalent for her. She helped Drew understand the ways she needed him to care for her in those hard moments. Drew risked expressing the hurt he had felt from Trish's rejections in the past and how he needed her to allow him to care for her. The darkness of their tomb filled with light as they admitted to each other and to God just how much they needed. They hadn't realized how much they had been trying to make it in their own individual strength.

The Risk

What a risky, painful process. But it is worth it. How frightening it was for this couple to hear God say to them, "I want you to listen to how much you want from and with each other. I want you to have great sex, and even more, I want you to know that your hearts are with each other." It was unthinkable. But this pious couple swallowed hard and found the courage to lean in and say, "We don't fully understand where you are taking us, Jesus. But okay, here we go." That's obedience. And this is what Trish says now:

> I now know that God sees me not stained and dirty, but beautiful and
> full of potential. I have learned that I am not justified by my proper
> theology, not sanctified by the death of my desires, and not purified by
> locking away memories of the past. I am no longer a slave to my story;
> I am freed by the endless pursuit of the lover of my soul.

What sensuality in her words! I asked them what caused the change. After a lengthy, solemn silence, they both said, "Our desire." And then they giggled like children. They had admitted their thirst and started to squirm with innocent need. They had listened to Love and had somehow, mysteriously, become childlike again.

It is a mystery. Love's call comes from a God humble enough to stand vulnerable before his accusers, abandoned in the garden, agonizing alone while his friends start to snore. It comes from a Love willing to be humiliated. It is a God willing to suffer the rejection that comes from giving us the freedom to love him. This God is simply past explaining. He must be *responded* to, not defended. And we cannot fully respond to him until we stop trying to speak for him.

Love asks for our dependence. Jesus invites us either to bow to shame or to be released into the freedom of godly sorrow with its desperate, middle-of-the-night cries and the wonderful, surprising embrace found just around the corner.

Four

LISTENING TO EACH OTHER

Relinquishing Our Autonomy

I can't *hear* you!
—SERGEANT CARTER to Gomer Pyle

We must prophesy, not simply to change the world,
but to prevent the world from changing us.
—HENRI NOUWEN

On my drive to work, I hear so many voices. It all sounds like background noise until I tune in to what each voice is trying to say. One voice tells me that if don't have a conservative view toward current foreign policy, I am "mindless and not thinking clearly." Another voice tells me that sexual experimentation outside of marriage is a great way to heat things up with a spouse. Another has bad news for me concerning my investments. Suddenly, without realizing it, the voices are more familiar, more intimate. I replay a conversation—actually an argument—I had with my dad. My heart tunes in to a familiar sigh, a sadness that we've found ourselves, once again, in a place that neither of us wants to be with the other. I replay sentences from the conversation until once again a particularly loud radio voice tells me that if I don't agree with legalizing homosexual marriages, I am a narrow-minded, bigoted, mean-spirited person. Later, a softer voice sings a beautiful song, but by the end of the drive, I want to take a shower. I wonder if I focused on anything that gave me life or reminded me of Love.

Voices careen into each other in the wilderness of my culture, all begging for attention. Think of the divergent voices in a day that I either tune in or tune out in order to discern the one voice that causes me to ask, "Is it you, Jesus?" Peter Jennings, Aaron Brown, Macy Gray, David Letterman, Oliver North, Sting, Kofi Annan, Colin Powell, Bill Maher, the president, Rush Limbaugh, Marilyn Manson, Billy Graham, Martin Luther King Jr., Franklin Roosevelt, Hitler, Marilyn Monroe, Billy Crystal. Can you hear them? I've never met them, but, like you, I know their background noise in my life. And, like you, I tune in most to the closer, more resonant voices of my family and friends. Your spouse, children, parents, and friends either pierce or bless you with words that carry particular weight for your heart. My sister's voice can put wind in my sails one week and deflate me the next.

So if the people in my life have power to bless or harm, why do I give the choice of whom to listen to about as much energy as I put into moving through a salad bar? Make a bad choice? That's okay. Just go back for something else. What is going on when I tune in to what my heart is saying about my relationship with my father only until I'm interrupted by a bombastic radio personality? Some days I'm too lazy to change the radio station. Some days I choose not to pursue a friend about what she really meant in a conversation or to ask my pastor to interact about something unsettling in the sermon. But most of the time I'm simply overwhelmed. Too many voices. Too few filters. So much so, I end up tuning out everything and everyone, including those I love, for a while. You can probably relate. We've got a problem in discerning which voice to take in, listen to, and follow.

LISTENING IN

Jesus was the Word made flesh so we could hear his voice guiding us into all truth. *Listen to me,* he says, *for the life of your soul is at stake.* He seems to think this problem is a matter of life and death, at least for our hearts. He knows that the question "Is it you, Jesus?" is the most important one we can ask. And he wants us to discover that sometimes the answer is found in those around us.

My brother Dick discovered this when he was given the words you never think you will hear. The radiation oncologist was sober, direct, and kind as he told Dick that his life was limited, that his cancer was incurable. Though his symptoms and the initial tests pointed in this direction, in the shock of a conversation like that, only a few words make it through clearly. Cancer. Metastatic. Liver. Incurable. Lymph nodes. Bones. What follows is a literal barrage of information: each specialist has a different idea about which palliative treatment is best; each nurse has his own "off the record" comment that leaves you puzzled. And then a stream of kind and wonderfully intentioned souls bring their own take on nutrition, health, prayer, and spiritual needs.

In the midst of this onslaught of voices, one particularly poignant moment came for Dick. As the gravity of the news started to sink in, he realized that fighting for life is one thing and trying to discern how best to spend his days is another. Aggressive chemotherapy and radiation to reduce the foreign growths with a goal to make him more comfortable, or forgoing these treatments and their nausea in order for him to be more comfortable? How should he ask people to pray? Should they pray for the miracle of healing or for the miracle of having strength to endure?

As he contended with these questions, Jim and Karen, who are friends to me but virtual strangers to Dick, came onto the scene. They showed up at Dick's house one day when a group gathered to pray for Dick, who doesn't particularly enjoy either gatherings of people or being the center of attention. Jim, an imposing man in stature, arrived at Dick's house donning his beaded skullcap, his trademark hat in the midst of therapy for his own incurable cancer. When he saw Dick, he said, "There's Dick, my homeboy!" and then proceeded over the next few hours to offer his presence and experience to Dick in a way that only one who has walked that road possibly could. Jim knew what it was to hear the word *incurable*. Jim knew the dark road ahead, chemotherapy or not. Jim knew what it was to be dying, and he knew what it was to continue to fight for life. When Jim and Karen heard about Dick through the grapevine of my social circle, they couldn't wait to get to him, simply because they knew. Without trying, they offered a voice that would matter so much to him. They came with the sensitivity of those who suffer, and they came with the hope of those who have not been crushed by suffering. The moments of asking, "Is it you, Jesus?" when contending with the fact that this would be Dick's final road found a fledgling answer as these two men, fighting a similar fight, knelt on the ground to pray, to face the One who was asking this of them. Jesus was responding, *It's me. I'm here. And I'm showing up to be with you through this man you barely know.*

Messages of Love

We need each other. Obviously this is more than a Hallmark card sentiment. It would be more accurate to say there are times we cannot hear God when listening only through our own ears. Isn't it wild that God would allow our feeble human voices—trembling, weak, and full of error—to speak his words? Isn't it crazy that he would use our ears—overburdened, selective, and foggy—to clarify his voice?

I think of myriad people who have been the voice of Love to me through the years. It sounds trite, but I honestly don't know where I would be if it weren't for them. Ms. Benjamin, a kind fifth-grade teacher, noticed that I might be having a hard time at home and became this message: "Someone sees you." Lisa, a friend from high school, came from a broken and alcoholic home, yet she would let me sit by her side on a piano bench as she sang, not about, but to the God to whom she clung. She ushered in the message "This is not all there is." My friend Lynne, amid her life-threatening battle with anorexia, showed me care and understanding as I struggled with my own eating disorder in college. She brought the message "There can be healing." Little Musa in Swaziland taught me about gratitude from his mud hut and wheelchair. My friend Vivian taught me about courage. After witnessing many family members being bludgeoned for their faith in Christ, she fled with her sister on foot through the bush of Central Africa to avoid Idi Amin's rampage. A man I know has trusted me enough to share the quiet torment of depression, helping me understand what it takes for some people to make it through the day.

When I scan these scenes from my life, again I find that the most powerful voices have been unintentional in their impact. The voices that matter the most are usually the ones who aren't trying.

THE CALL TO LISTEN AND THE CALL TO SPEAK

The "oh no" comes when we realize what is being asked of us in order to let Jesus speak through other people. It also comes when we're asked to let Jesus speak through us. Whether receiving the voice or being the voice, the "oh no" times keep us on our toes, dependent.

My brother had to let strangers into his life during his most vulnerable time, when it would have been easier to cloister and ruminate about the bad news. During the past many years, the voices of friends have nudged me to realize that the writing and speaking I do has an eternal purpose and I must continue even though I'd rather be home "baking bread, having sex, and doing a little writing on the side" (my self-proclaimed, futuristic mission statement). I am fiercely independent, and I have to let that independence go in order to listen to the voice of God through my friends.

The "oh no" also comes when we're asked to enter into every interaction, every relationship, with a fresh need to hear from God. Book knowledge, prescribed answers, even our experience with others in the past may not be what the heart in front of us needs. "Oh no, Jesus. I don't know what to do. You want me to walk close to your heart, so the way I respond to others reflects your heartbeat. Only you know whether silence or words are necessary. Only you know what this person in my life most needs. You want to offer your love even when there is nothing to say and no way to be helpful." The voice of Jesus keeps me on my toes, on behalf of others.

I felt this as I counseled two couples in one week who had similar scenarios in their lives. The data on paper was the same, the names changed to confound the counselor. Each wife had discovered her husband was being unfaithful to her with a friend. Each husband had a history of being overly dutiful and compliant and had bowed to his wife's wishes for years. It was a wild déjà vu experience for me, that is for sure. So what was I being called to? I was being called to listen carefully to what Jesus wanted for each of them individually. If I had pulled out the "counselor's manual on marital infidelity" or if I had dealt with one couple based on how the other couple responded, I would have missed their hearts. I had to listen carefully to them and for them.

Parents know what this is like. When my friend Beth relates to her daughter Jessica during a heartache, she does so with the voice and intent that comes from studying Jess over seventeen years. When Beth relates to her other daughter, Emily, the voice is Emily-specific. Love pauses, studies, listens, and finds a way to speak the language of the beloved.

How We Handle Each Other—with Space

How well we study and listen to each other sometimes determines how well the voice of Jesus is heard through us.

Please indulge me another story concerning my friend Brent and the days after his death, as they were full of treasure. Soon after Brent died, the veil of shock parted long enough to allow me to get away to regroup and refresh. I headed for the mountains by myself. As I did this, I was caught off guard—in a good way and in a bad way.

One evening at a small country hotel, as the scorch of the day gave way to refreshing pockets of cool summer air, I eased into a conversation with some strangers around a picnic table. They were kind, well-meaning folks who seemed eager to swap historical data, the normal vacation chitchat. As the conversation unfolded, we discovered our common faith. A comfort, I thought, in my fragile state to run across folks who would understand the hope of Christ. With unsteady spontaneity, I mentioned to them why I was out traveling by myself, needing time to grieve. Their response was not unkind, but it was scripted and disengaged, a well-rehearsed litany of God's being in control of all things. "What a tragedy for you. We are so, so sorry. You must be so glad to know he is in such a better place. And goodness, you have to be so glad that you'll look back and see all the reasons for this."

I cherish God's sovereignty, but there is truth in the proverb "Like vinegar on soda, is one who sings songs to a heavy heart" (Proverbs 25:20, NKJV). Their automatic response left me disheartened, wondering, "Did you even hear me? Were you *listening?*" Why did their words not bring comfort? Why did these folks leave me more weary than before? I certainly was not anticipating complete strangers to fully enter my grief; they were on vacation after all. So what was my problem?

Later that day at natural hot springs surrounded by granite, aspen, and deep blue sky, my mind wandered into much-needed oblivion. After a time I barely overheard a conversation that indicated to me the crowd sharing my sulfur-soda-near-nirvana was a Christian family. *Oh great,* I thought, feeling a twinge of guilt for my immediate rush to judgment and cynicism left over from my earlier interaction. I decided to keep my mouth shut, feeling that my heart could bear no more. They continued their conversation, and each sentence made my silence more of a struggle. Their daughter attended my alma mater. They spoke of South Africa, where I had lived for several years. I knew the lack of coincidence was compelling me to say hello, but I didn't have the energy. No matter, because the wife greeted me first. Our conversation quickly turned to things of faith. *That's fine,* I thought. *I'll let them talk but keep my grief to myself.* As the conversation unfolded, this kind woman stated that she was in the middle of reading the best book, called *The Sacred Romance* (the book Brent had coauthored), and she asked if I was familiar with it and wasn't it sad how one of the authors had died. I was stunned. I started to weep with this complete stranger. And with these tears I experienced Christian hope with another believer. She did nothing but look at me, tears welling in her own eyes. She said, "I can see you knew him. I'm so sorry. I'll leave you to have some time to yourself. We'll be over there if you care to join us later."

What a kind gift. It was not the providential meeting (though that tasted sweet) that poured life into my weary soul, prompting hope to rise up as a wellspring. It was the simple, loving presence of this woman who didn't know me but who *heard* me. She was listening. She didn't presume to know, and she didn't presume to have a perspective that would ease my pain. She listened with her heart, and in leaving me alone, she gave her presence to a stranger. So like Jesus.

The point is not that Christians perfectly handle those in pain. But can we lament that we who are most equipped to provide a sensitive presence of Love too often steal its beauty by not listening? We speak too quickly in order to keep from entering into his suffering with another. We would rather answer suffering than enter it. The whole encounter underscored Henri Nouwen's words: "The whole meaning of Christian community lies in offering each other a space in which we wait for what we have already seen."[1] The woman at the hot springs joined me in my waiting. She offered me space as she ached with me and listened to how God would have her respond. She was obedient, and I was the stranger she invited in.

How We Handle Each Other—with Respect

I sat around a dinner table listening to my father speak of his involvement at the end of WWII in the Manhattan Project. I'd heard the story hundreds of times, but as he shared this familiar piece of family history with some guests, I heard something new. What strengthened his heart was not so much the work itself, though the race against the Nazi war machine and the pressure to unlock the secrets of uranium and plutonium and the newly unleashed power of a split atom were a thrilling context for a young man in the secret city of Los Alamos, a mountain community where even his young bride, my mother, couldn't visit. No, it was the mission and the way the mission was led by Robert Oppenheimer that, after fifty-five years, still thrilled Dad's senses. Dad speaks of Oppenheimer ("Oppy," as he was known through the ranks of the project) with great respect and admiration. He was the brilliant physicist who was selected, through conversations between Albert Einstein and Theodore Roosevelt, to lead the civilian and scientific aspects of the project. A lithe, quiet humanist who was antithetical to the bellowing, bellicose General Groves, who led the military aspects of the project with an iron fist, Oppenheimer led the project with an attitude of respect for all voices.

What meant so much to Dad was the colloquial manner in which Oppenheimer brought together all the scientific minds from several major national laboratories, several nations, and several bodies of research and knowledge.

And he did this by simply making sure that every person—whether physicist, chemist, engineer, or technician—knew his ideas and opinions mattered. General Groves had wanted each division of the project to work separately, focusing on their own aspect without interaction with the rest of the community. Oppenheimer knew that if the secret was to be unlocked, it would happen in a context where all ideas and thoughts and knowledge were given freedom of expression. Dad watched as countless times a certain group of scientists would get hung up on a particular formula, and another group of folks from a completely unrelated field would say, "Have you tried this?" Sure enough, it would be the thing that was needed. The freedom was such that, as Manhattan Project folklore goes, it was a guy squeezing an orange and thinking, *Hey, this is what we are after!* that helped this gathering of international geniuses to envision an implosion type of detonation—something that had never been done before.

Would they have achieved their goal without this forum of listening? Of course no one can say, but it was the listening that allowed everyone's gifts—everyone's voice—to be a part of the mission. If any one voice had been predominant, the mission would have suffered.

How We Handle Each Other—Without Possessiveness or Pride

To handle the gifts, movements—and people—of God with such a free hand! What is it about us that once something beautiful or new begins to occur, we want to corral it, bottle it, keep it for ourselves or our own little group? We miss so much when we do this. George MacDonald once wrote to his wife when they were experiencing a movement of God in his community, "Our great danger is of acting on feeling as a party…. We ought never to wish to overcome because *we* are the fighters. Never feel—there is *my* Truth—the hardest lesson to learn."[2] If we don't listen to divergent, even contrary, voices, we can miss the voice of Love and follow other voices down a path cluttered with confusion and deception about ourselves and our God.

It takes many forms. The first is in thinking that our way is the only way. Indeed, what we've been given may be uniquely powerful, but could it be that the person who does not respond to *that* way may have something equally important to give to the bigger picture?

There's a little, repeated phrase in the book of Revelation: "Anyone who is willing to hear should listen to the Spirit and understand what the Spirit is saying to the churches" (Revelation 2:11). The churches being spoken to were a mixed bag, but Love was speaking to them all. Who is being addressed is a mystery, but the message is clear: they are a blend of glory and mess, and Jesus is faithful to them, no matter his grievance with them. Muse with me a minute about these churches. The church at Ephesus is lauded for its hard work, perseverance, and willingness to suffer (perhaps overloaded with missionaries, clergy, counselors, Peace Corps workers) but chided for doing all that hard work without their first love. For those in Smyrna, who are persecuted and impoverished, wealth and the crown of life are coming (I can't help but think of believers in China, Nepal, Kazakhstan). Those in Pergamum—said to be located at the very throne of Satan—have remained loyal to the point of martyrdom, but they tolerate those who trip up others (an understandable mistake given the spiritual oppression they must have felt). Sardis worked hard not to soil her white garments but had a reputation for being alive when she was really dead (the so-called religious right?). Thyatira, full of love, faith, and service, allowed idol worship and sexual sin (a vast number of Christians in the West, me included). God calls those in Philadelphia "the ones I love," saying they are protected from testing. And the more familiar Laodicea, who is neither hot nor cold, think they are rich when they are wretched and miserable and poor and blind and naked.

One church is asked to turn from its indifference; one is asked to turn from its feeling of being abandoned; one is asked to turn from its dullness to sin; one is asked to remember they are beloved. Sometimes I think I'm a member of each church described in any given week! The point is, none of us, none of our groups or movements, has a monopoly on the truth. We each have our strong points and our blind spots. Only Christ himself can guide us into the full Truth. MacDonald, again, says,

Every higher stage of Truth brings with it its own Temptation like that in the Wilderness, and if one overcomes not in that, he overcomes not at all. The struggle may be hard. I would I could be sure of the struggle, and then I should of the victory. But Jesus overcame in the truest spiritual fight—So shall we overcome, too. Our God will surely help us attain to that which he himself loves most.[3]

We are myopic creatures. Sometimes when I am in Sam's Club and see the wire rack of Christian books marked down for quick sale, I get a glimpse of how much we try to see faith through a Western, modern, evangelical frame of reference. Thankfully the quick sale rack doesn't contain the writings of saints from the fourteenth through sixteenth centuries. The major themes of Christianity, after all, have been handed down by Love from group to group, century to century.

There is nothing wrong with being Western. I'm grateful for it every time I'm at the store and have a gazillion choices for cereal. There's nothing wrong with having a contemporary lens; we are living in the twenty-first century, after all. But our view becomes stunted and distorted if we see our faith only through this limited lens. We read what the apostle Paul has to say about our being one body and many members of that body—all equal in significance and equal in the functioning of the whole—yet in our pride we think of this only within our own little spheres (1 Corinthians 12:12–30).

C. S. Lewis speaks of an inner circle that begins to develop in every community or group—the mindset that some are "in" and some are "out." A spiritualized version of that is to think that our truth is "it" and others' perspectives are "missing it."[4] What would it be like for our group to consider itself the little toe on the body, while the group we are most ready to dismiss has some heart or lung function that we are sorely without and don't even realize it? We forget that Christianity did not begin with our group, our culture, even our generation. Carol Davis said, "Don't give yourself too fully to your generation lest you become a widow."[5] Stated another way: when we listen only to what our present society, time, church, or movement has to say, we lose. We lose our history, our foundation, our mission, our focus, our passion, and our authenticity. And we lose our heritage. I want to know that a conversation I have with someone today might affect a generation twenty-five years from now. I need to know the craziness of writing a book might reflect the face of Jesus for someone down the line, just as I rely on saints of old to instruct me on what I'm missing in my current spiritual language. Few things could cause me to despair more than to think that Christianity as it represented in the language of my culture in this decade is all there is. Is Christianity in your neighborhood and community, this year, a language expressing the fullness of God?

LISTENING TO THE POWER OR POISON OF INFLUENCE

Because we need each other so much in order to hear Love, and because each little voice is necessary in order to get the full Truth, it shouldn't surprise us that the temptation that comes to us is to be or have the most influential voice.

Anyone who has lived through the impact of interpersonal blowups knows it is not too strong to compare them to a destructive explosion. When any of us tries to "capture" the voice of Love rather than respond to it, countless people are left shocked, numb, and bewildered. Something life-giving becomes the catalyst for explosive harm. For example, I love it when someone says, "I love what you wrote about…" But a string of those moments over time tempts my heart to pride. It makes me want to "write with impact" instead of writing from my heart and leaving whatever impact there may be to the Spirit. No wonder there is a warning in the book of James for anyone who has influence through his words, for anyone who comes to love her influence more than the message. Influence can be a powder keg detonated by the once-thought-innocent tongue, and it can leave ashes of relationships and the coated veil of disillusionment. Hear the difference between that kind of harmful power and the power of a stranger in a hot spring who had influence simply because she was listening to Love and not trying to influence?

I live in a world of words and people. The circles I've run in put a high premium on relationship and teaching about relationship. And I've known some pretty rare people—each one expanding my heart. I've watched young families uproot from the American dream to serve in places of need. I've seen older couples following God's voice—sometimes from continent to continent—teaching and influencing. Eager friends from college have blossomed into theologians, pastors, and teachers. I've been spoiled being around some of the keenest minds in the world of spiritual direction and counseling. I've known people in publishing, social work, political activist groups, corporate leadership. The common thread woven through each is their influence over peoples' lives. And sadly, there's another common thread: the blowups and falling-outs, the severed relationships. In the fabric of the relational human heart, influence seems to be the thread that can cause discoloration and the unraveling of the fabric unless it is handled with the greatest of care.

So the question becomes, Why do people with good intentions and a desire to love suddenly find themselves in the midst of strife-filled, ugly, interpersonal problems that hinder their effectiveness and shroud the beauty they were intended to display? What is Love trying to say as we survey the damage? James 3:1–4:17 offers a look at the disruption that takes place specifically among influential leaders and teachers due to internal and external forces. Fallout in relationships occurs when humility is pushed aside and false wisdom—a wisdom that is rooted in envy and selfish ambition—is relied upon. Simply put, one woman wants to be "the one" whom people seek out for advice about parenting; another woman wants to be more creative than her fellow author. One man wants to be more astute and effective than the other guy; another man sees people respond to his visionary leadership abilities and begins to forget the people in his life who aren't in a position to applaud him.

This stuff doesn't show up overnight or in overt ways. The "earthly wisdom" attitude percolates over time in words spoken to and against another person. These words have the power of destruction in them. You can hear the mockery—the Word speaks life; false wisdom breeds words that destroy "in the name of Love." Without humility, those of us who believe we are acting in wisdom are in fact being propelled by dark forces, resulting in disrupted unity and "confusion and every evil thing" (James 3:16, NKJV). When confusion and strife show up, Love is pleading for us to love the Word more than the power of our words. Again, Ignatius's thoughts ring true: when strife is present, the dark spirit doesn't sound like water hitting a rock, because our own spirit is filled with the noise of ambition. James writes particularly to those in a position of influence, emphasizing that when selfish attitudes are not dealt with, confusion will be the inevitable end. Humility is the only attitude that crushes the destructive blast of selfish ambition.

It would take a separate book to think through what it is to be humble. But it was the attitude in Jesus, who wasn't swayed by his influence and position but "emptied himself, taking the form of a servant," the attitude that welcomed a desperate woman as she matted her hair with tears at his feet (Philippians 2:7, RSV; Luke 7:38). It is the fragrance of heaven given up for soiled straw. It is why the most verbose journalists shut up when they were around Mother Teresa. It is what Aleksandr Solzhenitsyn experienced when his keen mind finally had no answers for the atrocities he had witnessed in the gulag and, more important, no answers for the impotence of his own influence:

> You have come to realize your own weakness—and you can therefore understand the weakness of others. And be astonished at another's strength.… In the intoxication of youthful successes I had felt myself to be infallible, and I was therefore cruel. In the surfeit of power I was a murderer, and an oppressor. In my most evil moments I was convinced that I was doing good, and I was well supplied with systematic arguments. And it was only when I lay there on rotting prison straw that I sensed within myself the first stirrings of good.[6]

I think of Karen, a woman I respect who was at a gathering where we were discussing the truth in 1 John that there is no fear in love, that perfect love casts out all fear. We also discussed Paul's prayer in Ephesians 3 that we would all be able to grasp how loved we are and, therefore, have the power to love. We reflected quietly on this for a while, and then Karen said earnestly but somberly, "I am not sure I've ever loved in my entire life." She was not being maudlin or falsely humble. Karen was simply pierced with the vision of the kind of love Christ releases us into. Her comment has haunted me since.

LISTENING TO A SEEKING HEART

My friend Peggy has a saying I like: "It's so easy to forget what it's like to be without Jesus." So true. Maybe the best antidote to spiritual pride is to listen to those who don't know Jesus. They will, after all, tell us what is important. I was driving on a road trip with a young man I care a great deal about and who is in a very honest search process. He's got a pretty big beef with God and has many understandable reasons for that. He is honestly struggling with Christianity, wondering what the answer might be for him. He likes the Dalai Lama's teachings, and he's drawn to the seeming peacefulness of many Eastern religions. He's vocal about the hypocrisy he sees in Christians, but he is asking about Christianity, and I was so honored that he would ask about my reasons for being a Christian. With the scenery flashing around us, I told him some of my story, the ways God had sought out my heart through the years, and the questions I had and still have. It was so good for me to realize again that even in the middle of the most dense theological question, one thing is crystal clear: Christ loves me, even when I do not deserve it. Grateful tears came to my eyes as the simplicity—the confounding simplicity—of Love once again showed up.

This young man then began to question the differences between the denominations in Christendom. "What *kind* of a Christian are you?" he asked. For a weak moment or two, I found myself describing the difference between mainline and reformed Presbyterians, a Baptist, a charismatic, an Episcopal, a Quaker, and a Catholic. It was wild. As I painted this tapestry, I thought, *Who could ever find Christ in such a jungle?* I found myself able to laugh at how diverse we all are and joked with him about our various quirks and traditions, our various errors and strong points. But the beauty of the conversation was that he, after hearing it all, said, "So the one thing you have in common is a belief that you need Jesus." Once again I teared up, knowing this wasn't always the case, but, yes—that was the point.

This Love we are listening to is simply too big for any one person, group, theology, movement, or teaching to contain. Can we celebrate the way in which we carry this gift and marvel at the way others carry it differently? We are not the ones to originate it, and we will not be, unless Christ returns in glory soon, the last to carry this treasure in earthen vessels. It is our story—woven into the individual life of every person given the gift of understanding this scandalous, confounding, simple Love. It is our story—collective, international, regional, passing through generations, defying even governments that forbade it, through the writings of Tolstoy, Dostoevsky, and Hugo. It whispers in the humor of Charles Schulz and through the music of Handel. It is carried on through the hearts of scientists, housewives, firefighters, and street bums.

LOVE'S TABLE

I'll never forget a gathering I was a part of—eight folks around one table. We were all connected in some way to our host, but there was the slight awkwardness that comes from dining with strangers. I had only one dear friend there with me. As the evening unfolded, one gentleman who had spent quite a bit of time in Japan and has friends there began to speak caustically against the atomic bomb. I listened to his thoughts and his reasoning, keeping my family heritage to myself. I heard arguments I've heard for years as to why the civilian atrocities of Hiroshima point to our mistake in using the bomb. I was quiet, because I knew this man was speaking on behalf of his friends, on behalf of those he loved. I was content just to take it all in, listening without revealing my father's role in what this man deemed an unconscionable act. But after a short while, the dear friend of mine went over to the gentleman who was defending his Japanese friends. Putting his hand on this man's shoulder, he said, "Gary, isn't it an amazing thing how big the table of God is?" Gary agreed, not quite sure where this was going. "Isn't it an amazing thing that this table, Christ's table, can hold a man who loves his Japanese friends and a woman whose father was involved in a project that both killed Japanese and ended the war?" The whole table fell silent as the reality of what he was saying sank in. It is a large table. Big enough to forgive all mistakes, big enough to hold the most mysterious, ethical dilemmas of history, and big enough to provide a place for us to listen to each other.

It is Love's table. Each of us brings to the table our own depth, reasoning, revelation of glory. We've all thought about life, at least a little. And we all have questions. When our little pocket of glory gets revealed, we assume everyone's glory should look like ours! When our glimpse of the masterpiece is called into question, we rise up with vehemence rather than listen to what might be noteworthy about another's perspective. Maybe we're simply meant to learn from one another and actually enjoy that process. Maybe it isn't possible to experience a full meal without others serving us or isn't possible to take in the complete, intended work of art without another's eyes. G. K. Chesterton said, "Christianity got over the difficulty of combining furious opposites, by keeping them both, and keeping them furious.... One can hardly think too little of one's self. One can hardly think too much of one's soul."[7] Maybe we're being asked to take a step back and consider each other's life, giving space for the Voice to be heard.

Five

LISTENING TO REALITY

Losing Our Religion

That's me in the corner. That's me in
the spotlight—losing my religion.
—R.E.M.

Don't you want to cry when you see how far you've got to go
to be where forgiveness rules instead of where you are?
—JACKSON BROWNE

We're not in control as we thought we were. And this is good news. We're more childlike than we knew. This is even better news. Once we start to clue in to these realities, we naturally want to be around others who understand. Then we look around and think, *Is there anyone else who thirsts as I do?*

I know I'm not alone in this experience: it seems the more I know I'm loved by Jesus, the more I'm left dissatisfied in just about every church body or group of which I'm a part. And I don't think I'm alone in trying to reason with myself about it. "What is wrong with you, Jan? Can't you just be content and grateful with what you're given? Maybe you should concentrate on all the positive things instead of thinking about the gnawing, unsatisfied feeling you have as you drive away from church on Sunday or from your home group on Tuesday." I honestly don't think I'm a perpetually dissatisfied woman, so why can't I be *satisfied* with the church, gathering, or group of people I'm a part of at any given time? What are we to do with our internal squirming in even the best groups of people?

I must, of course, learn how to bear with and love those around me, and I know it is good to look at life through grateful eyes. But the good news is, I'm learning that my dissatisfaction can be an indicator that Jesus is beckoning. I'm learning that when I begin to squirm, it is a great time to ask, "Is it you, Jesus? Are you the reason for the discontent?" I'm finding he usually comes with a clear answer of yes. Why? Because religion—which shows up in even the most life-giving and passionate groups—is not meant to satisfy.

An older couple I know, loved by many because of their depth, warmth, and commitment, has been a part of a rare Christian community for years, a group in which they have experienced a movement of God in their own and other peoples' lives. I have always respected them, but I respected them even more when I heard them say the other day, "Our group is not big enough to hold up our hearts." They discovered long ago what it is like to live in the delicate tension that all of us face. They have admitted they want people to walk with them through life; they have risked and opened themselves to relationships. And they have been let down. They have wanted something authentic and trustworthy from their community, and though they have been disillusioned by the people, ideas, and emphases of their community, they are learning not to put too much pressure on their group to be everything for them or to never fail.

Another young woman I know has been involved in a small group that includes many people who have been either burned or disillusioned by the church. This group has been a life-giving haven, giving the members a chance to mend their wounds and discover a Jesus they never encountered in their parents' religion. This woman has been committed to these people for several years and has been struck by the tenderness and commitment they all have for each other. But now she is discovering the limits of even the best of fellowships. Though strong in support of each other, her group has a developed a core belief that Jesus is committed to keeping us from shameful experiences or anything that would cause us to suffer.

This woman is being asked to enter into a delicate tension—the place between the life her community might provide and its failures. She is being asked to listen for the good things her group teaches yet also to value her own personal journey of leaning in and listening to Love. For instance, as this woman leans in to listen to God, she knows Jesus is calling her to talk to her mother about her mother's choice to remain in a verbally abusive relationship with her father. By doing that, this woman runs a high risk of being shamed by her father. Her group members question the wisdom of this, saying she should shelter her heart and draw thick boundaries around it so her father cannot harm her. Instead, she knows Jesus wants her to risk being wounded in order to invite her mom to something different. As this woman enters this tension, she says, "It is amazing how we, a little band of renegades committed to not being shamed by religion, end up making a religion out of running from the experience of shame—even shame that lets me share in the sufferings of Christ in order to love someone, something for which Jesus said we would be blessed." This delicate tension is the place where intimacy with Christ is found, where he shows himself to be the only source of life, the only source of true religion.

Whether in a church, a small group, a home church, or an organization, the tension where Christ is, is often the first thing to be swallowed up by one of the greatest enemies of our hearts: a false religious spirit. Listening to Love requires great discernment when navigating the realm of religion and Christian culture. And the hardest thing to discern is how we ourselves become falsely religious without even realizing it.

ENTER THE PRESSURE

We are all prone to make a religion out of something good. If there was one target for Jesus's wrath, it was religion that lost sight of the point of Jesus's love: to release us from the pressure of keeping the law in our own strength or conforming to a set of standards and to free us into the life found in him alone. He burned against religion that was external and pressured and that stole people's joy. Many world religions fit this category, yes, but when pressure and fear pulse through the veins of Christ's followers, I can understand why Michael Stipe and millions of others have been losing their religion.

The truth is, I *am* grateful for the small community of people I'm a part of. We encourage and challenge each other. I have the benefit of being in a church that is young enough not to have formed its own culture yet, and I plan on being around when it does. That's the thing. It will. All groups and churches and movements of Christianity do, over time, develop their own culture, language, and standard way of doing things. And it's not unusual for the language and way of doing things to be powerful at first, only to take on a "life of their own" that is laden with pressure.

This crops up in our Christian lives like a weed we don't even recognize is thriving. This weed has grown up, unnoticed, during different times throughout my Christian life, slowly choking the life out of my ability to hear Love. Again, I'm confident I'm not alone.

I have been impacted by some of the most life-giving messages in the world, and yet I turn them into something they're not. As a counselor, I've been trained to see both the restored dignity and the residual depravity in our hearts. This has allowed me to look at my own life and the lives of others with a confidence, an anchor to my beliefs about people. But as I counsel people, I can easily make a religion out of this—and become presumptuous. When I do this, I place a heavy requirement on a person's heart. ("I know what is true about you, and I'm waiting for you to clue in on what is true about you. What's taking you so long?") What is going on for me when I make a religion out of something good, killing its power?

My Christian life began in a conservative, Reformed community that was focused on the sovereignty of God. I came to love the security I felt as I learned the unshakable anchor of God's grace. My heart was captured by the thought that it is God who seeks me. After a time, though, I took this beautiful truth and turned it into something it is not meant to be—a Christian life that is more like pablum than living water or new wine. God was completely in control, and Jesus was the initiator of everything, so I didn't really need to ask for anything more than patience as his sovereign plan unfolded. I turned the truth of God's initiation into passivity on my part. And ironically as I did so, I judged other friends who were more aggressive in their faith—those who were the seekers after God. The weed had sprouted. *Fools,* I thought. *Don't they know they don't need to work so hard?*

Fast-forward about ten years. By this time, all the passivity had made me weary. I longed for the life of the Spirit, so I begin to search, to seek, to press to find all the things I heard Jesus speak of but hadn't experienced. I witnessed healings, had prophecies spoken over me, saw spiritual gifts given through the laying on of hands. I tasted those parts of the kingdom feast that show up only as we ask for it. I discovered the Jesus who asks me what I want and if I want to seek for it like hidden treasure. It was a beautiful time of going after life.

Again, we make religions out of even the best things. I can't tell you how, but over time I made *going after* the kingdom into something heavy and burdensome. I turned it into a fearful Christianity where I always wondered if I was I seeking enough, doing enough, fasting enough, serving enough. I turned the truth of searching for the kingdom of God into another kind of backward pressure. This time I judged my more Calvinistic, rest-in-God-type friends, thinking, *Fools. Don't you see the riches you are missing in your passivity?* The burden I had made out of the search escaped me. The weed had reappeared without notice.

In both of these spiritual seasons in my life I had made something true, something Christian, into something full of pressure. We easily recognize this kind of pressure in legalistic, performance-oriented religion, but I believe we all create this kind of pressure—taking beautiful truths and making them heavy—along the way.

Thankfully, this pressure is swallowed up over time by the love of Christ, the only language strong enough to make it from movement to movement, from generation to generation. Love is the only language that can answer the questions "Is it you, Jesus? Are you more than my religion or group has taught me? Is it you that I *glimpse* there, and is it you telling me you are so much more?"

The movement of our hearts as we contend with Christianity sounds something like this. The first posture: "Is it you, Jesus? I've been introduced to you by religion, but could it be, as I hope, that you are so much more than I've been taught?" The second posture: "Oh no, it really is you, Jesus. You are so much more than the safe God religion has taught me. What you allow to come into my life in order to capture my heart does not bring comfort. You seem to be after me—my heart—and your desire for me scares me. I've never been loved like this. I'm thrilled to be yours, but I'm also finding myself uncomfortable because sometimes you want me to trust you in the delicate tension, and I don't know if I'm ready for that." And finally, the third posture: "Oh good, it is you, Jesus. Religion is not big enough, because it cannot contain the vast nature of your heart and your love."

OUR UNCOMFORTABLE INHERITANCE

What a mess, religion. Or rather, what a mess has been made of the Christian religion. For some reason, I feel more apologetic about being associated with the Christian religion than ever before. I am grateful I can be called a follower of Jesus, but so much bears his name that I don't want to bear my name. We all know moments of feeling apologetic about our belief in Jesus in light of how religion has been misused and mishandled throughout history. There's nothing like having to respond to the injustice of the Crusades, the blindness in the papal system, the violence in the Middle East, militant Islam, and the hypocrisy of televangelists before having a conversation about Jesus. A graduate degree in debate is helpful when engaging those who oppose Christ, but it provides little help when trying to talk to someone who is curious about Jesus but doesn't want anything to do with the Christianity she sees in the headlines, the media, or on the freeway. At that point, forget debate. Only one force is powerful enough to persuade the heart: love. Love is the central pulse of Christianity. Anything contrary to love is the pulse of false religion.

The word *religion* comes from the Latin *religio,* "to rebind," binding together us and God, releasing from captivity the "us" that has gone missing, raising to life the "us" that was dead. Of course this word is worthless if we don't admit that religion itself is not a strong enough mediator to accomplish this. For God so loved the world he gave our mediator. For God so loved the world he gave us *true* religion.

Religion exists, with all its little cultures and languages and distortions, because Jesus is so vast—and so unmanageable. There is no religion in heaven. On the vast, timeless plane, Jesus's death, resurrection, and ascension are surely not set on a linear, historical time line. What would happen if we thought of them as perpetual? His resurrection and ascension do not negate the Cross; they fulfill the reasons that blood was shed. The Cross does not negate his resurrection, but rather it stands in holy memory of what it took for Jesus to purchase our freedom. To follow him is to partake in his life, burial, and resurrection, all at once, in a finite world. God's secret plan, Ephesians tell us, is to bring everything in heaven and earth under the authority of Christ. The Holy Spirit within us (our "inheritance") lets us know that everything is *already* under Christ's authority. But we are given this eternal gift in a land locked in time.

That's the nature of any inheritance, isn't it? We have a sense of its value, have perhaps even held portions of it in our hands, but it is not time yet to receive it in full. If this is not uncomfortable, I don't know what is. This is why the communion table causes me to pause; it is a strange, dissonant sacrament when I've spent weeks and weeks concentrating on the new, full resurrection life within me. Conversely, a friend may need to remind me that Jesus is ascended and actually pleading my case before the Father when I've spent days too focused on my own failure. The life of Christ is found both in the place of remembering death and remembering resurrection.

Delicate Tension

So how do we turn the gift of the rebinding love of God in Jesus into the falsely safe, stale, misshapen thing we call religion? How do we so easily lose our focus on love? It happens whenever we try to remove the delicate tension from our lives. When I make Christianity completely about God's sovereign ways, I miss the tension that comes from Jesus's more proactive admonitions (ask, seek, knock). When I make Christianity completely about pressing to the things of God, I miss the tension that comes from remembering Jesus is fully in charge, even when I fail or am assaulted by evil. We try to nail down God's message of love, and it evaporates in our hands, leaving us in a tension that says to our hearts, *My love is too big to be explained fully.*

The apostle Paul says, "God's way of making us right with him depends on faith. As a result, I can really know Christ and experience the mighty power that raised him from the dead. I can learn what it means to suffer with him, sharing in his death, so that, somehow, I can experience the resurrection from the dead!" (Philippians 3:9-11). To be a follower of Christ means that we straddle two realities: death and life. Somewhere in the threshold between the two, or somewhere in a combination of the two, Jesus is. He is found in the full places—when we walk with buoyant hearts away from the graveclothes of our selfishness in marriage, fear of what others think of us, sexual choices made without thought to what God wants, or pride over whom we have become. We leave the tomb of our self-sufficiency and shame, amazed that it has been obliterated by the same power that brought Jesus out of death.

And he is found on a path that looks and feels very much like the desert temptations toward resignation or addiction, Gethsemane experiences when our dreams are handed over in blood and tears, and even Golgotha when we're asked to experience the same isolation, abandonment, crises of faith, and rejection that he did. It's not terribly easy to control or predict, is it? And it definitely makes it hard to know the "right" path. We have to be *led* through, following close in dependent trust that the story is his and that he will tell it the way he wants to tell it.

Am I to trust that the struggle my son is having at school is going to be woven into his life to strengthen his character, or am I to intervene quickly and proactively, to be his advocate as I talk with his teacher? Am I to let the part of the sermon that doesn't sit well with me roll off my back, or do I listen to the nudges that tell me to discuss it with the pastor? Our need to be led through shows up in countless moments when we must lean in and ask, "Is it you, Jesus? It isn't so clear to me right now."

Wildness Revisited

I'd like to visit another snapshot from the life of my friend Brent in order to illustrate how we're led through this tension. Brent was killed while securing climbing ropes for a group of men for whom he and our friend John were leading a retreat. It sounds so feeble to say, "The rocks just gave way that day," but that is the truth. When death comes, it doesn't really matter how. Five years have passed, and much life has happened. But as those of you who have lost friends know, it was just yesterday.

It has been over five years, though, since I listened to Brent on tapes recorded at the very first Sacred Romance lecture series, a series that spanned twelve weeks and was the "test drive" for the book he and John Eldredge would write. These tapes never made it to market, and there is something about their unpackaged, raw form that reminds me of Brent, even before hearing his voice. I took a road trip recently and, on a whim, grabbed one of these old tapes from a closet to listen to in the car. What I heard blew me away. Brent was teaching on "The Wildness of God," on just how much God will allow us to be hurt in order to capture our attention and our hearts. As Brent spoke about the story God is telling and how orthodoxy teaches that God writes the script, he said, "There is something powerfully comforting in the thought that my sufferings (at least those not from gross sin) are redemptive." The problem, he said, is that we are not given a whole lot of information apart from our own scenes and part, and we're even asked to feel privileged for the part we do have!

All of this set the tone for the story that, for me, is suspended in time. He breezed through this story in less than three minutes and then was on to the next. But the foreshadowing in his words is haunting. Brent said this:

> I was working for the Park Service at the age of twenty-four up at
> Rocky Mountain National Park. On the weekends we would all go to
> seed. One weekend I was all alone, so on this beautiful Colorado day
> I went up to Shadow Mountain Reservoir and found a monolith of
> rocks. Those of you who know me will wonder why I ever leave solid

ground (laugh). I climbed up the rocks and quickly discovered I could neither go up or down; I could not move. At first I said to myself (voice shaking), "Be calm, be calm. You can find your way out." And then I realized, "No, I can't."

I don't know if you have ever passed that place where the shock hits you: you might actually be allowed to die. No one will intervene to save you. The rock will not offer a protuberance to grab. The sky is blue and the sun shines, but neither one stoops to help. What a surprise it is that this is actually allowed to take place.[1]

The Love found in true religion gives us space in which to live with, wrestle with, and listen to all the unanswerable losses that are allowed to take place.

As I heard my friend speak of "being allowed" to be where no one stoops to help, I smiled. Please don't think me heartless. I'm not glad for his trembling, his fear, his predicament—I just know my friend. I smile, knowing he wanted his audience to understand that even in abandonment and assault, God is very much in control, writing a story to which we are not privy. He wanted his listeners to know that despite betrayal and seeming abandonment, he found a resting place in God's story even when all the evidence says God's story is flawed. He knew that spiritual opposition can take us into an even deeper abiding place with Jesus; he wanted us to know that God allows far too much (for my comfort) in order to fulfill the story he's telling.

Brent was allowed to die. But his posture toward God—his willingness to wrestle with *and* surrender to him—showed the humanity and otherworldliness that comes from being met by Jesus in the real tensions of life. It produced the kind of Christianity you want to tell your friends about; it can be trusted.

There is no explanation for Brent's death. For all I know, Satan himself could have pushed Brent from that rock ledge on his last beautiful Colorado day. (I'm not being flippant here; I'm sober beyond words at the thought.) But isn't it mind-blowing to think that such an assault could be scripted *by God* into the story? Evil thinks it has gained the sweetest victory, while the Author holds the secrets as to how the whole thing will be turned on its head for good.

Yes, Brent, what a surprise. What a surprise that, in the story God is telling, this is allowed to take place. "Oh no, it is you, Jesus."

TENDER WRESTLING WITH SOVEREIGNTY

I don't think we give ourselves or others the space necessary to wrestle with the "Oh no, it is you, Jesus" experiences of our lives. And because of this, we aren't led through the experience of leaning in and listening to Love, discovering God's heart for us in the tension. Isn't it a surprise that God wants me to contend with him about this? My immediate reaction when Brent died was to rush to other people who knew him well as I puzzled about the whole thing. When no answers surfaced that satisfied, I wanted to fight with the one who steals and destroys. I wanted to curse, blame, and proclaim revenge against evil for what it had taken. Of course all of us wanted to slaughter evil at that point. How could we not hate its cruelty?

But all of this missed the point. The Author wanted me to do business with *him.* Jesus wanted me to contend with the fact that his father could have stopped this tragedy and didn't. This is tender, tender business. It is the business of the second posture of the heart. It is the business that keeps us in the tension where Jesus is found, resisting the complete clarity that false religion offers in its explanations.

We become too sure of ourselves when we stray from the tension of suffering and resurrection, when we stop engaging God with our "What are you talking about; what are you really saying?" questions. I still want to blame someone, even the devil himself, for Brent's death. But the deeper reality (as it was the deeper reality for Job) is that my beef is really with God. For me, the immediate thought is, *No! This is* not *good. A rare man has been taken, leaving countless people without a trustworthy shepherd.* Where are we to go with thoughts like that?

I can't think of a more vulnerable moment inside the human heart than the moment when we must ask, "You mean…Jesus…you *allowed* this?" It is betrayal to some, abandonment to others, like acid in a wound. It is almost impossible to reside in this question, waiting for the answer. Usually we move quickly on, fearing that the answer will be yes and that we will have no category for that kind of a seemingly reckless and uncaring God.

But God invites us to go with him there. He knows we cannot enter the question of his seemingly capricious ways on our own, so he goes with us as we ask our question. His answer is not what we want to hear. This is the crisis of our faith: can we open ourselves to the strange comfort that comes from accepting that he is fully in charge and yet invites us to wrestle with his sovereign ways?

As we listen to Love, we find that this crisis can be a beautiful one, if we let it. We are asked to acknowledge that he alone holds all knowledge, power, and authority over what he is doing and what he allows. And because he wants our hearts more than anything else, we're asked to lean in and contend with him when his sovereign way confounds or confuses us. In this place where we wrestle with God's sovereign ways, we have the "what I have feared has come upon me" experience as our illusions about God are shattered. In this place, he is introducing himself, perhaps for the first time. When Aslan in C. S. Lewis's Narnia tales finally introduces himself to the boy Shasta on the road to Anvard, he does so by explaining that he was the lion who had been present during each of Shasta's horrific adventures. But he also reveals himself to be the lion that had wounded Shasta's friend Aravis.

> "Then it was you who wounded Aravis?"
>
> "It was I."
>
> "But what for?"
>
> "Child," said the Voice, "I am telling you your story, not hers. I tell no-one any story but his own."
>
> "Who *are* you?" asked Shasta.
>
> "*Myself,*" said the Voice, very deep and low so that the earth shook: and again "*Myself,*" loud and clear and gay: and then the third time "*Myself,*" whispered so softly you could hardly hear it, and yet it seemed to come from all round you as if the leaves rustled with it."[2]

Have you noticed that God doesn't often feel the need to explain himself? He holds our wounded hearts, revealing himself as Love, but a Love beyond our comprehension. Not much explanation is given; he seems to be perfectly at peace with who he is. His way of offering comfort isn't always what we think it should be. *Myself* is enough, and we realize we don't really know this God. Here we can say with Hosea, "Come, let us return to the LORD! *He has torn us in pieces; now he will heal us. He has injured us; now he will bandage our wounds.* In just a short time, he will restore us so we can live in his presence. Oh, that we might know the LORD! Let us press on to know him!" (Hosea 6:1–3, emphasis added).

So much of our religion is structured so that we don't have to contend directly with this One who scares and confuses us. Or better said, we construct a God we like better, one we can explain and who fits into our categories. George MacDonald says,

> There are those who in their very first seeking of it are nearer to the
> Kingdom of Heaven than many who have for years believed themselves
> of it. In the former there is more of the mind of Jesus, and when he
> calls them they recognize him at once and go after him; while the oth-
> ers examine him from head to foot, and finding him not sufficiently
> like the Jesus of their conception, turn their backs and go to church or
> chapel or chamber to kneel before a vague form of tradition and fancy.[3]

I would give anything to be able to construct a fanciful religious paradigm in which God does not allow friends or brothers to die. I and many friends have tried. But we cannot stay there, not if we want Jesus. Because, again, Jesus is found in the resting place of letting the unknown parts of the script be firmly held in the hand of God.

We All Do It

Our resistance to enter this delicate tension shows up everywhere—not just at church. It shows up in communities like mine where freedom in Christ is emphasized; it shows up in movements where the family is emphasized, and in house churches, and where the emphasis is the heart or prosperity or morality or liturgy or the mind. And this is not just a Western thing. Two-thirds of world churches and communities are equally prone to making smaller stories out of anything glorious, choking the life out of what we offer, making religious nooses out of any one perspective rather than allowing Love to open up the vastness of the truth.

So with your permission I'd like to indict the whole of Christendom—your community as well as mine. We are all guilty. Well, that's great—nothing like global indictment. Actually, I'm hoping you can smile with me as we admit this so we can look together at our foolish ways and be amazed at the loving patience of Christ with his church.

TIGHTROPE BALANCE

True religion—or living, breathing, orthodox Christian teaching, the core truth about the rebinding made possible through Jesus's burial, resurrection, and ascension—has gotten a bad rap in the past fifty years. We've come to view it as mundane or somehow so terribly unpostmodern—yawn. When we think of Christian teaching, we glaze over, thinking it a necessary evil, like having to show up for a conversation with a contractor. He wants to show us the blueprints and foundation measurements when all we want to do is throw a party in our new, finished, beautiful home. Doesn't he understand we just need him to get on with the good stuff?

Orthodox Christian teaching *is* the good stuff, but we believe it is boring on its own. (I mean, look at how we try to spice things up, trying to entice people to church with Starbucks coffee and Krispy Kreme doughnuts!) Nothing could be further from the truth. Chesterton calls Christian orthodoxy a "discovery of the new balance—an irregular equilibrium."[4] I don't know about you, but I've come to dislike intensely the word *balance*. Now there's a word that *has* become mundane and boring! We use it as a word for maturity when in fact it usually speaks of a milquetoast attempt to please everyone. This is *not* what Chesterton means by balance. His term speaks more of the daring, skill, and agility necessary to navigate a tightrope with pillars holding the rope in place on either side.

This irregular equilibrium is the place where Jesus is found. It is the delicate tension between engagement and surrender. It is what I experience as I watch my brother with cancer. Some days I fight—fasting, pleading, praying, rousing others to ask for healing for his body and spirit. Some days I surrender, knowing that God is in control of his life and the disease. It is what a friend feels as he longs for more intimacy from his spouse who is shut down. Some days he knows he must fight, engaging her about it. Other days he must lay off, quietly praying for change to come. You can hear that we can't stay in one posture; the irregular equilibrium brings us back to a place where we have to lean in and ask, "What would you have today, Lord?"

Chesterton explores how the early generations of the church in Europe had to contend with this tension in their lives. He says:

> The church could not afford to swerve a hair's breadth on some things
> if she was to continue her great and daring experiment of the irregular
> equilibrium. Once let one idea become less powerful and some other
> idea would become too powerful. It was no flock of sheep the Christian shepherd was leading, but a herd of bulls and tigers, of terrible
> ideals and devouring doctrines, each one of them strong enough to
> turn to a false religion and lay waste of the world.[5]

I love this image. It takes a brave (albeit foolish) person to get on a tightrope, and I know a groundswell of people willing to be brave today, willing to be fools for Christ. I'm also encouraged because it tells me that the terrible ideals and devouring doctrines of today—and we *all* succumb to them at one point or another when we're passionately following Jesus—can be held in Love's hands. The early church was a herd of bulls and tigers because they were willing to introduce the wildest ideas to a self-sufficient world that wasn't really asking. The foundations of the faith are just as wild today when you think about it; they aren't rational and can still be distorted when overemphasized in any one direction.

So there are two questions for us to ask. First, have I so tamed my Christianity that I can predict and manage it? Is my faith so milquetoast and rational that the idea of my being a bull or tiger is laughable? Second, if I've allowed the wild passion of Love to find me, am I now running headlong in one direction without any thought to a delicate tension I might be crushing in the process?

Bulls and tigers are preferable to milquetoast, sleepy religious people. I love that I'm in relationship with some bulls and tigers whose wild passions behind orthodox truths are being rediscovered. The gospel was never meant to be tamed. But Love does *constrain* these divergent ideas, not allowing the slight touch on one emphasis to shroud the vastness of Christ's heart.

For example, the church in the fourteenth century emphasized worshiping the Creator and not created things, including art of any kind. Chesterton reminds us that this "would have broken all the best statues in Europe" if it had been allowed to be the *only* emphasis. Similarly, if we today allow the only emphasis to be on morality—religiously defined by us as antihomosexual, antiliberal, pro–American Dream—we fail to be constrained by love, and Jesus is represented as an ugly, angry face plastered over the Internet, on the airwaves, on *Letterman*, and in Times Square. An emphasis on watching over the heart, which I cherish because it is imperative, can easily lead to a commitment never to be hurt if it becomes divorced from other aspects of the kingdom. An emphasis on prosperity can lead to assumptions that those who live below the poverty line are not "believing enough." If we only emphasize the *journey* of the Christian life, it can keep us from being forthright or proactive with one another for fear that we might not be honoring others' process or meeting them where they are. In other words, we end up never challenging each other. If we only emphasize Christ as the Man of Sorrows, we can get stuck in despair. Yet if we only emphasize victorious living, we can spill over into naive optimism, refusing to believe that suffering is part of life with God.

Not all at once, of course. A venture out of the tension in any direction can look and feel exhilarating at first; the free fall can feel like life. But again, the wonder of it all is that the Jesus of history will faithfully nudge us *back into* the tensions of our grand faith before we end up on late-night television, distorting the face of God.

OUR LITTLE WAYS

When I was in college, it was all about "being a woman of God," which was supposed to mean living with integrity but often got translated as having a Bible study in your dorm and making chocolate chip cookies for the men. In an Episcopal youth camp in the seventies, the emphasis was on having an "encounter." I am sure the original intention was to foster intimacy with Christ, but by the time I came along, it was just a great excuse to head out into the woods to make out. "I Found It" bumper stickers gave eager believers a chance to explain themselves in parking lots just before the era of "earning the right to be heard." In my conservative Presbyterian upbringing, the important emphasis on being transformed by renewed thinking (for which I'm extremely grateful) was taken to Olympic levels of intellectual competition between Sunday school teachers. Cross Talks were beautiful until they became over-emotional. Being missions minded, we sent thousands of workers into the harvest field, only to realize that we had as much to learn from the "lost heathen" as they had to learn from us. In the charismatic realm, wondering whether or not you had the second blessing got in the way of the blessing itself. In more contemplative circles, it has been about living in the mystery to the point of resignation. For those in academic settings, it is living honestly in a postmodern world to the point of having no separation from the world. I hope you're smiling. I am.

We are no different from the generations before us as we try to listen and follow. "The church in its early days went fierce and fast with any war-horse; yet it is utterly un-historic to say she merely went mad along one idea, like a vulgar fanaticism. She swerved to left and right, so exactly as to avoid enormous obstacles."[6] The church has been swerving, all right. I've swerved with her, and I'm a bit dizzy from it. Lately I've been swerving between two truths. One day I realize that Jesus, with one touch, can bring complete physical healing, and I'm compelled to pray for this for my brother. Other days I swerve and realize that Jesus can do, ultimately, what he sees is best, and this very well may mean death for my brother. I've been a little bit embarrassed by my swerving until I realize that it keeps me in the place of greatest adventure in my life of faith—the risk of having to lean in, every hour it seems, and to discover what Jesus is saying to me. If Christ's followers have swerved like this from the beginning, then maybe I'm not so crazy.

We have to remember that when the culture or language of our tradition becomes *the* thing, instead of Love, it can be damaging. Without Love, we can so easily think we are right without considering how this attitude implies that *everyone else must be wrong.* The Pharisees seemed to know they were right. At least *they* were convinced of it. They were convinced they were godly, mature, and spiritual while they were actually crushing people and preventing them from entering the kingdom (Luke 11:46–52).

The beauty of the law, for them, became a thing to be mastered and displayed rather than being the tutor to lead them to Christ (see Galatians 3:24). But what about the disciples? Didn't they *have to* know they were right? After all, weren't they following a man who said he was the Way, the Truth, and the Life and that there was no other way to the Father? Yes, the disciples had to look the arrogant Pharisees in the eye and contend with their Old Covenant pride. But what carried the followers of Jesus was not an attitude of "You're not right; *I'm* right" but an attitude of "I'm confident of how Jesus has changed me with his love."

THE MIND OF CHRIST

When I try to be *right* all the time about God, when I attempt to explain Brent's death or try to make what is happening to my brother clear and understandable, I reach for the fruit that I think I deserve—the fruit of a full and clear explanation of God's ways. Jesus did not die to give us the knowledge of good and evil; he saved us from the devastation of eating from this tree.

So what am I to do when 1 Corinthians 2 tells me that the secret wisdom of God is revealed to me by the Spirit, that "his Spirit searches out everything and shows us even God's deep secrets" (1 Corinthians 2:10)?

The curse of God came after we reached for the knowledge of good and evil; we wanted to be like God. Jesus came to answer that curse. I can't know all that God knows, but he humbly and lovingly grants me the wisdom of the Spirit to see into his kind intentions, to understand his heart.

I think of my friend Allyson, my counseling partner once a year in a weeklong ministry to women who have been sexually abused. Every year Allyson and I have the opportunity to work with ten women in an intensive setting as they think through their stories in light of the gospel. It is, as you can imagine, a challenging week and a beautiful week as Jesus calls these women to follow him. For Allyson, it means taking a week away from her husband and three young boys. Prior to the week, amid a frustrating situation at school with her son Jordan, Allyson heard Jesus speak to her: "I will give you the mind of Christ for your son." Puzzled by its meaning and thinking it sounded extreme ("It's not that big a deal, God, but thanks"), Allyson simply tucked those words away. During the middle of our week together, she received a phone call that, back home, her son had had a seizure, the third in a growing trend that she had hoped would not continue. Knowing her mother's heart was breaking, I watched as she grieved both the seizure and the distance between her and her son. I watched as she "sowed in tears" on behalf of the women we were counseling. The words she had been given held up her heart in a mysterious way. Time will reveal exactly what Jesus meant in his words, but within days of her son's seizure, Allyson reflected the mind of Christ as she entrusted Jordan's care to her God. Her tender fingers were being asked to place him in another Palm. As she did this, she was luminous.

Allyson was in the tension-laden threshold where Jesus is found. She had the mind of Christ: she understood that Jordan was in God's care, but she didn't understand why he had to suffer or why she had to be so far away during the seizure. She received some assurance but no clarity.

In this threshold, the Tree of Knowledge of Good and Evil bends its branches only to a Sovereign God. As Allyson stayed in this tension without demanding clarity, she was able to bring her heart and her wrestling *to* God: *Lord, why does this have to happen when I'm so far away from my little boy, when I can't run to hold and reassure him?* Yet she was able to trust: *Lord, he is completely in your hands. You love him even more than I do, so since I can't be there for him, you must be there for him, fighting for his body and fighting for his heart.*

As Allyson reached for the Tree of Life, its branches humbly bowed to reassure her that although much is hidden, all is well. She could have easily reached for the Tree of Knowledge of Good and Evil, trying to convince herself that she knew what God was doing or what the outcome would be. But if she had done this, she would have missed intimacy with her God. The mind of Christ allows us to choose the Tree of Life, a place of rest amid uncertainty, even though we're tempted to choose the path that requires no faith and no tension.

Love is the pulse of our faith, and it is the sap pulsing through the Tree of Life. Think of it this way: God alone held the knowledge of good and evil in the garden. He wanted us to work and play and learn of him, enjoying him. We grabbed the branches and said, "There's more!" in stubborn rebellion and fell hard as the weight of too much knowledge crashed on our hearts. Too much knowledge was *death*. Jesus makes a way for us to be restored without the death sentence that is rightfully ours for presuming to be creatures who can handle what only God can handle. He sets our captive hearts free from this presumption and heals our hearts that are broken over our foolish choices.

Jesus died to restore us, to rebind our hearts to his. And through his Spirit he reveals things to us that we would never know otherwise. He reveals the most limitless power on earth—Love. Love often brings answers to the hard questions, but Love does not bring the full knowledge of good and evil. The primary answer that Love brings, over a lifetime and over history, is this: the love of Jesus is enough to hold up our hearts in the tension of all that is unanswerable.

A couple I know had raised two children. They had sent the older one off to college, only to find that they were expecting another child. In the shock they prayed and searched for a shred of openness to this new child. Their hearts did open, and they began to anticipate and plan for this baby. And then they miscarried. A month earlier they might have been relieved, but now they were devastated. What can possibly carry our hearts through such madness? This couple made it through, bruised and befuddled but ultimately comforted as the mind of Christ gave them an openness to be given answers and also to be left without them.

When Love is the source of our religion, I can trust Jesus's intentions as the anchor for my heart even when I sit with my brother, a man who may be given life through death by cancer or may be given life by a divine healing. I can sit with my brother in this tension, knowing that much is unclear but that all is well. Similarly, with the security of sovereign love being my North Star, I can navigate through the vast terrain of emphases in the Christian life with an unthreatened heart, not needing to cling tightly to one doctrine as if it is life itself. I *want* to learn the secrets of God, to seek them like treasure. I *want* to be prepared and alert in the spiritual battle, learning all that Jesus wants to reveal to me. But the mind of Christ tells me that these secrets will be given as I need them, and it is not up to me to root them out. The fullness of good, all that God is, cannot be known to us until we are like him, seeing him face to face.

SLAVERY ISN'T ALWAYS WHAT WE THINK

Paul wrote a chiding letter to the Galatian church when they were "adding on" to the gospel of saving grace by faith in Christ by forcing men to be circumcised as "proof" of their faith. We add the same kind of weight and pressure to our faith when we seek to "prove," or at least gain a little reassurance, that we are in the right with God. This is why asking, "Is it you, Jesus?" is so important. Is it you, Jesus? Or is it you and some added, unnecessary burden that I have attached to you? Faith seems too simple; we figure there must be more. So we add on to the gospel. We don't circumcise, but we might as well! Our scalpel cuts away the foreskin of a childlike freedom in our faith by communicating to people that they are not "holy enough" or "free enough" or "missions minded enough" or "victorious enough" or "reverent enough" or "worshipful enough" or "in tune with the interior world enough" or "parenting God's way enough." You get the idea. The result is a new job assignment: work, work, work. In theory we acknowledge that you don't have to work at keeping the law to be saved, but in reality we preach that you must work, work, work to attain all that Christ has for you. The result is a low-grade Wall Street kind of pressure. Stay on top of it at all times. Paul calls it "bewitching"; he was furious over it. He was watching as God's children, who were meant to abide and rest in God's loving embrace, slowly succumbed to a new religious taskmaster.

Was it for freedom that Christ set us free? Absolutely. But again, we must define our terms. Paul says,

> So I advise you to live according to your new life in the Holy Spirit. Then you won't be doing what your sinful nature craves. The old sinful nature loves to do evil, which is just opposite from what the Holy Spirit wants. And the Spirit gives us desires that are opposite from what the sinful nature desires. These two forces are constantly fighting each other, *and your choices are never free from this conflict.* But when you are directed by the Holy Spirit, you are no longer subject to the law. (Galatians 5:16–18, emphasis added)

Can you hear the tension? We have been given a life source, a power that beats with the heart of Love through the Holy Spirit. Yet on this earth, locked in time and space, we are never free from our sinful desires. We put pressure on each other, breaking God's heart as we try to convince ourselves and one another that we can be free from this struggle, instead of celebrating the freedom that comes from a God who wants to embrace us even though we continue to clothe ourselves with sin that doesn't fit our new, redeemed hearts.

Paul's emphasis is on the fact that we are no longer subject to the law or its consequences. There is no longer any *penalty*—none!—for our sinful desires and choices. The desires that God sees in us are the desires he places in us. He no longer views our sinful desires as something that indict us. He grants us this freedom. Freedom is deliverance from the *judgment* that should be ours due to our sinful nature. "When we place our faith in Christ Jesus, it makes no difference to God whether we are circumcised or not circumcised. What is important is faith expressing itself in love" (Galatians 5:6). Another way of saying this, depending on your community, is that it makes no ultimate difference to God whether we homeschool or don't homeschool; what is important is faith expressing itself through love. It makes no ultimate difference whether we have altar calls or no altar calls. It should make no difference whether a person is a lover of *The Sacred Romance* or not. Should it matter whether or not you enjoy liturgy? It makes no difference whether we are debt free or have some debt. It doesn't matter if we know perfect inner healing or not. What matters is faith expressing itself through love.

THAT'S ALL

Staying dependent and humble in the tension of life when I have been given access to the secret things of God—remembering my need when I realize I've been made alive with Christ—makes me want to put a banner up on the nearest freeway overpass: True Religion—the Impossible Task. Thankfully, Jesus knows me, and he knows that the impossible task is *a mercy.* First Corinthians 13 says it is something only he can accomplish—moment by moment as his Spirit breathes patience and kindness and as he sloughs away jealousy, pride, demands, irritability, and keeping score. Love is breathed into hearts that have none, and since it comes straight from Jesus, Love never fails.

There is one mediator between God and man, Jesus Christ the Righteous One, the only one worthy of binding our hearts back to God. He holds us in the tension until the day when "we will see everything with perfect clarity. All that I know now is partial and incomplete, but then I will know everything completely, just as God knows me now" (1 Corinthians 13:12).

Six

LISTENING FOR THE
THREAT OF LOVE

Relinquishing Our Naiveté

Who will say, "This far, no further!" if I die today?
—JAMES TAYLOR

Be strong with the Lord's mighty power.
—THE APOSTLE PAUL, to Christians in Ephesus

I was at Sears standing at the checkout counter in the dark corner with all the big-screen televisions and electronics. The young girl who waited on me seemed robotic and oblivious as she punched in the codes and made a phone call to the warehouse. As she did this, I watched as the twenty-five screens played videos from the country music channel. I listened as a "good love gone bad" song ended and was followed by a "bad love gone good" song. The lyrics and stories went on with no one paying much attention. I watched the girl waiting on me and realized that no amount of loud, blaring music would disturb her oblivion. I watched her robotics and was actually jealous for a minute. Not jealous of her deadness, but jealous of that numbed-to-the-world state, where not a whole lot matters. *I lived that way once,* I thought. I thought about all that has clued me in to the story going on behind all stories, to the God who loved me too much to let me continue sleeping. It was God who woke me to see that I had an enemy poised against my heart.

Entering the Battle

I've had my hand forced in this department. I never liked scary movies, and if I saw the bully on campus, I'd walk the other way. But my life has been orchestrated, as I'm imagining yours has been, so that I've had to open my eyes. At first, I viewed the things that happened to me solely through these lenses:

Lens 1: This is happening as a test of my faith.

Lens 2: This is happening to reveal God's glory; he wants to be seen in this.

I still look at life through these lenses. I have to; 1 Peter and Romans tell me these things are true. I cherish these lenses; they comfort me as I think of God's being in complete control.

But now I look at life with an additional lens, a lens that brings into focus the breadth of this story we are living in:

Lens 3: This is happening *because I'm hated.* This is happening because Jesus has revealed his love to me, and the Adversary will not relent until he gets me to stop looking at Jesus with adoration.

Evil wants the attention, like a spoiled child screaming, "Look at me! Look at me!" If he doesn't get the attention, there is, quite literally, all hell to pay.

I've glimpsed how evil stops at nothing to get to me as God's beloved. It might sound like science fiction, but I've a hint of how evil has worked to destroy me, even before I was born. Evil's ways are generational, researched, intentional, and cruel, and at the same time they are as predictable as the snow in the high country. In hindsight I can spot the condemnation and isolation intended for me. But walking through an average day, I don't find it so easy to recognize. I'm grateful I don't have to recognize every assault and every scheme, but why should I even open my eyes to this stuff?

When we start to clue in to how passionate Jesus is about us, then the warriors poised against our hearts rumble like a pack of coyotes stirred by a whiff of fresh meat. When we start to clue in to the unseen world and the battle that rages over us *simply because we are loved by God,* it is as if we subscribe to satellite channels we never had before. We become aware of fallen angels who have nothing else on their radar screen but a desire to bring a scourge to Jesus's reputation as they answer only to their wounded, pathetic, pride-soaked leader.

It's becoming clear by now—responding to Love is not easy. We have to have a growing confidence in Love's ways in order to let go of our pride, control, manageable religion, and independence. And when we start to have confidence in Jesus's affection for us, that is when we most come up against the enemy of God.

Jesus has changed me, and through his blood, resurrection, and ascension, I am sealed in the very life of Christ. That can't be taken away. Through the new nature he's given me, I am given the ability to trust his heart.

All this sounds like good news, but it is a glorious problem. A heart that tastes of God's goodness is never unopposed. In the movie *The Fellowship of the Ring*, Saruman, formerly a good wizard and friend to Gandalf but now seduced by the powers offered him by the dark lord Sauron, tries to get Gandalf also to "enlist" in Sauron's dark army. Gandalf resists, calling Saruman a fool for having given in to Sauron's enticement, and tries to flee. Saruman blocks Gandalf's escape and, in a classic clash of powers, pins Gandalf high against the wall. Saruman says this: "I gave you a chance to join [in the power of the dark lord Sauron], but *you chose the way of pain*."

Satan hates us for not joining in and will do anything to eradicate our allegiance to and trust in Love. Saruman was right about one thing: saying no to evil is *the way of pain* because it is an actual relinquishment of power. We relinquish not only the "full understanding" we spoke of earlier but the power that accompanies it. Not exactly a winning marketing line: "Come follow Christ and become powerless!" I can see the faces of men, especially, grimacing at this point. But this is the surprise: the life we have been missing is found where we least expect it. When we seek to save our own life, we are bound to lose it, and in losing it, we will find it. *Is it you, Jesus? Are you truly asking me to give up my power, trusting yours instead?* This startling Voice does ask us to be powerless, as Christ relinquished his power in Gethsemane. The surprise comes in that we get to share in the power of his rising. He asks us to become as humble as a child in order to be the greatest in his kingdom. We're asked to share in the Crucifixion, so that resurrection life can flow.

The powerless don't fare so well in this world, have you noticed? We have some idea how much we are hated because of our allegiance to Jesus. Evil—the enemy of God, the Adversary, the accuser of all who belong to Jesus—is our nemesis who rarely tips his hand that he is even there until we begin to grant Jesus access to our world. When we begin to respond from the heart, all hell breaks loose. And it is in this battle that we learn the truest things about Love.

When we tune in to our heart's posture, it first sounds something like this: "Is it you, Jesus? You're asking me to trust your power, but are you even there as I see evil's assaults on those I love and as I feel the taunts in my own life? Are you really greater than all this?" Then we move into "Oh no, Jesus. You don't provide complete and total protection from this enemy. What exactly *do* you promise to protect?" And then, in just the nick of time, it becomes "Oh good, Jesus. Because of who you are, I really don't need to fear, because even in the darkest onslaught against my heart, the Enemy cannot have my soul." As we move through these postures, some things about us are revealed: how we choose to be naive about evil and how we tend to fear rather than resist this one who hates us.

I See Nothing, I Hear Nothing

Years ago I heard naiveté defined as "chosen blindness." I know a woman who was harmed as a girl by someone in a position of trust. Now, as an adult, she is interviewing a day-care provider for her own daughter. The financial charges are reasonable, but the day-care worker is evasive when it comes to offering references. This woman is enrolling her daughter anyway. "I'm sure it is fine," she said. "They are just too busy right now. I'm sure they'll get around to showing me references." Should this woman live in paranoia all her life? Of course not. But for this woman to turn a clear, open eye to the vulnerability of her child, she'd have to remember her own life. She'd rather choose blindness. I also know a man who was mentored in business by a leader who he now notices is making unethical financial decisions. Choosing blindness is easier than a confrontation and facing disappointment in someone he's wanted to emulate. Chosen blindness can be cultural, too, like the movement on some college campuses to teach that the Holocaust didn't really happen—evil *couldn't possibly* exist in such ways. There's no question that this blind choice is the easier path.

One redemptive thing to seep out of the ashes of September 11 is a renewed awareness that evil does exist. As a culture, we had allowed the veil of tolerance to cover our eyes to evil, but now the global community has been forced to root out "evil schemes" wherever they are brewing. Terrorism is hardly the comprehensive face of evil—it shows itself just as much on television or in my own judgments against others—but at least we're cluing in.

The temptation to turn the other way, whistling while darkness plunders, is a historical one. Atrocities prior to Rome's demise are comparable to what we now witness on CNN or MTV. Pol Pot, Milosevic, and Kim Jong Il were *allowed* to rise to power. During the genocide in Rwanda, millions were slaughtered in the early nineties as the whole world, it seems, kept living their lives, choosing to look the other way. The Russian soldiers who went in to free the surviving Jews at Auschwitz certainly wished they could choose blindness when they uncovered the ovens that incinerated millions and the buildings filled with human hair, which was used to weave rugs for the Nazi elite.

And, as has been true in reigns of terror throughout history, the rise of evil brings to the surface the truest things about Christians—that our lives are imperative and chosen for such times as these. I have not gone looking for some of the people and situations I've encountered in the past twenty years. In some of these situations as a counselor or as a friend, I have royally messed up. But there have been other situations that made it clear that my life *is* for such times as these. I am nothing but humbled as I say this. Why would a woman I had never encountered before show up at my office and within six months have memories of praying for me when she was living on the streets in Texas and I was living in Africa? She had visions to pray for me as she was trying desperately to extricate herself from a cult. God was preparing *both* of us for her to get help. And just as the wonder of all this began to set in, the cult began its meddling, mean retaliation for her getting assistance. Threatening phone calls were made. My sweet dog was poisoned (she's fine, but it was awful).

In the late 1990s Brother Tom Wolf predicted, "As this generation of Christians [in the West] connects with the global church in the twenty-first century, they may be the first that shed blood."[1] Though it might seem like it, it is not a militant war cry. It is a beckoning to move outside of ourselves, quietly counting the cost as we open our eyes to anything that opposes Jesus. For every fairly dramatic story in my life, there have been a thousand unseen moments where I was asked to make a choice, either in my thoughts or in my behavior, to choose Love's path or my own power. Jesus doesn't distinguish; they are all moments when he knows we are making a choice to either step into or lean away from how much he wants us to be present in this world on behalf of Love. Love asks that we be willing to lay down our lives in simple and, if called to it, profound ways.

Open Eyes to Ourselves

Today the number of sexual assaults, especially against children, is rising, as is the number of children harming other children. The flow of sexual slaves from Eastern Europe and Asia, fueled by a supply-demand vacuum of bored traveling businesspeople in the West, is growing in mind-numbing percentages. Federal funding is designated to assist in the formation of a synthetic DNA, which scientists hope to use to create life out of nothing. Crimes committed by adolescents have increased. Video games are available that depict assaults with gold clubs and automatic weapons and allow the player to participate in gang rapes. Every day I'm tempted to let the love in my heart grow cold.

So why choose to see these things? We must, because it shows up in subtle ways in *our own* lives. We don't want to see our own capacity for it. Unless we are willing to recognize ways that we join in with evil through the hardness of our own hearts, all the hype about evil falls mute like mounds of celluloid outtakes. Another way of saying this is that if I'm not willing to grieve the jealousy in my own heart, then battling against the one who is jealous of God rings hollow. If I'm not disturbed by my own selfishness, then railing at my supremely selfish enemy falls flat.

When Eve "was convinced" (my least favorite phrase in Scripture), she chose to join with the dark offer to know and see *all*. Had she not been convinced by the deception, she and Adam would have remained in a garden so powerful that Africa's Victoria Falls couldn't compare, a place so tranquil it would make the Sonoran Desert seem chaotic. Evidently it was just too much for her—letting God keep his secret things, the knowledge of good and evil, and resting, trusting that God was revealing to her just what was best for her. She reduced the lavish gift of God as she set her eyes on her own power.

How I am convinced to set my eyes on my own power is not so different. It shows up when I try to manipulate a friendship or when my heart secretly burns with jealousy as I see someone else lauded and appreciated. My tendency to reduce God's lavishness shows up in my attitudes. I have walked with God for several decades now, and though I'm still young in many, many ways, I have observed this to be true: we as Christians like to think we know much more than we really do. I believe this is when we are most vulnerable to evil's whispers against God and our own hearts. I can so easily live from an attitude that sounds like this: "I am so glad I am not like others who haven't clued in to the spiritual battle yet. I can see the Enemy coming a mile away. I'm so glad I'm not blind." When I slip into this attitude, I have taken God's lavish gift—his mercy to make me as wise as a serpent and as harmless as a dove so evil can't win in my life—and reduced it to something I own, I achieve, I attain. Once again, notice the ease with which I reach for the Tree of Knowledge of

Good and Evil. We all do it. We want it to be clear so we don't have to lean in and trust someone else's understanding.

DELIVER US FROM...

Evil wants to steal and destroy, and Jesus's love for us is more powerful, promising to bring life where evil meddles. Notice I didn't say Jesus would rescue us from every meddling encounter. Jesus told us he came to give the abundant, full life that a Good Shepherd wants to give to his flock. Anyone who has tended to a flock of any kind of animal can tell you that attacks from the outside happen. Jesus acknowledges this. He speaks of the thief in an "of course there is a thief, and he'll kill you if he has a chance" way. What he emphasizes is how we are to recognize his good voice, trust it, and follow.

Years ago I lived on a small sheep ranch. Too many mornings to count I would wake up to the most hideous sound: the bleating of sheep that were stuck in the fence. I'd look out my window and laugh. It was like clockwork, their stupidity and stubbornness. These guys had lush, green pasture to roam around in, and the field on the other side of the fence was a mess of tumbleweeds, old tires, and windblown trash and was vulnerable to the predators of the nearby hills. Those sheep just *had* to get to that dry, messy, unprotected field. It was the other side of the fence, and that seemed to be all they cared about. They'd stick their necks through the wire and get stuck, and then their whining and crying would begin. I'd watch as the man who tended those sheep would go out and gently pull them backward. (They didn't realize that the whole time they were crying, all they had to do was back up!) He'd nudge them, they'd rediscover green grass, and they'd be content again, for a few hours.

The abundant life is obviously not safe pasture without attack. If that is true, then I'm doing something terribly wrong. What Jesus lets happen inside his gate is too much for me at times (okay, most days). But he promises to *lead me out* into the pastures that he knows will be best for me. In the vulnerability of these days of watching my mom and brother in the dying process, and as I've sought to finish this book—a project that, at moments, seemed impossible—the wolf has been prowling. Last night is an example.

Friends have prayed specifically and intentionally for the protection of my home and my sleep. They have prayed authoritative, passionate prayers. But last night I was awakened with a deep sense of dread, a foreboding that caused my blood to chill. I felt very alone and vulnerable. I wrapped myself up and went downstairs and said, "Jesus, why is this happening? You know how weary I am of being assaulted. We have asked you to protect me. Please, please remove this thing that is pressing on my heart and mind." Nothing seemed to change. After a long while, the darkness dispersed, and I was able to go back to sleep. If I'm honest, I was disappointed in Jesus for not protecting me better. The next morning I got a phone call from friends I'd not heard from in quite some time. "Jan, we wanted you to know that both of us were awake in the night last night, and both of us felt Jesus compelling us to pray for you. It's a strange way to keep in touch, but please know we battled for you last night." As I listened to their words, I was silenced by Jesus's message to me: *Even when it seems there is no protection, I am moving heaven and earth to keep your heart well.* He knew it was best for me to be reminded of this, even if I had to suffer for a short while.

I want Jesus to say to me, "I am the Good Shepherd, and I will lead you out to the place where there is no enemy, because I could never bear to see you wounded." He never says it. So again, I have to lean in, wrestle with a God who is beyond my understanding, and follow into deeper levels of trust in his love. Jesus promises the abundant life even as the thief lurks in the brambles, even as the thief gains access in the night. When our focus is on the thief, we become captives in our own green meadow. With our hearts attuned to the Shepherd, we can know the freedom of recognizing the Enemy's presence without succumbing to the captivity of fear.

THE POWER OF HUMILITY

My first obvious encounter with the thief happened in my friendship with Andrew Sanker, a man who left Hinduism to serve Jesus Christ in the East

Indian areas of coastal South Africa. With the smell of curry coming strong from the kitchen, I was visiting with Andrew and his family in his home one afternoon. An urgent cry came from the front garden. A member of Andrew's small group was more than distraught and needed help. Our little entourage followed the man to his home just a few blocks away in this crowded neighborhood that could easily have been mistaken for a neighborhood in Calcutta. My Indian friends and I were so sad to see this man's fourteen-year-old daughter tormented by evil spirits. She was being physically bound and gagged by the spirits and literally tossed across the room by the cruelty of evil. She could say nothing; she was at the mercy of this assault. The man explained that this sweet girl had become a follower of Christ just a few months earlier and had been devouring Scripture like food. This attack was the first of its kind in the home.

Was I seeing things? I didn't know how to respond. As I watched it all, scriptures flooded my mind. I remember thinking, *Oh, yeah—Jesus "cured many people of their various diseases, and he cast out evil spirits and restored sight to the blind."* But these weren't pages on my lap in a church pew. Reality jumped out of a book and into the present, awe-producing moment. I wondered how or if Jesus would intervene. I felt a mixture of faith, anticipation, and sheer doubt that anything would stop this assault. Think for a minute about your personal torments that no one can see. Isn't the heart response the same?

My Indian friends were not shocked. To them, this was a predictable assault against one of God's children. In a Hindu environment, power and fear are the language of life, and my friends knew that evil desired only to push this point.

Jesus had other things in mind, and maybe one of the greatest was to shatter my categories of what evil can and cannot do to a believer in Christ. That day evil was allowed to do way too much. I could not reconcile it. How could this Christian girl be the playground for such darkness? But I watched as Andrew and the others began to humbly pray, confessing that although they had been given authority over those demons, they did not rejoice in that power, but they rejoiced that Jesus already had this girl's heart, and their own. They read scriptures about Christ's authority over all rulers and authorities in the unseen, heavenly realm and truths about this girl as his child. There was no dramatic show by them (to match the drama of the dark spirits), just humble pleading and confession of truth. After a long, agonizing time of "reminding" evil of its place and its eventual destruction before the living God, the grip started to loosen. But the girl still could not speak. It took her community, her family and friends, and those in the body of Christ who could speak that day to speak for her. After many hours, the dark power broke, and this precious young woman collapsed in a heap on the floor, thanking Jesus over and over, with tears, for releasing her.

Had she been set free from captivity? No question. This girl would live with the gratitude that comes from having her life delivered from bondage. But through her struggle, those of us watching were freed from a different kind of captivity. We were confronted with our complete inability to do anything; we were set free from any presumption about our own power. My Indian friends, who witness this kind of overt craziness frequently, had a humility about their authority in Christ that I haven't witnessed since. Sounds kind of backwards, I know. We would think that those who encounter evil and see it flee would grow broad shoulders when thinking about the true commission Jesus gave his disciples to cast out demons (Mark 6). But that was not their posture. These friends fully understood their authority; they understood they were *necessary* in order for this girl to be released. What anchored them was not their authority but the humble thought that their names are written in the Book of Life.

EVERYDAY DELIVERANCE

Many of the assaults we face are as damaging as what the Indian girl faced. But we think of it as *normal* life. We believe condemning messages without a blink, never once thinking that they are throwing our hearts up against the wall, trying to steal our belief in Love, or accusing us for our unbelief. Let me give you an example from my own life.

Not-So-Obvious Evil

There is a spirit of pride that runs deep through my family blood. It shows up when my father and I lock horns on a ridiculous subject, only because we don't want to give the other the pleasure of being right. It shows up in isolated relationships (we rarely call one another) and misunderstanding. So what does this say about us?

It can be stated differently, depending on your tradition. My charismatic and prophetic friends would say, "Your family bears the generational sin of pride, and the blood of the Lamb is the only thing sufficient to break it and keep it from being passed down to the next generation." My counseling friends would say, "Your family's self-protection shows up most as you hide behind your own resources. This must be repented of in order for there to be change." And other friends would simply say, "Have you ever noticed your family is hard to be around?" All of the above is true. All of the above speaks about the *spirit* of my family. Forget the semantics. It would be naive to look at my pride and its interplay with my family heritage through only one of these lenses and try to nail it down with language and a system of "undoing" it. I must continually search my heart for the ways my pride is causing harm. For me it shows up in a cross-armed attitude of "Fine. I'll be okay without them."

As I think about how my pride brings harm, Love also asks me to consider how this pattern is keeping me safe. *What am I afraid will happen if I admit how much more I want with the members of my family?* Finally, it invites me into a prayerful, intentional intercession on behalf of my family. I pray that all dark intentions set against my family line will lose power and that Jesus will deliver us from evil. Can you hear what starts to happen inside of me as Love beckons? My own heart's crust begins to fall away, a dependent posture comes, and a spirit of humility rises to wash over the pride.

I have a good friend whose demons produce an empty momentum. He's always moving, never stopping long enough to be really intimate with anyone. He joins hands with the demons of pressure and pride as he chooses to believe that people in his world will fall apart or think less of him if he is not being productive on behalf of everyone else. Author Kathleen Norris understands this. She says:

> Anger is my best demon, useful whenever I have to go into Woman Warrior mode, harmful when I use it to gratify myself, either in self-justification, or to deny my fears. My husband, who has a much sweeter nature that I, once told me that my mean streak grieved him not just because of the pain it caused him but because it was doing me harm. His remark, as wise as that of any desert abba, felt like an exorcism.[2]

How do we choose to see our inner demons, to keep our eyes open to evil's ways without getting overwhelmed? And how do we find the courage to walk in the way of pain without despairing? The answer is in our willingness to die. *Oh, no.* When we aren't afraid to lose everything, then nothing can threaten us, including—no, make that especially—evil.

Our Not-So-Obvious Responsibility

You can see how the reality of evil and our response to it are woven loosely together, like a rope hammock. When I focus only on my response to evil, it leads to pressure: "I have to be alert! I can't let my guard down!" or "I have to make sure I repent perfectly so Satan has nothing on me!" When I focus only on how much evil has taken from me, I quickly lose heart and don't engage my will: "What's the big deal? My ability to hurt a friend is nothing compared to how I've been hurt, so why bother even thinking about it?" But Jesus binds these two realities together, giving me a resting place, a place where I'm in need of him. As we walk through each day, it is a resting place of knowing that sometimes we need to be alert to Satan's schemes. Sometimes we need to repent, and sometimes we need to chill out. It is a rest that comes from listening to what Love wants for us at any given moment. This rest allows us to respond without so much pressure.

We've all known people, perhaps walked in relationship with them, who have been victims in the truest sense. They have really been hurt. I'll not forget the first time I needed to call such a person on her meanness and stubbornness. It felt crazy. How could I ask anything of such a wounded heart? Jesus respects us so. He never treats us solely on the basis of the harm done to us. As the two ropes of the hammock came together for this person, we grieved the ways evil had tried to steal her joy, and she grieved ways she had, in her stubbornness, shut out love. The ropes, together, allowed her heart to feel secure in the tears of God and in the good heart Jesus had given her, which she was covering over with her hardness.

THE TRAP OF FEARING EVIL

Sometimes we're blind to our level of fear of the Enemy. Can we, as we enter the battle, be willing to see the fear we live under that actually becomes worship of the enemy of Christ?

A few years ago my counseling partners and I had the privilege of working with women who had grown up in homes where religion was practiced during the day and satanic cult rituals were performed with and against their precious bodies and hearts at night. This was daunting work, as you can imagine, but it also gave me glimpses into the eternal realm more than anything else of which I've been a part. Nothing has taught me more that only the power of Love can crush the serpent (Romans 16:20) that is behind the dismantling of children's innocence.

Sheri was a lawyer with a prestigious firm in another state. No one in her practice would have any idea of the fractured internal existence she held together through disassociation. She was a savvy lawyer in the marketplace but a terrified, cowering ten-year-old in our office. One day she came into our offices trembling. She was holding a small, ornate gold box. As she sat with it, she stroked it as if it were treasure, but she looked at it as if it were fire. It took a long time for her to explain that this box held some of the choice "instruments" used in the ritual that shattered her psyche but also promised her power from darkness. We're talking about real power—not imagined. These rituals were used to initiate her into a high level of leadership in the cult structure, promising and providing her money, power, and esteem. Sheri sat before us, terrified to hand over this treasure that tormented her with memory but afraid to keep it around. She felt it held evil power.

It's what happened to my partners and me that I really want to communicate, though. Here we were, knowing that it was right to invite Sheri to hand over this box, this object that represented pain and falsehood. As she did so, we were left with figuring out what to do with the box. As we stared at it, a strange thing began to happen. We began to *fear it.* I'm not talking about the kind of fear that prompted all of us to crush our "evil" LP records in the seventies; it's similar, but not the same. We began to fall into the trap that delights evil so much; we suddenly felt pressure to handle the box just the right way, with just the right words, expressing a strong enough authority to keep it from causing problems in our office. I'm putting this into words, because it is a common trap. Do you see what we were doing? We bumped up against something that evil had used, and we felt we must "disarm it" like a bomb, with the correct CSI intelligence and equipment. In our fear of this object, we became momentary animists, forgetting that "God disarmed the evil rulers and authorities. He shamed them publicly by his victory over them on the cross of Christ" (Colossians 2:15).

What we fear, we will serve. If my counseling partners and I had stayed with the fear, that object would have ruled our daily routine (praying just the right prayer before entering the office) and therefore would have become our object of worship. Thankfully, Jesus nudged us out of that posture. We invited Sheri to have a new ceremony, one where she picked out a new box and some new contents for the box (not "instruments" but treasures) to signify Jesus's love for her and her place in the kingdom. We all went with her and buried the old box. You can imagine the spiritual opposition surrounding that one lovely afternoon gathering. But the true battle is the battle over Sheri's belief that evil's power is dead compared to Christ's love for her. I believe Satan shrieked more as Sheri lavished some new gifts upon herself than if we had remained terrified of all the potential demons in the room. Why? Because there is no fear in Love (1 John 4:18). Now there was a tangible reminder of evil's attempt to destroy and the disarming, healing power of Love.

Kathleen Norris speaks similarly of the delight she has in her Benedictine medal, given to her upon becoming a lay associate. The medal bears these words: "Begone Satan! Tempt me not with your vanities! What you offer is evil—drink the poisoned cup yourself!" She treasures the prayer and the power of the words, but she says this of it: "I value it as a reminder of God's daily care for us. But it is not magic: while putting on the medal is a good way for me to start the day, I do not panic if I forget to wear it, or to say the prayer. *That would ascribe too much power to the forces of evil.*"[3]

ONE LITTLE WORD

The spiritual momentum in the late seventeenth century was strong, when many were forced to see the church they loved lose its power under a structure of greed and secrecy. As many started to say no to things that grieve God's heart, they became targets, both in their private lives and through the unseen assault, as the subterfuge of the true things was uncovered. I think the greatest spiritual-warfare song ever penned was written during those days by Martin Luther, who had the guts (or any similar word in German!) to set off this warfare by pounding his Ninety-five Theses to the doors of the Wittenberg Cathedral. Luther was up against the Catholic Church itself, and he was up against the enemies of his own heart. I love that he wrote "A Mighty Fortress Is Our God" in the midst of this personal mission, fueled by love of Jesus's saving grace through faith. Read the song in its prose form (sadly, we rarely sing the whole thing anymore, and it loses its punch without the story it is telling):

> A mighty fortress is our God, a bulwark never failing. Our helper, He, amid the flood of mortal ills prevailing. For still our ancient foe doth seek to work us woe—his craft and power are great, and armed with cruel hate—on earth, is not his equal. Did we in our own strength confide, our striving would be losing. Were not the right man on our side, the man of God's own choosing. Dost ask who that may be? Christ Jesus, it is He—Lord Sabaoth His name, from age to age the same. And He must win the battle!
>
> And though this world with devils filled should threaten to undo us, we will not fear for God hath willed His Truth to triumph through us. The prince of darkness grim, we tremble not for him—his rage we can endure, for lo, his doom is sure. One little word shall fell him—that word above all earthy powers, no thanks to them abideth. The Spirit and the gifts are ours with Him who with us sideth. Let good and kindred go, this mortal life also. The body they may kill, God's truth abideth still. His kingdom is forever!

God is limitless. Evil not only has limits, but it operates under the strictest, most suffocating hierarchy you can imagine. Because of this, it is limited not just by the authority it is under with Jesus ascended and reigning, but it is limited by its very nature—a fallen, rejected defiler at the helm, who holds memory of untold beauty, charisma, and power ("on earth, is not his equal") but who will one day shrivel like a star-gazer lily in a desert inferno. When we become naive to evil's limits, we are saying that we live in a dualistic universe—God and his enemy battling it out on the same plane, and we hold our breath to see who will win.[4] I fall into this trap so quickly when I'm in the midst of a battle with contempt, because the battle is all I can see. Dark lies feel too real, too big. But it really is true—"one little word shall fell him."

Laughter and Lightness in the Face of Evil

How is it, do you think, with all of this being true, that Jesus has the audacity to say, "My burden is light"; "Do not be anxious about your life…. Consider the ravens: they neither sow nor reap…and yet God feeds them…. Consider the lilies,…they neither toil nor spin." And he ends it by saying, "Seek first his kingdom" (Matthew 11:30; Luke 12:22, 24, 27; Matthew 6:33, RSV). Jesus knows his kingdom is deeper, far deeper than the war we are in. In this kingdom, resurrection life is the final reality. This kingdom and your heart made alive for acts of love and service are what the war is fought over.

I know a woman who is looking evil in the eye as she confronts the fact that her father and stepmother made extra money by handing her over as a child to older boys in the neighborhood for sexual favors. She's facing their harm of her, but she is also facing how Satan has wanted to use her past to enslave her to false messages about herself and about Jesus. Sharon said, "I can walk around the rest of *this* day within the close, safe confines of his living white cloak. Life is within me." This is not naiveté; this is the lightness of the kingdom. Sharon knows the reality of the thief gaining access; she can't be naive because evil stole from her and continues to try to steal every day. When she says "close, safe confines," she is talking about the safe enclave of God's love upholding her in resurrected, ascended lightness—a lightness that comes from knowing there is a power greater than evil at work on her behalf.

This is why Jesus's audacity is more than justified. It helps me understand how Jesus can say to me, "Fear not." Ted Loder states, "I passionately believe that our deepest longing is for the freedom Jesus spoke of, lived out, and calls us to share: *the freedom not to be afraid.* Even small doses of that freedom will enable us to live in the world differently."[5]

Our Bumbling Authority

I fully believe in the authority given to every believer in Christ. His authority is our authority. We no longer belong to evil, and we have a restored dignity that words cannot capture. Now, this might sound like a contradiction, but can we be honest for a moment and admit that *the working out* of our authority looks a lot more like Barney Fife than an NYPD police chief? We hold the badge, and we get the job done, but we bumble along more than we're flooded with confidence. I think God takes delight in this. God sees Schwarzenegger as we muddle along like Columbo. He sees Kristin Scott Thomas when we're all over the map like Lucille Ball. God sees heroes in bumbling hobbits. Even as I write this, I see an office cluttered and disheveled. I know I have it in me to be Isabel Allende, typing her novels on an immaculate desk adorned with fresh flowers (on the Argentine coast, no less), but the glory and authority that seep out of me comes as a surprise to me, under protest—and under a few piles most times! When we do have wonderful, full-glory moments, our hearts are flooded with the *yes* of eternity, yet we know it is fleeting. So the question we must ask is, How can our hearts rise with the fullness of no longer belonging to evil, but rest knowing that the working out of our new identity may be, shall we say, less than lustrous?

I love the authoritative buffoon in the book *The Fellowship of the Ring*. His name is Tom Bombadil, and he is part court jester, part powerhouse. In a fearful encounter in the Barrow-Downs, a dark figure (a Barrow-wight) puts an icy grip on Frodo and his friends, leaving them in a slightly frozen fog (which is where, if we're honest, we find ourselves most of the time). But Frodo knows they cannot remain frozen and survive, much less complete their mission. Frodo remembers the face of Tom Bombadil and his merry ways as he ruled the forest. He remembers Tom's lilting attitude about himself and his authority in the woods:

> None has ever caught him yet, for Tom he is the master:
> His songs are stronger songs, and his feet are faster.[6]

Tom understood that he was the master of all powers within his sphere. But he wasn't taken with himself or prideful; the authority just made him glad! Frodo was strengthened by this thought and quoted Tom to the thing that gripped them: "Get out, you old Wight! Vanish in the sunlight!"[7]

We're told that "at these words there was a cry and part of the inner end of the chamber fell in with a crash. Then there was a long trailing shriek, fading away into an unguessable distance; and after that silence."[8] When we listen with the ears of our heart, we can hear that long, trailing shriek, the clamor and fog of condemnation giving way to the silence of grace. We hear this whenever we remember the authority Christ has given us, and it simply makes us glad. We are not to be enamored with the authority given to us, but we are to present it as a humble offering to the One we're now indentured to, in love. This way we can walk with Tom's confidence and Tom's humility.

There is an old story in the desert fathers' tradition:

> An elder…went out to cast a demon out of someone who was possessed. The demon said to the elder, "I am going to come out, but I am going to ask you a question. Tell me, who are the goats and who are the sheep?" The old man said, "I am one of the goats, but as for the sheep, God alone knows who they are." When he heard this, the devil began to cry out with a loud voice, "Because of your humility, I am going away," and he departed.[9]

We are in a war and must show up for our place in the war. But this is a war where all soldiers—men and women, support personnel and Red Cross employees—all have one thing in common: we all, at one time or another, carried the flag of the enemy. The minute this is forgotten, we lose our power. We resist evil in humility, drawing near to God in awe of our change in allegiance. We lean in and ask if Jesus could possibly want us to give up our own ability to protect ourselves in this war, and we hear his startling reply: yes. He, in fact, does want us to stop fighting in our own power, but he doesn't leave us unarmed. He bestows his power on us as we humbly remember *his* power and authority. There is spaciousness in this, allowing us to say, "Oh good, Jesus." I can watch a crimson finch outside my window and find a knowing smile grow inside me that says, *The one who created this playful little bird is the same one who has crushed the head of my Enemy. Somehow, in ways that confound the wise, he has this battle fully in his control.*

The Response of Grace

Even when I remember the authority Jesus has given me, or when I think of the fullness of his life inside me, or when I am anticipating my full restoration, I still find that I exhale the most, find the most relief, in admitting my capacity to hang with the goats, the pigs, the convicts, adulterers, and murderers. The problem is, demons understand my capacity for it too. They are legalists to their core. They will call us on every shred of evidence they have gathered from human history, from our family lines or from the wandering of our hearts in this past hour. How do we want to reply? By trying harder not to hand them any evidence? Or by handing them a full affidavit of guilt, amazed because we know the indictment and sentence should be ours, and instead our God gives us a feast. Do we want to scramble to clean the mud from our face so the demons have nothing on us or even to scramble to match wits with them, making sure each accusation is rebutted with a statement of truth? When we try to meet their legal demands, we end up exhausted. Maybe the thing to do is to stand, mud stained, in stunned silence that there is laughter from heaven as the aroma of the meal hits our nose, as the Father runs down the road to kiss us. There's nothing that can prompt the laughter of heaven more than agreeing with a demon about your sin.

Even in Stumbling

It isn't about power. I mean it isn't about our finding and maintaining power. It is, of course, about Jesus's power. He is, after all, the one who makes a way for the Father's feast on our behalf. I'm reminded of Moses's words to the sweat-matted, exhausted, and forgetful Israelites in the desert: "And remember the miraculous signs and wonders, and the amazing power he used *when he brought you out* of Egypt. The LORD your God will use this same power against the people you fear" (Deuteronomy 7:19, emphasis added). We have been delivered out of the bondage of our own captivity. The power of cancelled guilt, the power of covenant love—we can trust this. Trust in his promise is perhaps the most effective weapon we have against our enemy.

I'm not talking about perfect trust. I'm talking about a direction of trust…
the leaning-in, listening, responding, screwing-up, laughing, falling-on-our-
face kind of direction. Not perfection, but a heart set on obedience. Remember Screwtape and his instruction to Wormwood in Lewis's *The Screwtape
Letters*? Screwtape says in his lesson about God:

> He cannot "tempt" to virtue as we do to vice. He wants them [his
> followers] to learn to walk and must therefore take away His hand;
> and if only the will to walk is really there He is pleased even with their
> stumbles. Do not be deceived, Wormwood. Our cause is never more
> in danger than when a human, no longer desiring, but still intending,
> to do our Enemy's will, looks round upon a universe from which every
> trace of Him seems to have vanished, and asks why he has been for-
> saken, and still obeys.[10]

My favorite thought from 2 Timothy says, "If we are unfaithful, he
remains faithful, for he cannot deny himself" (2 Timothy 2:13). He's brought
me out from under the judgment of my faithless, doubting ways. He knows I
doubt, I wander, I daily break his heart. But he cannot deny the Spirit, which
resides within me as an inheritance. He cannot deny *himself*. He has bound
himself to love me, and there is no shame in that. That is the nature of a
covenant. I break it. He keeps it. The best marriages understand this.

I'm not sure how it is for you, but the phrase "putting on the spiritual
armor" feels contrary to all of this. Yet when I remember his faithfulness to the
covenant, the spiritual armor isn't so cumbersome and heavy. The breastplate
reminds me that the righteousness is his, not mine. The helmet reminds me
that he saved me; I couldn't save myself. I'm girded up by truth even when, to
use Screwtape's words, Jesus "seems to have vanished." My feet are prepared to
obey even when I feel forsaken. And the sword…well, it cuts into my own
hard heart, dividing and convicting, as often as it is plunged into the heart
of evil.

You are marked for all eternity to be his delivered one. As you live, relinquish your own power and lean into the authority of Jesus, because even as you listen carefully for what lurks in the brambles, you can rest. You can stumble along, sometimes strong, sometimes weak, but always loved.

Seven

LISTENING TO OUR EXHAUSTION

Relinquishing the Pressure

Doesn't anyone…think this sounds like a definition of hell?
—HOWARD STRINGER, chairman of Sony America

I like my neighborhood. It has big, mature cottonwood and aspen trees and lots of open space. A trail system runs along a stream, meandering through comfortable homes and quality schools. If you hate suburbia, you wouldn't love it, but there's enough wildlife to keep even an outdoors person happy. Seems like this would be a wonderful place to let down, to chill a bit. You would think. But when my nineteen-year-old neighbor two doors down comes home at 1:00 a.m., forgetting the volume level on his low-to-the-ground car stereo, I don't have to describe what happens to my peace. I don't have to describe how the tranquil atmosphere evaporates when the beagle four houses down lets out his (consistent and predictable) moan from the torments of hell. He sounds like a peacock. If you've ever heard a peacock, you wonder why God made them so beautiful. I don't need to tell you about the lawn mowers at 6 a.m., the backyard parties until midnight. We can collectively grimace about noises like these; we bear with them, and they eventually go away (well, with the exception of the moaning beagle).

But it is the distant, growing-louder-every-year noise from the nearby interstate that is most hard to bear. I recently realized it is never going away. I have to tune it out, or it will drive me crazy.

Most of the pressure in our lives is like the freeway noise—if we don't learn to tune it out, it is crazy-making. This is why knowing Love's voice is so important—so we can hear how it contrasts with the pressure-filled voices that push to have a say with us and how it contrasts with the pressure we put on our hearts to be something or do something that Love never asks of us.

Just today I've pressured myself by ignoring Jesus's nudges for me to take a nap. My desk is now cleared of a pile of paperwork, but I feel an exhaustion that has been creeping up for weeks. Now I realize that responding to Love's wise admonition would have refreshed me, and the pile would have been taken care of anyway. Today I've spent energy worrying about what the family of a client is thinking about me. And today I've raced across town to check on a friend who had surgery, not so much because I knew Love was calling, but because I knew other friends would be checking in, and I didn't want to appear to be a slacker.

When we're pressured by habitual movement or by the desire to please people, we simply miss the point. It is again what Canon Barnett said about our busy, useful-in-appearance lives that are actually burying our hearts. Love may mess up our lives by what is asked of us, but Love never pressures us or pushes us to prove ourselves to him or to others. For Love, the point is to release us into full, abundant lives that are hallmarked by, as Oswald Chambers says, "simplicity and leisureliness."[1] When our lives are hallmarked by lots of movement but little leisureliness, we can be pretty sure we've ceased leaning in to ask, "Is it you, Jesus?" and we've either been living on autopilot or in response to pressure.

THE PRESSURE IN EMPTY MOVEMENT

I like to think of myself as someone who lives with simplicity and leisureliness, but pressure shows up for me in the people arena. I have kept a numbing pace in my attempts to maintain relationships. My movement in this realm is, no question, habitual at times. We all have certain areas of our lives where pressured movement shows up—in business, ministry, parenting, even hobbies. You know how frantic it can be when you pressure yourself to have the "best" day skiing, playing tennis, even snorkeling; the enjoyment evaporates in the harsh heat of pressured competitiveness against yourself.

Thomas Friedman wrote these thoughts in Davos, Switzerland, while attending the World Economic Forum. During a panel discussion about the twenty-first-century corporation, participants described an "age of digital Darwinism": "The key to business today is adapt or die, get wired or get killed, work twenty-four hours a day from everywhere or be left behind." Friedman reported that Howard Stringer, chairman of Sony America, stood up and said, "Doesn't anyone here think this sounds like a definition of hell? While we are all competing or dying, when will there be time for sex or music or books? Stop the world, I want to get off."[2]

Me too, Mr. Stringer. It is a vision of hell. A hell that is becoming the norm rather than the exception. Howard Stringer was a courageous man to voice it, but I'm imagining a collective sigh of relief as the leaders in the room realized how mindlessly they had been pushing to produce. Not all momentum in business is mindless, but you get the point. They may have momentarily realized that their electronics get more attention than their children, that they recognize airports better than their own neighborhoods…or the face of their spouse. They may have realized, as they paused, that the numbers don't add up; the bonus they'll receive this year does not square with the amount spent on the new mortgage, car payment, childcare bill, private school tuition, overseas vacations, insurance, retirement, and taxes. Maybe, in a momentary understanding, they realized they have imprisoned themselves to a life of payments and due dates and a grading system that always says, "Not enough." Maybe they tried to remember the last time they were completely *inaccessible*—no e-mail, no phone, nothing. The lucid moment Howard Stringer gave them may have caused them to reassess how much they've given themselves to the pressure to make the business succeed, rather than simply investing in it and enjoying the process of risk. Maybe some went so far as to realize they didn't have to break their back in order to pay college tuition—that their daughter might do just fine working her way and paying off loans. As C. S. Lewis said in *Mere Christianity*, "The Christian and the Materialist hold different beliefs about the universe. They can't both be right. The one who is wrong will act in a way which simply doesn't fit the real universe." I imagine that the men and women at the World Economic Forum realized for a moment that digital Darwinism doesn't fit the real universe.

I hope for more lucid moments, like the one in Davos, for all of us. We're simply too busy. For example, my neighborhood is nice, but it is also on the edge: it could quickly go the direction of either junky or nice. There are weeds along some stretches of sidewalk, some neglected paint jobs. The people who live here—maturing families with teenagers and school-age kids mostly—would, I believe, love to be tending to these things. They'd all love to have a nice lawn and manicured garden. But because digital Darwinism has crept into most all our lives, there is simply no time. In fact, the volunteer home owners' association board recently sent out a letter saying they all quit because they weren't getting enough help! I'm sure that when the pleas for help are heard, most think, *Come Saturday morning, let me sleep in—at least until I have to get everyone to the soccer field.*

I'm tempted to say this reality is not about our schedules, but of course it is about that. We want our kids to be well rounded and intellectually challenged, but we've forgotten that the word *scholarship* comes from the Latin word *schola*, "to recreate." When you look back on your own life, don't you find that the unstructured, lazy times when you could be imaginative and explore were just as formative as the rigor of fully scheduled days? Dr. Richard Swenson says, "We have come to believe that activity is all that counts, everything else is sloth. If we are not busy, we are not of value."[3] Isn't that tragic? I would ask where this notion came from, but it seems obvious: our enemy takes something wonderful and good—hard work—and, like a desert temptation, turns it into a way for us to prove our worth.

A very simple assessment of how this looks in your life is to—are you ready?—take one day, just *one* day, in the middle of the workweek, one that is not part of a planned vacation. Take this one day and recreate in the way you love best: take a long walk, go golfing, window-shop, go to a mountain lake and swim, go into the city for a movie. As you do this, listen a bit to what's happening internally. It won't take long to hear the messages: *I really shouldn't be doing this. I wonder what they are thinking about me. I had better check in when I get home to make up for this.* This exercise is not completely detached from reality. You might be thinking right now, *You don't understand how much I have going on right now.* Right, I don't. So the question is, if the same proposition were put in front of you in six months, in all honest assessment, would your response be different? What pulls on us rarely ever goes away. Thomas Kelly says, "God will not guide us into an intolerable scramble of panting feverishness."[4] No, God won't, but the one who hates us wants to see us scrambling so we don't have time to hear from God. Talk about pressure. We're so quick to join in.

Our feverishness comes from economic pressure, of course, but it also comes from the internal pressure of proving ourselves. It's sobering to realize that we now associate the word *disgruntled* with those who kill coworkers with unexpected gunfire. I used to hear the word and think of Archie Bunker. This, of course, cannot be "blamed" solely on either the economic situation of these disgruntled workers or their internal pressure. But as we see the growing trend (this form of violence has increased significantly in the past ten years, with six major incidents of its kind in North America alone), what can we learn? We can't know the experience of these folks who—and it's fair to say it this way—cracked. But we can make a general assessment: Job stability and economic security are no longer viewed as good things; they are viewed as *imperative*. Dr. Swenson says, "Progress is not misbehaving. It is not evil. We are not talking about a conspiracy here. Progress is, after all, only doing what we asked it to do. We just did not realize the downside would feel quite like this." The noise on the freeway is only going to increase. "Because progress isn't going to change, *we* have to change."[5]

THE BEAUTIFUL INTRUSION OF REST

It would take a separate book to discuss how this change can come. But a good place to start is by asking how we can unplug and not push so hard. How can we, along with Howard Stringer, respond to the pressure differently—choosing life rather than choosing the pressure of hell? One of the ways is to be intentional to reintroduce rest into our lives. The concept of rest shows up in two words in the Hebrew language: *shabath* and *menuchah*.

Shabath is of course the notion of Sabbath. It has a multitiered meaning: "cease or desist," "to stop," "to take a break." My favorite, which will be no surprise to you, is "to celebrate," which means to have a party as we admire God's creation. When we're pushing too hard, we miss out on this celebrative rest, either in watching light dance on the water or watching light dance in our spouse's eyes. The other word, *menuchah*, means "abode, a settled home, a place to be." As we start to reintroduce Sabbath realities back into our lives, we remember more the thing we really miss in our movement: an intimate, abiding, relationship with Jesus, our Home.

But there is another tier to the meaning of *Shabath*: "to suffer what is lacking." Think about that for a minute. When you think about taking just one day away from all that pulls on you, *shabath* is exactly what is being asked of your heart. Jesus, in his love, is saying, "Please allow something to be lacking. For just a little while don't consider yourself imperative to the progress of the world. And don't consider yourself complete without me." As Sally Breedlove says, "We find rest in the incompleteness of what is and as we trust what is needed for the future will be added at the proper time."[6] That is internal rest, and it is found in the middle of a very busy workweek.

You may have picked up that I'm often convinced I'm imperative for the world to function properly. So I have had, as you can imagine, a difficult time living from this kind of rest. Recently, after several weeks of nonstop counseling, writing projects, and caring for my brother on the weekends as he deals with his chemotherapy, I heard Love beckon me to the worship service at my church. As I've already acknowledged, I often find that church is not a place of rest, so I prepared my mind, knowing Jesus wanted me to simply come to a corporate place to remember him, to rest with him for a while. I got to church, all right. And then the whole time I let my mind wander: I ruminated over the prescriptions that needed to be picked up for my brother; I thought of a client's situation and mused over what needed to be addressed; I rewrote portions of this book in my mind. You get the point. I was beckoned into rest, but when I was called into this place of "suffer what is lacking" rest, I refused to suffer what was lacking, because I figure nothing should be lacking as long as I'm around. It is this kind of daily "let go of it all and rest" moments that feels so dissonant to us—whether from a strong work ethic or subtle conditioning or pressure from our life stories.

RELINQUISHING OUR REPUTATION

It is also hard to let go of our reputation. This one is a sacred cow, I'll admit. One of the hardest things in life to let go of is what people think of us, their estimation of us.

I had an amazing gift given to me this past year. A group of six couples got together, at the urging of one dear woman, to provide a four-month sabbatical for me. Can you imagine? Those sabbatical days started out as a "crash and burn" and slowly opened up into long, lumbering days filled with reading, walks, music, and friends. During those days a quiet, deep healing occurred inside my heart—healing from heartbreak and from years of expending myself as a counselor. It was so kind of God to come like a gentle wind, tending to my wounds and weariness without my having to "go after healing."

Something else happened during those days, something more difficult to face. A few years ago I would not have been able to write about this for fear of what it would do to my reputation. Even now, I share it gingerly. And I'm trusting you, the reader, to hold what I share with honor. During those months when nothing was required of me (no counseling, no writing, no speaking), I experienced dips and mood swings that I had previously written off as residual consequences of my schedule and the nature of my work. Years ago I had to face that the mood swings that had so profoundly debilitated my mom were in fact carried in my body, and in a process that was profoundly humbling, I began a course of preventative medication to ensure this would not get out of hand later in life. I had spent many years facing my story and had asked others to pray for spiritual intervention to break generational patterns or anything that might not be from God. I experienced the Holy Spirit's strength, allowing me to feel as if I could live "above" this struggle. But this surrender to using medication was on a deeper level; it was confessing that, in essence, I walked with a limp and needed Christ's strength in my weakness.

During my sabbatical the extent of my limp frightened me. Here nothing was pulling on me; there was little stimulus other than the wonderful, lazy days. And yet I continued to experience the ups and downs. For those of you who have struggled with your moods, you know the ups and the downs have both a weight and edge to them. I leaned in and wrestled with what Love was trying to say. His reply was not, "You need to believe me more fully, and I will deliver you," but rather a quiet affirmation of his love: "Jan, this is your limp. This is where I have been found by you from the beginning. It is in this struggle you have tasted my love for you. I delight in you regardless of your moods. This is not your identity. But you do have to live carefully. You must give yourself more time and space than most people need. You need more rest than many. Continue to listen carefully to how I view this need, and I will tend to you and keep your heart." Can you hear what happens in the face of such Love? I felt as though I had lost ten pounds. God was not asking me to battle for relief. He was asking me to allow him to be present in the very thing that torments.

I share that story for a few reasons. One is obvious: God's estimation of us is never what we imagine we'll receive from others or from ourselves. The other reason is that we spend too much time in our Christian lives trying to impress others with the ways we have navigated around our suffering and calling that godly. I do think it was right for me to ask, seek, and knock—for years—for this dread thing not to be a part of my life. It was good for me ask, as Paul asked for relief from his thorn in the flesh. But there also came a time when, for the sake of intimacy with Christ, I surrendered to whatever he thought best with regard to my health. Again, you can follow the progression we seem to go through. The Spirit rouses us enough to remember our dreams and desires (I wanted nothing to do with depression; my dream was to be free of this struggle), so we begin to ask, seek, and knock. Sometimes the door opens as we hope; sometimes it remains dreadfully shut. But beyond the anticipated answer to our dreams, Love is always there, longing to love us, to care for us in the midst of our lack of belief and in our weakness. Freedom from reputation can be best found in the simple prayer of the disciple: "Lord I believe, but help my unbelief."

THE PRESSURE IN PLEASING PEOPLE

Similar to protecting our reputation is the pressure to please particular people in our lives. Five years after his divorce John was beginning to have stronger footing than he'd had for a long time. He'd charted the waters of shared custody and loss of extended-family relationships better than most men, but John's heart was still held captive by something. His former wife would often call him to talk about their children—usually to tell him that he was letting them down in some way. John was all there when it came to his kids; he was on the scene with them as much as he could be with the time limitations dictated by the agreement with his former wife. But it wasn't the needs of the kids that shut him down. He shut down in his hollow place whenever his former spouse would begin her cruel, albeit cordial, attacks about his failings.

John had always felt strong in every arena but his marriage. When he was young, his dad was not the kind to be ahead of him on the trail, telling him when he fell, "It's okay. You're doing great. You fell, but you are really strong!" His father lit up a bit only when John would excel. So the trail was not pleasurable and full of companionship; it was filled with pressure to be the best— honors classes, student leadership, Dartmouth undergrad, Harvard Business School. John knew his way around success because there was a gleam in his father's eye when John was sailing above the crowd. It never crossed John's mind that he longed to know his father loved him just for who he was. No accolades, no trophies, just John. John had always wanted to be a poet. He had a strong artistic and expressive side that his father never engaged. Being the classic handyman, his dad ran the tightest ship—no room for the seeming fluff of creativity. The voice John heard was pressure and condemnation when he entered any arena that he couldn't nail.

Well, when was the last time anyone nailed it perfectly with a woman's heart, let alone mastered the world of children? In other words, in the precarious and mysterious world of family and relationships, John felt lost, like a little boy. When his ex-wife launched into him with her criticism, he faded away, thinking just as he had a thousand times in their marriage, *I don't know what she needs. I will never be able to nail this. I'll just give her what she's asking for. I might as well give up.*

So he did, at least in his marriage. He continued to conquer in the world of business and finance, but John gave in to the voice of condemnation every time he allowed his ex-wife to berate him without responding to her. He just took it. He listened to the internal voice that says, *You have to get this right, John, or you are worthless. You have to figure out what is being asked of you and provide it perfectly.* Jesus's voice, all along, had been saying, *John, I see you. I created you. You are a strong man with a good, creative heart, with love to pour out on your wife, your children, and the world around you. Relax. Enjoy yourself as you give to them. If you miss it with them every once in a while, that's okay. They don't want your perfection. They want you. Your presence is the life-giving force they want. I believe in you. Rest.*

THERE FOR US TO ENTER

The book of Hebrews speaks clearly about all this.

> So God's rest is there for people to enter. But those who formerly heard the Good News failed to enter because they disobeyed God. So God

set another time for entering his place of rest, and that time is today.... There is a special rest still waiting for the people of God. (Hebrews 4:6–9)

On the surface it seems that if God asks us to rest, it would be the most natural thing in the world to comply. Evidently this is not the case. Disobedience is actually a failure to enter God's rest. We miss the point of what Love wants for us when we fail to lean in and wrestle with what he is after in asking us to rest; we never get to the point of realizing "Oh good, it *is* you, Jesus. You want to give peace and rest where I've chosen pressure!" When we choose pressure, we allow ourselves to be robbed. When we let a frenetic pace call the shots for us, our lives soon become a living hell. When we allow ourselves to be pressured by reputation, we can miss the intimacy found in hearing what Jesus thinks of us. When we are pressured by what others think of us, we fade away, missing the most important opinion of all.

Eight

RECOGNIZING HIS TOUCH

Relinquishing Our Ideas About Healing

How fragile we are.
—STING

But for you who fear My name, the Sun of Righteousness
will rise with healing in His wings.
—GOD, through the prophet ISAIAH

I come to the subject of healing with ambivalence.

As a little girl, I relished life. My earliest memory is of being on a swing set with my friend Mary. We were swinging in her yard on a bluff overlooking hundreds of miles of high desert plateau leading to the purple Sangre de Cristo mountains in the distance. As the wind rushed through my four-year-old curls, I remember thinking, *This is the most beautiful place in the world. I am so happy.* Winsomely independent but secure even at four, I remember meandering two houses down to my home and walking in to the smell of my mom's sugar cookies and her smile.

That kind of open heart is pierced hard when life brings its wounds. My heart was first pierced when I started to notice little changes in my mom's behavior. It was a gut sensation; I learned to know when all was not well. I can't tell you when the cycle started, but by the third grade I came to expect that she would be home and "fine" for a few months, and then things would change. First she'd stay in bed for days, and then I would hear her talk about the voices she heard—voices that told her she was a horrible person. Then she'd become erratic and unpredictable. One day I came home from school, again to the smell of cookies, but the cookies had been left unattended in the oven. Every appliance in the house was going—the washing machine, the vacuum cleaner—and water was running in the bathtub. And no one was home. Hours later, after our frantic phone calls and searching, the police found my mom wandering in the mountains, not knowing where she was. My heart deflated into an increasingly familiar place of emptiness. I knew that once again she would be taken to the hospital for a long while, and I would be left without her.

We called these Mom's "bad spells" because we didn't know what else to call them. Now we recognize them as severe manic-depressive episodes, in an era when medical treatment for this was slipshod, and also as torment from the Evil One, who was kicking a dear woman when she was most vulnerable. Often during these spells, before she would be hospitalized for long periods, I would find myself, as an eight-, ten-, or twelve-year-old girl, sitting on the couch and talking to my mom about her interior world. I learned early that I was actually *good* at it. She opened up to me in ways she didn't with others, and this gave me a feeling of connection with her—and the only sense of control I had. She'd share her desire to die, and I, as a young girl, would find the words to talk her out of taking her life—at least for a little while longer.

I'm sure, as you think about my young heart, you can feel the weight and pressure that began to settle on me, crushing my winsomeness. The message I learned was this: "You must be enough. You have to come through for her. Jan. *You* must keep her alive."

This wound, and the deception and pressure that it brought, is where I have most needed the healing touch of God. I've begged for this wound to be wrapped in the bandages of Love, and I've sought to be delivered from the deception of having to come through for my mom or anyone else.

And I have known healing. Jesus has touched me, consistently speaking love to me even when I *choose* the false power of being sufficient for others, nursing it like an old drug habit, with no thought of him.

So if I have begged and Jesus has answered, what is the ambivalence? I've touched the hem of Jesus's garment, as the desperate hemorrhaging woman of Luke 8 did, in my quest not to be so bound up with believing I have no worth unless I'm coming through for people. I've been on the receiving end when Jesus says, as he did to this woman, "Power has gone out from me," and God has spoken to me of my worth. But I've also been the frustrated old woman of Luke 18, pounding on the judge's door and pleading with him to heal my brother's cancer—knowing that he promises to weary of my pounding and answer me, but experiencing only what seems to be a cold, closed door.

And it's these closed-door prayers that have led me to realize there has to be something deeper going on at all times than specific answers to my prayers for healing.

CAPTIVITY, FREEDOM, AND THE LONG ROAD TO HEALING

This chapter is a hard one to navigate because the subject of healing is tender —laden with joy for some, disappointment for others. When you saw this chapter's title, I'm guessing you didn't have a neutral response, especially if you or someone you love has been sick or has struggled with physical or emotional health. You may have a miraculous story. You may have a story of disappointment.

There isn't much resistance at first. Opening the door of our hearts is relatively easy when we first hear Christ proclaim his intentions toward us as he stands in his hometown temple, saying,

> The Spirit of the Lord is upon me,
>> for he has appointed me to preach Good News to the poor.
> He has sent me to proclaim
>> that the *captives will be released,*
>> that the *blind will see,*
>> that the *downtrodden will be freed from their oppressors,*
>> and that the time of the Lord's favor has come.
>>> (Luke 4:18–19, emphasis added)

We don't hesitate too much when we hear his kind offer of healing: "I want to make you new; I want to set you free from judgment and restore your true identity." But as Love moves one or two steps beyond the doorway, there we find our own fear, confusion, and ambivalence, if we're honest. When Jesus comes with intimate and personal offers—"Tell me what it is *you* want"—opening the door can feel frightening and threatening. Two things simultaneously go on in me: "Is it you, Jesus? Do you really care enough to see me? You want to touch me?" and "Oh no, it is you. You're asking me to *ask*. I'm afraid to ask, because I'm afraid my request will fall on deaf ears, or worse, that you'll ignore it."

The offer of healing and the questions that surface differ for all of us. The thought of healing may bring a quiet hush to you. The wound in your heart following a breakup may seem as though it will never heal. The emptiness of a miscarriage may haunt you at unexpected moments. Addiction may have lessened for you because of prayer, allowing you to "live into" the healing with ongoing support. For another with the same addiction, the conclusion is "This kind only comes out with prayer and fasting," and they are fasting still. For some of you, healing prompts rage because the answers have not come, not in ways that brought relief from pain. You may be the man who vigilantly tries to rise above the feelings of failure following divorce. You may be the woman who is weary of the constant inner voices telling you that you are not beautiful, compelling, or intelligent enough. For one, healing means prayer in the midst of a chronic illness; for another it means acceptance of the illness, a daily surrender.

The word *healing* has been tossed around in such a way that its meaning has become muddled, even as we try to make it clear. So where do we start? Healing is a mystery, but Jesus wants to give us Love through it all. In this chapter we are going to see how Jesus comes—offering his release, his sight, his freedom—in our process of healing. He comes in *kindness,* showing us our wound really does matter to him ("Really, Jesus?"). He beckons us to *repentance,* showing us that our wounds are never the final determination of who we are, that our wounds are never the bottom line ("Oh, no, you're asking me to move beyond a belief that I've lived with for so long"). And he offers us *restoration and renewed life,* showing us that his gifts of release, sight, and freedom are ongoing ("Oh good, Jesus").

Allowing Love beyond the doorway of our wounded hearts is worth it to see the treasures hidden there—kindness, repentance, and renewed life—offered regardless of the outcome of our specific requests. Allowing Love beyond the doorway allows us to glimpse the deeper, most true story that is going on at all times, despite the outcome.

KINDNESS: SEEING JESUS AS HEALER

Jesus's definition of healing can't be pinned down. For years I looked for the "one way Jesus heals," but now I'm glad there isn't just one, because I'd always be afraid of missing *it.* He is too personal for formulas, though a common thread does show up when we meet the people who sought out Jesus in the New Testament. Sometimes the answer is swift and clear, like it was for the hemorrhaging woman ("If I can just make it to the hem of his robe"). Sometimes we're caught off guard by their faith, humor, and audacity, like the woman who sparred with Jesus in Matthew 15, saying basically, "Jesus, I know my begging is bothering people, but help me because even dogs are permitted to eat crumbs that fall from the master's table" (see Matthew 15:27). Sometimes we're caught off guard by their creativity, like the guys in Mark 2 who believed "If we can just get this hole in the roof big enough, we can get our friend to someone who heals!" Sometimes it is a lifelong process, as with Paul, taking him to an answer he would have never guessed, to what truly ailed him: "I can't plead anymore for this torment to be removed; Jesus's intention must be for this thorn to take me deeper into humility and grace."

Can you hear the common thread? These people are *desperate,* begging him for healing no matter what others might think (or how crazy they felt). They have seen Jesus as healer, and they do whatever it takes to get to him, regardless of the outcome. Desperation takes us to the edge of the garment, through the thatched roof, and into conversations where we beg, telling Jesus of our need. These are good things. Surrendering the answer is, of course, a different story and impossible in our own strength. This is true when we pray for our back pain to lessen or when we pray to shake off the wounds of a painful argument or when we yearn to be released from childhood wounds and deceptions.

Complete and Ongoing

In Christ, we are completely healed. Now, before you respond, you have to know I've wrestled long, wondering if I believe that. I do, even with my own half-covered wounds, with friends who limp through this life spiritually and physically. Imagine sitting in a gathering of people who follow Christ. As you scan the faces, you may see (whether you know it or not) a man who struggles with pornography, a girl in a wheelchair, a woman who has a biopsy scheduled, one who goes to therapy regularly for depression, a man who feels crippled inside because he can't face his father, a man who is feeling his age, a woman who experiences no pleasure in sex because of past abuse, a couple about to declare bankruptcy. So where's the complete healing? I'm more at rest now than I've ever been, but I still have to fight off feelings of pressure and worthlessness—often. Shouldn't I be done with all that by now?

It is a mystery, but the Sun of Righteousness, as Malachi refers to Jesus, comes to all of us with healing that is complete, full, and binding when the judgment for our sin is taken from us. This is kindness. And this is where the best definition of healing begins: it is release from the weight of sin that keeps us in the tomb of self. Peter says that Jesus "personally carried away our sins in his own body on the cross so we can be dead to sin and live for what is right" (1 Peter 2:24). And Paul says, "Since Christ lives within you, even though your body will die because of sin, your spirit is alive because you were made right with God. The Spirit of God, who raised Jesus from the dead, lives in you. And just as he raised Christ from the dead, he will give life to your mortal body by this same Spirit living within you" (Romans 8:10–11). No disease, struggle, or oppression can touch this *life in us* because it is found in the deepest, truest, part of us—our spirit. The life of Christ rises in my heart as consistently as the sun, even on days when I cast a shadow on it with pressure. My sin is simply not enough to stop the life of Christ. The power that blew the stone of death away is now my life, granting daily power to say no to the pressure my wound brings.

I cannot tell you that I am completely healed. I wouldn't try, because the healing Jesus has accomplished in me (through his atonement he has healed my broken heart and set this captive heart free) is too vast and wonderful to be lived into in this lifetime. I will need an eternity to live into it.

In the meantime, I continue my search for healing, and I continue to bear with my ambivalence about healing. It is a bit comical that I am a counselor, because this is where the ambivalence shows up. The life of Christ is the final truth about me, and yet there are days I walk into my counseling office and feel gripped with the old messages: *Jan, you realize, don't you, that the person you are about to be with has a life that is simply way too much for you to handle? Are you going to produce what it takes to come through for him?* The pressure shoots through me to find that old drug. At those moments I become either more determined to come up with something "really good" to impact this person, or I just want to give up.

Yes, I'm completely healed in the life of Jesus, but I must live into this healing on an ongoing basis. Living into this healing means that when the old messages come, I can answer them with the life of Christ: *Yes, I know the person coming for counseling has a life that is way too heavy for me or anyone else for that matter. So the Spirit of God is going to have to carry me and is going to have to come through for this person—loving him, giving him the sight and release I can't give.* Our restoration *is* finished (our complete healing), and yet the restoration is happening each day (our ongoing inner healing).

My inner healing over the years would not be what it has been if it weren't for the confidence I was given, early on, in the ultimate, complete healing of being united with Christ through his blood, resurrection, and ascension. I'm so grateful that I was taught early about God's grace, helping me understand that Jesus is the only faithful one, that my faith begins with his pursuit, and that he is responsible for completing it. When disappointment and confusion pierced my heart, the intellectual knowledge of being a new creature in Christ quickly became *sight* that Jesus wants desperately to meet me in my internal world, loving me and having relationship with me, even when I'm filled with doubt, unbelief, and rage toward him. Jesus opened the eyes of my heart, as Paul prayed for the Ephesians (1:18), to show me that he never tells me to "get over it" when I'm confused or angry about the circumstances or wounds. He points me to the new, perfect life inside of me and always welcomes me home.

When I protest and try to bring out all the evidence against myself—"Don't you see, Jesus? I am unworthy. I am furious, and I'm not even sure I trust you"—he seems undaunted and simply invites me to come and dine with him. Sometimes he is a strong disciplinarian; sometimes he is a tender lover; but he is always patient with my heart, and he is never harsh or condemning toward me as I am with myself.

There's no analogy that can capture this, but the rebuilding of the temple after Solomon's was plundered and burned by the Babylonians is a good picture. Solomon's temple was a painstaking, architectural, and artistic marvel that pleased God and mirrored his requests down to the minute detail. And then it was destroyed. Cyrus was prompted to have it rebuilt, and it was, but with inferior workmanship. The priests who had seen the first temple had eyes to see all that was missing in the second temple. Listen to their reaction when they saw it: "Many of the older priests, Levites, and other leaders remembered the first Temple, and they *wept aloud when they saw the new Temple's foundation. The others, however, were shouting for joy.* The joyful shouting and weeping mingled together in a loud commotion that could be heard far in the distance" (Ezra 3:12–13, emphasis added). That's the way it is with us who are the spiritual temple of the Holy Spirit: Our hearts are new, have been restored—that's worthy of a good shout. We've been rebuilt after plunder, after all. And, in the ongoing restoration, we are worthy of tears—we're not like the original. Our sinful nature continues to weaken our foundation, and we're not yet fully glorified. We are glory and ruin mingled together. God displays his power by restoring our hearts, and he humbly resides in the imperfect temple of our bodies until we see him face to face and become like him.

The Long Process of Healing

I am glory and ruin mingled together. Jesus has not a shred of ruin in him or in the life he's infused in me. No wonder my healing process is clear (I love how much freedom I have from pressure now), and no wonder it is ongoing (I know how far I am from the winsome lightheartedness that was intended for me). No wonder kindness, repentance, and restoration have been intermingled along the way.

No wonder no one can know why healing comes to my friend Mari's inner world as she surrenders to and copes with her MS, while healing comes to Susan's inner world as she begins to exercise an atrophied faith muscle by believing for—begging for—a full recovery from breast cancer. Healing wings spread over us in personal, intimate ways *as we see Jesus as healer, as we beg, and as we surrender the outcome.* This is a lifelong process, and whether we're being called to beg or to surrender varies with the seasons. Usually it's a faith-building blend of the two. We're never done with our healing, not here. And it is rarely the healing *we think* we need. But the process is beautiful, taking us into even more—more of our need, more healing, more Jesus.

REPENTANCE: THE INNER ACT OF FREEDOM

This beautiful process often takes us where we simply must choose to live in the freedom already given to us, even if all the evidence says we are not free at all.

A man preached to a sober, frightened group just a few months after the Nazis had occupied Norway in 1941. Eivind Berggrav offered to them, "Obedience is not submission to a state of serfdom—not at all a passive condition. Obedience is the inner act of freedom, a decision I take. The whole life of Jesus is therefore an encouragement to us to believe trustfully in God. Rely upon His presence even when we cannot see Him."[1] Mind-blowing posture, when you think about it. Foreign, cold, mind-controlling forces have laid siege to your land, and you find inner freedom by choosing to trust what you cannot see.

When my brother, Dick, was given the news that, from a medical standpoint, his cancer was not curable, his response silenced me, showing me what it is like to choose freedom. As we walked out to the parking lot, I felt as if someone had punched me in the stomach and could only imagine what he was feeling. I said, in that feeble way you do when you have not a clue what to say, "Well, there's heaven." Dick said, "Yes. And it is wrong for anyone to say that this is hopeless. Even if I die tomorrow, I have Jesus." After about a week, the shock started to wear off, and Dick went through all the understandable tidal waves of fury and emotion. He would tell you that he hasn't been the greatest guy to be around in his despairing moments. But that initial choice to turn toward inner freedom did sustain him, and all of us who love him, through the long, dark journey. Death had no ultimate threatening sting.

One day, when it got especially dark and the only thing real to Dick was the physical consumption and the spiritual oppression, a friend came and spoke these words: "There is always hope, and victory is always certain." Because Dick had chosen freedom, these words had a landing place inside his heart; they strengthened him for one more day. Chosen freedom always provides healing, even when we cannot see anything good.

Right in the Middle

Take a moment to think about this internal posture of freedom and apply it to your inner world. You may not be facing death, but what has laid siege to your world? What deceptive messages have grown up in your heart? What kind of serfdom is familiar to you? Are you a professional worrier (*I have to stay one or two steps ahead of anything bad that might happen*)? Do you spend the quiet hours in the middle of the night ruminating over how you might fail (*I can't let up; I have to stay on top of things*)? Are you pulled toward hidden eating (*If I feel ashamed of myself, then I don't have to wonder if anyone thinks I am beautiful*)? Do sexual images crowd your mind, leaving little room for those you love? Does Gestapo-like pressure push on your chest and your pulse, causing racing thoughts and sweats? Do you secretly nurse thoughts of your ugliness and all the reasons you are unchosen?

The most natural thing for us to do when imprisoned by deceptive messages is either to give up (submit to a state of serfdom) or to think we have to overcome the thing by force. This is so important to think about, especially in communities that emphasize healing. There have been times in my community when I have felt a subtle embarrassment that I continue to struggle with some internal battle—assuming I am doing something wrong or not following Jesus correctly or haven't asked hard enough or passionately enough. I know I'm not alone in this. We see other people experiencing freedom and release from things that bound them, and so we determine to find a way out of our struggle as well. We ask questions: "How am I going to bust out of this prison? What have I not tried yet?" or "How am I going to outwit or oust my tormentors?" or "How can I defeat my weakness?" In the midst of the addiction or struggle, it sounds more like, "I'm going to get on top of this thing, once and for all."

The really good news is, we aren't meant to escape. We're meant to be *delivered.* We usually think of deliverance as being taken out of the struggle, and then all is well. Actually, the most powerful deliverance comes by the renewing of our mind in the middle of the struggle. Not mental gymnastics, but the renewing that comes from either passionate asking or passionate surrender. Jesus transforms us into a new person by changing the way we think, renewing us as we give our mind and body to God (see Romans 12:1–2). If I wait until I'm "over" my internal pressure or until I've "defeated" the struggle, then it will be a long, long wait before I offer friendship to anyone. I will never have the joy of sitting with people, talking about their lives, and learning from them along the way in the midst of my struggle, seeing Jesus strong in my weakness. This is where Berggrav's posture is so powerful—finding, choosing peace of mind *in the midst of imprisonment* as we surrender our body, our self, our well-being to the hands of God.

We're not to escape? Does this mean that when anxiety presses on our mind we should resign, saying things will never change? I hope the answer is clearly no. Tearing down every speculation and everything that sets itself up against the knowledge of Christ, taking every thought captive to the obedience of Christ (see 2 Corinthians 10:5) is a proactive thing. The healing Jesus offers transcends any escape route we can plan on our own because it is offered to us right in the middle of the worst of the worst. The best posture we can take, the most beautiful question we can ask, right in the middle of our imprisonment, is, "What kind of inner freedom do I want midst this oppression?" If I can remember Jesus's love the moment after an eating binge, there is a growing inner freedom that will one day match the depth and breadth of the freedom of Christ. If I can enter the quiet place of his love as torrents of anxiety hit my heart, that is inner freedom. When a family member rips into me with contempt, and I choose to remember the love of Jesus instead of nursing his condemnation, that is freedom. Sometimes all there is to choose is the inner freedom of allowing Jesus to say, "I see you. I love you. You are mine."

There will always be another intruder coming across our borders; there will always be something new (like a binge, a drink, a chat room, or a clean house) to offer us a false sense of control. There will always be a new enticement to bitterness or jealousy. The renewing of our mind does not bring immediate change. It is a long and learned process. But how much better to know that we can choose freedom at any time, rather than succumbing to the pressure of believing we must outwit and overcome our infirmity.

I imagine you might be thinking, *Yeah, right, easy as that. Just choose internal freedom. You obviously don't know my internal struggle.* No, I don't know your internal struggle. No one but God does—not even you. Often the most respectful things we can bring to the process of healing is to allow the dignity and the life of God to surface in our hearts or the hearts of others when all we want to do is make pain, our wounds, the bottom line.

Once I sat with a woman whose heart was ripped in two by her husband's betrayal and a barrage of painful memories. She was in torment, and she had clearly forgotten that she could choose or engage her will. She saw herself only as a victim. I remember quietly asking Jesus what should be said to her. His answer: "You will not die." *What? Could I possibly have heard you? Jesus, how cold and heartless.* "She needs to know the struggle and pain will not kill her." So I told this woman she would not die. After she was initially offended, over time she was also deeply honored and grateful. She said that without the anchor of chosen freedom, she would have felt disrespected and would have despaired in the midst of the worst of her pain, believing the pain was all there was.

The Hollow Place

The flip side of this beautiful process of healing comes from *honoring* our wounds. Sometimes we don't know what act of freedom to take or what choice for healing to make, because we really haven't faced how much we've been hurt.

One of my favorite novels is *The Power of One* by Bryce Courtenay. Set in South Africa during the Boer War, it tells about a little English boy named Peekay, who was orphaned, raised by African women, and sent to live in an Afrikaans (Boer-Dutch) boarding school. This was not a good thing. The British were considered as heinous to the Dutch as Jews were to the Nazis, and the tormenting tactics of the Boer children reflected this. Peekay was a target. He spent his boarding-school days in fear of relentless, vile abuse by the older Dutch boys who considered him vermin and nicknamed him Pisskop.

At five years old, Peekay prided himself on never crying. Reading about him, we wish so much that he could let down, like so many little boys, in the privacy of his mother's arms or the strength of his father's reassuring smile. ("I know it hurts, Son. Let it out. You'll be okay. I'm here for you.") Peekay never had this. He had to hold himself together with mustered courage while the Dutch boys took his only friend, a rooster named Grandpa Chook, who was his imagined comrade in the Boer War. They killed the bird in front of him. When Peekay was able to escape, he finally let down all by himself:

> After a long while, *when the crying was all out of me and the loneliness birds had entered to build a nest of stones in the hollow place inside of me,* I carried Grandpa Chook to the orchard and laid him in the place I had made to keep him from the rain.... South Africa's first victim in the war against Adolf Hitler was safe at last.[2]

What a picture Peekay gives us of what happens internally when we are wounded. Peekay's words are our words, or at least his words call us to consider our own hollow place. We might think it takes great trauma, like Peekay's, to produce wounds worthy of "a healing." But we have all had moments when the loneliness birds entered—a shameful glance (or no glance at all) from our father or someone we love, an inappropriate touch, a moment of confusion, or rejection—telling us, "This is not the way it is supposed to be," that we were not going to be safe anymore. And we have felt the weight of the stones being built up inside—maybe a pile of bitterness, fear, bewilderment, shame, or betrayal.

The weight of the stones in my life has often been the pressure of being enough for people. The loneliness birds entered my life, making their roost in the hollow place, the terrain of my internal world, and there is more room in there than I had any idea.

We generally avoid our inner world (with the exception of occasional journaling and prayer or an occasional retreat). It is vast and has a God-designed ache; we'll do anything to avoid the ache because, if we're honest, we just don't know what to do with how big it is. David Wilcox compares the interior world—the heart (our desires, our will, and affections)—to a castle that is drafty with loneliness because *it is just too big*. He sings, "If I feel hollow, that's just my proof that there's more for me to follow—that's what the lonely is for."[3] So it follows that when the loneliness birds set up something hard and heavy in this place, it takes up room meant for more of Jesus and more of what Jesus wants with me.

Hiding Behind the Stones

Removing the stones that take up room for Jesus is not as easy as we might think, and—are you ready to admit it?—we want to keep them around. Here's another way of saying it: being hardhearted is easier than responding to the voice of Love. Of course we don't want to keep memories of sexual abuse, harm by a spouse, backhanded slaps, unexpected medical results, or crushed promises around. But the hard stone nest that I make after I'm hurt gives me a false shelter, a block to the flow of God, and in my own fear and stubbornness, I'm happy for it. As long as the stones are blocking me from the light and life of God, I don't have to experience streams of life I'm not sure I want.

A good friend and I were reminiscing about the past five years, during which time I've walked through the death of a friend, two broken relationships, the wildfires, my mom in hospice care, and my brother suffering from the pain of liver cancer. During the losses of the past five years, I have longed for broad shoulders to lean into. This longing is a true and beautiful thing that God has placed in me. When I admit this longing, I am admitting that I am not enough on my own. I can honestly say that I don't have huge illusions of marriage. I don't think marriage would take away pain, and I'm pretty clear on the added suffering that would come from it. But I still long not to have to walk through hard seasons alone. When I take this tender ache to God and let him meet me in my sadness and aloneness, it sounds like this: "Jesus, this continues to get harder and harder. Now more than ever I need to remind you of what I've asked for as long as I can remember—please bring someone who will both love me and will want to expend the energy needed to navigate situations like this with me." The other choice is to harden up, buffet myself, and grumble from behind the hard stones, "A little strength in this world would be nice."

Having hard stones to hide behind gives us something to point to when we need an explanation for why we're not responsive to Love. As long as I'm grumbling about there being no strength in the world for me, I don't feel I have to respond when Jesus gently nudges me to be honest with him. Even as a teenager, I remember first hearing the words, "To all who mourn…, he will give beauty for ashes, joy instead of mourning, praise instead of despair. For the LORD has planted them like strong and graceful oaks for his own glory" (Isaiah 61:3). My immediate gut reaction was not to be encouraged. My honest thinking was, *I want joy, but I'm not sure I'm ready for it. I'm not sure I want to give up my mourning.* Being a strong, graceful oak was a beautiful vision, but the tug back behind the heavy wall was more secure. The God of my Worst Fear, crouching behind a hard stone wall, seemed a much more rational deity.

Seeking and Surrender

Coming to Jesus as desperate beggars—asking, seeking, knocking—can be healing in and of itself. You know what it is to come to Jesus with something specific, only to find that the answer comes in a package you'd never expect. I pray for someone with whom to share life, but when I send guests out the door of my home after a full evening, I am alone. I will keep on asking, *and* I am more and more okay in my aloneness. It is no different with healing. Jesus alone knows what the healing should look like; the answer is held in the hand of Love. Somehow the healing we really need comes through the begging and through surrendering the answer to that hand. As Dallas Willard says, we find peace only in surrendering the outcomes to God. We know by now that the road to that surrender is saturated with desire and risk.

Please hear the difference between these statements: "Jesus, you're the one in charge, so do whatever you want to do with my anxiety, and I will thank you either way" and "Jesus, no one sees me the way you do. No one knows how crippled I feel inside, how much I hate missing out when people get together. I wish I could be in a conversation without feeling so overwhelmed. Jesus, I want so much more than this. Do what it takes to release me from this thing that torments me."

The first choice looks like obedience, but it is a lifeless, detached honoring with the lips while the heart is far from God. The second is the intimate engagement that delights the heart of God. We immediately feel the risk of living like this. We feel like fools, thinking *this is setting me up for great disappointment.* And it just might. But we're asked to surrender ourselves (engage ourselves in faith *and then* let go of the answer), not resign ourselves to a detached, impersonal, fearful god.

I have a friend who has felt the fool for begging his God for healing of a serious back condition. After several major medical procedures and countless hours of prayer, he still has chronic pain. But he also has the kind of relationship with Jesus that you can trust; in that wild, mysterious way, he loves God more now than ever before. Berggrav adds, "Obedience alone can free us. In this faith, liberating obedience is formed."[4] Remember, if we're talking about a choice we make internally, my friend understands liberating obedience, even though he's frustrated every Saturday afternoon when he can't play rough with his sons. Surrender means we plead and beg and pray and cry; we bring our desperate need to Jesus, *then* we begin "accepting that we do not," as Willard says, "have in ourselves—in our own 'heart, soul, mind and strength'—the wherewithal to make this come out right, whatever 'this' is. Even if we 'suffer according to the will of God,' we simply 'entrust our souls to a faithful Creator in doing what is right' (1 Peter 4:19). Now this is a major part of that meekness and lowliness of heart…what rest comes with it!"[5]

RENEWED LIFE: THE DILEMMA OF THE INNER WORLD

So how do we face our stories and remember the broken places, opening ourselves to the healing hand of God without succumbing to the pressure to go after each and every wound? How do we stay open to what Jesus might have in mind rather than demanding a healing that we ourselves define?

The posture of begging *and* surrendering is a good one when thinking about our brokenness and wounds. Otherwise we become professional excavators, miners of the vast quarry of inner stones. We can become narcissistic without realizing it, focused so fully on our healing that we lose sight of living, giving, and love. As my friend Cherie said the other day, "I'm so tired of thinking about myself." Boy, we all hear that. J. I. Packer says, "Often during the past thirty years, I have found myself publicly lamenting the way in which the twentieth century has indulged unwarrantably great thoughts of humanity and scandalously small thoughts of God."[6] At the threshold of surrender we say, "God, your anything might not be the anything I have in mind." Sometimes healing comes in the sweet honey of the Promised Land, sometimes from a desert journey where hope and manna are our only food.

This is so clear to me in my own life. I've wanted, and asked for, complete release from self-contempt and pressure. Along the long road of healing, Jesus has woven himself into my life in *kindness, repentance,* and *renewed life,* but his answers to my prayers have not been what I imagined. First Corinthians 13:11 provides a great framework for looking at this.

When I Was a Child

Remember, I was the winsome little girl who loved being outside. The woods called to me; the river comforted me; the cliffs were a familiar playground. When my mom got depressed and I couldn't seem to find anyone interested in my little life (Dad, too busy and preoccupied; Mom, too locked inside; my siblings tending to their own wounds), the loneliness birds came. The weight of their stones came with each season of hospitalization, craziness, and abandonment. (When Mom was doing well, we would bake and hike and pick cattails and make flower arrangements. Then she'd "slip away," and I would be crushed.) I learned early that "heavy" feeling inside.

I Spoke and Thought and Reasoned As a Child

In my little-girl innocence, the reasoning I came up with was that something must be terribly wrong with me for God to leave me alone so much. Where else can a little heart go but to this common misconception? I guessed that I would have to be on the lookout all the time for the next thing to hurt me. I figured it didn't do any good to get angry at any of it, because you couldn't change it anyway. The weight of this would find me when I was alone. I knew intuitively that my friends didn't have the same kind of weight inside, so I stayed pretty quiet about everything, not talking to anyone about how scary it all was. I lived my life at my friends' houses and told them only cursory things about my family, although they of course knew all was not well.

But When I Grew Up

As I grew up, I made some terrible choices out of my childhood reasoning. I was filled with intense anger, which I turned in on myself since I had resigned myself that nothing could change. I struggled with compulsive exercise, eating, and body image and threw myself into being a "nice girl." Much of my life was hidden; my heart was veiled, and my behavior was deceptive and desperate. Later, when those things were no longer as effective, the anger came out sideways, in contention and violence with those I loved. I became intoxicated with control and manipulation, but always with a smile and always in the name of being helpful. When my heart beckoned for me, I found a way to stay one or two steps ahead of it through lots of wholesome Christian activity and missionary work. I *had* to stay ahead of it; I hated how much fear and rage were inside it.

I Put Away Childish Things

Healing for me has been a comprehensive, ongoing, mixed bag of repenting of deception, self-sufficiency, the bite of my anger, a willingness to receive the kindness of others, and the unexpected intervention of God. It wasn't until my late twenties that I realized how my choices were impacting people. Through some strong words from friends who cared enough ("faithful are the wounds of a friend"), I had to see how false my "kindness" was, how arrogant I was in assuming the whole world needed my help. My friends' words lanced through me, calling to the true life of Christ inside of me. I experienced a depth of forgiveness I had never known when I understood just how unloving my childish ways were. This was the beginning of healing. In the years that followed, as I continued to be involved in peoples' lives, the reality of spiritual opposition became clear. I started to be intentional in praying against dark things set against my life, in the authority of Christ. This began to free me up from a veil of condemnation and contempt I didn't realize I was under. It was like oxygen coming back into my world. I experienced the gift of having some good people pray with me to break the patterns of my family line, especially pride. But even now I have to turn, literally every day, from independence.

Healing came to me through long, dark treks through the desert, including the years when I had to face the depression I inherited from my mom. The kindness of God has come through strong words from others and through countless opportunities to repent whenever someone wants to give me something or enjoy me.

Fast-forward to the present. As I walked through the initial days of caring for my brother in his battle with cancer, all the circumstances seemed to conspire to make the old message of "*you* need to keep this person you love alive" surface. My brother lives alone, and I'm the only family member near him. His sons and other members of the family began to make plans to come and help—we even had an entire schedule set up—and then the doctors expedited everything, scheduling two surgeries and the first chemotherapy in one week. Dick's good friend Rae was unable to help because she was having her own major surgery that week. For ten days and then many unexpected weeks afterward, it was, quite literally, up to me to be friend, companion, nurse.

You can imagine how these conspiring events surfaced the old pressure. Gratefully, I sensed the freedom that Jesus has brought to the enslaved heart that, years earlier, would have been crushed under the weight of being the one to come through in a terribly difficult situation. As I've walked through these dark days with my brother, I've had a quiet gratitude as I notice the hour-by-hour choice my heart makes when it hears the message "you are the only one, and you have to be enough for this." When I believe that message, I am crushed. When I resist it, I hear the invitation to lean into the power of the Holy Spirit to be sufficient where I can't and was never intended to be. I am carried, sustained, and loved along the way.

I've begun to glimpse the life Jesus has for me and the depth of his grace, but I'm so grateful that I can say Jesus is accomplishing this in me. I'm not perfectly healed or free, but I have a well-kept heart.

The Surprise of Healing Love

Something took place for me during my four-month sabbatical while I was on the island of Kauai. I had gone into the sabbatical knowing that it would be a time of deep restorative healing. I figured this meant I would have to do quite a bit of processing, thinking, praying, journaling—you know the drill. God had other ideas. For the first two months of my sabbatical, I couldn't pray. It wasn't that I didn't try. Whenever I was intentional to pray, it was as if Jesus blocked my path. He knew better than I just how soul weary I was from years of engaging myself in others' lives. He wouldn't let me "engage" myself in anything other than receiving. It was humbling beyond words.

So I found myself surrounded by colors I didn't know existed, encountering fish of the most comical shapes and hues, and hearing nothing but surf and marine birds. I was lost in the beauty of it and lost in the love of God. There were surprises around each corner—the monk seal, the stray puppy on the beach, the conversation with two elderly Hawaiian women—and I knew they were *all for me.* My friend Peggy, who was with me, told her husband, Mark, that the best vacations are when she is with Jan and Jan's Husband. That's how it was; it was a playground for me and my Love. As I hopped on and explored the volcanic rocks and coves of crabs, something quiet but powerful began to happen. Jesus began to call to the youngest places inside of me, those hiding behind their own little stone nests. He called to the one-, two-, three-year-olds, "You don't have to be abandoned anymore." He called to the four-, five-, six-year-olds, "You don't have to be deceptive in order to be loved anymore." All the way up through teenagers and young adults: "You don't have to be traumatized and rage filled anymore." Again, it all happened in a timeless, eternal moment, all while I was playing with seashells and starfish. Then Jesus turned me to look out on the aquamarine sea, the beauty of which took my breath. "This is how a True Father loves." It was the healing I've needed my whole adult life. I didn't lift a finger; I didn't "go after" anything. He came for me. It was time.

I can imagine what you are thinking. *Well, sure, anyone can know healing like that on Kauai!* There's some truth to that. But I'm convinced this encounter could have happened at home in Colorado as I was taking out the trash. Kauai was just one of those lavish, undeserved gifts that Jesus gives sometimes. I am grateful beyond words for this quiet, strong surgery. I believe I've opened my heart and my hand to this kind of intervention, should Jesus want to bring it. He brought it. It was time. But if I communicate nothing else to you, I hope you hear this: Healing is never merely about our wounds; it is always about Jesus inviting us to drink in his love.

Stunted Glory

Sometimes the pain is so piercing in that hollow place that it causes us to be in two places at once as our hearts are rent. Later in life the broken places often provide us a spot to hide. During the worst of Peekay's abuse, he had a little secret. As the Dutch kids blindfolded, taunted him, urinated on him, and told him he'd be driven into the sea with the Jews, he had a refuge no one knew about:

> But I was alive, and in my book, where there's life, there is hope. What they didn't know was that behind the blindfold I had learned to be in two places at once. I could easily answer their stupid questions while with another part of my mind I would visit Inkosi-Inshosikazi [the African lady healer who had cared for him].[7]

By learning to be in two places at once, Peekay had learned to disassociate. It would take an entire book to talk about the process, but all of us disassociate on one level or another. Imagine a man daydreaming at work in the midst of a tedious project as being on one end of the spectrum and a man with multiple personalities on the other end. It is a merciful gift from the hand of God to be able to go somewhere other than the pain. A little girl being abused is provided a way of escape from confusion she's not meant to endure. And yet somewhere on the journey, that escape becomes a place of false refuge, the double-mindedness spoken of in the book of James. Dallas Willard calls this a "stunted" soul, where we find something, some other part of us, "to take over our thoughts, feelings, behavior and social relations."[8]

This side of the garden, when we are in the presence of anything violating or contrary to glory, especially as children, it splits through our fragile hearts in ways we don't even realize. As I listened to my mother's torments when I was a girl, I didn't know I wasn't strong enough to handle the pain. But internally when I was being crushed, I found ways to be two places at once by daydreaming and fantasizing. I had one of the most lucrative imaginations of any kid in my neighborhood. And when I was in pain, I *fled* to these imaginings;

they were my refuge. As our lives take us into adulthood, disassociation increasingly becomes something we choose, although it rarely feels like a choice.

But, as Willard says, "The soul will strike back." In other words, we are meant for wholeness; we are meant to be unified in our deepest place; Jesus desires truth in the inmost parts. And he desires us to be fully present in the present moment. Love keeps us in the present, inviting us to wholeness by blocking our flight into places of false safety. Only when my path to being a dependable, functional, "I'm there for you" woman is blocked, do I realize how much healing I need even today.

I think of Joan, a gracious woman with an endearing way about her. But it is hard to keep Joan's gaze. She can engage you for a bit, and then she must look away. Joan grew up with a rage-filled father who "chose" her sister to abuse sexually and "chose" Joan to throw down the stairs. She grew up in a chaotic herd of extended family members, with little to no supervision. She had cousins who would tie her up and throw her into the swimming pool for kicks. You can imagine the confusion in the littlest parts of Joan that were left behind on her journey—so relieved not to be the chosen one, yet so ashamed for *not* being chosen. As an adult, Joan is a lovely woman who disassociates by fantasizing about things she can do to finally get her father's attention. You can imagine the shame in this. *I want to get my father's attention? So I want to elicit notice from my father, the sexual abuser?* Remember, the flight is away from something and into something. Joan's flight was away from her pure desire for a good, trustworthy father—the desire set in her heart from eternity. Joan's flight was into thoughts that kept her stained so she wouldn't have to face her sorrow over her good desires not being fulfilled.

Kindness, repentance, and *renewed life* looked like this for Joan: Joan had to be confronted on her flight into fantasy. Her husband and good friends had to tell her that her shame was robbing them, because she was not really with them when they were together. They wanted more of her. God used these conversations to convict Joan of her hiding and her disrespect of those she loved. As she grieved this, she felt the kindness of God showing her that the "more" of her—her good desires and the hidden places inside—were important. She started to be more present with other people as she thought about her story, and this was an invitation for them to weep with her. As she continued in this blend of kindness and repentance, Jesus began to tend to those places inside that had been left behind.

This is the long path of healing: Kindness comes to each wounded and broken-off place and invites us back to being "present." We repent when we choose to be present, and renewed life comes as we are surprised by how much Jesus wants to tend to us in the present.

JESUS TOLD ME

Keith, the brother of my friend Vance, experienced a physical healing after many men prayed for him when he became severely ill on a men's retreat. He was in bad, bad shape and was set for an ambulance, but the touch of God released him from the illness. Do you know what he said to Betsy, the first person he saw when they came off the mountain? "Jesus told me he loves me!" He didn't say, "Jesus healed me!" or "I experienced a miracle!" All that mattered was that Jesus loved him.

"Jesus told me he loves me" are the exact words that came from my weary lips when my fever broke during a critical case of dengue fever in the Philippines. My Filipino family hovered and prayed all night long; my friend Precioso Dalisay sang over my bed. Jesus made his way into the delirium of the fever and held me close, whispering his love. There was nothing else to talk about but the fact that Jesus came. Dengue fever sapped my energy for over a year, but I experienced the nearness of the love of God. When we say, "I was blind but now I see!" what we are really saying is, "I finally get it! Jesus told me he loves me."

Sometimes the healing is obvious. Sometimes it comes in a package only God understands. Does surrendering the outcome to God sound like a contradiction to the fact that we, as Christians, are overcomers? I suspect it might. But actually this process of ask, seek, knock—wait, listen, surrender—ask, seek, knock—wait, listen, surrender—takes us into the kind of overcoming spoken of in Revelation.

> It has happened at last—the salvation and power and kingdom of our God, and the authority of his Christ! For the Accuser has been thrown down to earth—the one who accused our brothers and sisters before our God day and night. And *they have defeated him because of the blood of the Lamb and because of their testimony. And they were not afraid to die.* (12:10–11, emphasis added)

As the shock of my brother's diagnosis wore off and the reality of the fight before him hit him, my brother received a phone call. The man who called him is a self-proclaimed "hesitant infidel," so I was amazed to watch what transpired in the conversation. This man, an expert in oncology, heard about Dick's severe diagnosis and was predictably concerned and gave little hope. Dick listened and engaged the conversation, taking in this opinion. He then proceeded to tell this man that he was filled with peace, no matter what happened, because of Christ. Dick told him that he would fight hard, but in the end, he had a true hope because he was not afraid to die. The man was quiet for some time and then said, "It is clear that what you believe in is real. I wish I had that." My brother, between sharp pains, told him that he could have it just by receiving it. And then he went and took a nap. What a perfect response. A response like that can only flow from a heart being healed, even if the body fails.

THE ULTIMATE HEALING

I've watched with interest in recent years as inner healing has become more prevalent in the larger mosaic of counseling and restorative ministry. It has played a beautiful role in my own life and thinking, as well as how I approach my counseling. But it's important to remember that when we make our inner healing the goal, the ending point, the *reason* for Jesus's life inside of us, it loses its intended power. Why? Because often we become so focused on wholeness that we lose sight of the communion that Jesus longs to have with us. Eve's problem was not that she was wounded. Adam was not blocked from the garden because he had been harmed. The angels posted as guards to keep them—and us—from going back to Eden were not responsible for the lost beauty. The beauty had been *squandered.* Communion had been broken.

God desires communion with us. It was an *idea* that enticed Eve to break this communion: "There's something more, Eve. God isn't shooting straight with you. He's withholding something from you. Take the fruit and get the rest of the story, stay on top of it, stay in control. Isn't that a good idea?" Eve was happy to agree.

Imagine what keeping communion would have meant. During the cool of the day, as she walked with God, it would have meant inquiring of him, questioning, wrestling for the purpose of keeping the trust, wondering *with* God, not behind his back. "Holy Trinity, I know you created all this for us to enjoy and to work and to think of you. The tree you forbid is troubling me. It makes me think you are withholding something. Is this true?" We can only imagine, but surely God's reply would have been loving and patient. He would have been glad their communion was not broken and glad to have engaged her question.

It took the power of the Resurrection to overcome Eve's decision to be persuaded by that one idea. The New Covenant is a blood transfusion of the most glorious kind—new life for the dead, sinful nature. It was God doing everything to reestablish the pulse of communion.

It is communion with Jesus that most powerfully touches our wounds. Jesus did come to heal my broken heart and to set my captive heart free. Could it be that the deepest healing happens when I'm broken over my own flight from him, my lack of belief in him? Could it be that freedom comes in being set free from the captivity of all my communion-breaking ideas about him and that Jesus has opened a way for me to once again engage myself with him in ways Eve never risked?

I imagine Jesus whispering to Jacob, while strong-arming his elbow behind his back, "I know this is the truth you most resist, but, yes, my blessing is the fact that I am stronger than you." And I imagine Jacob, sweat beading his face, limping and leaping, limping and leaping away from the whole thing thinking, *God apparently loves to wrestle with me. He may let me win for a moment, but in the end he is the stronger one. What a relief!*

I think of the little boy in an iron lung who was interviewed by Robert Coles. The boy said of his incurable suffering, "Job didn't know what to make of it and I don't either."[9] These are not words of resignation but words that come from seasons of asking, seeking, knocking, and surrendering.

There is a surrender, a state of healing, that comes after years of begging. Not one of us, if we've even come close to asking for healing from God, has been immune from thinking, *Jesus, I don't understand your definition of blessing, and I'm not sure I like it.*

Jacob became Israel, "the one who struggles with God," but he had to contend with the divine all night long before walking away with his healing— a limp and a new name. We might limp away from our encounter with God, but if we contend with our God, we'll understand that our new name fits both our struggle and our place in his story. Living like this makes us more human, as God introduces us to himself, not our image of him. It gives us the courage to live into our new identity.

Nine

LISTENING TO THE CALL

Living into Our New Identity

The movement of faith is unceasing,
because no explanation it offers is ever finished.
—JACQUE ELLUL

You do not know the road;
you have committed your life to a way.
—WENDELL BERRY

What keeps us going, what keeps our hearts open when the road is so hard? Samwise Gamgee, Frodo's bumbling but devoted friend, says the tentative words we so often feel:

I don't know how to say it, but...I feel different. I seem to see ahead, in a kind of way. I know we are going to take a very long road, into darkness; but I know I can't turn back.... I don't rightly know what I want: but I have something to do before the end, and it lies ahead...if you understand me.[1]

I do understand Sam, as I'm guessing you do. You have something to do before the end. And you, like Sam, "see ahead, in a kind of way." Something is nudging you from behind, and you suspect it is God's intention for you. Something is beckoning from up ahead, and you suspect it is the love of God calling you onto a path best suited for who you are, a path meant for no one else. But if I were to ask you where you're going, you would say you only know it lies ahead.

I don't have to tell you that the road to living into your purpose can be long and confusing. Peter, the unlikely rock, discovered his calling only after slamming headlong into his capacity for three-time betrayal. Paul was knocked off his pharisaical horse and lived with a torment no one understands in order to find his calling. I had my first clue about my calling as playground companions would talk to me about their lives and wounds and as I found refuge in crafting words in a notebook to describe it all. By sixth or seventh grade, I had a hunch, a sense about myself that compelled me in two general directions: people and words.

I could not have known what it would take for those clues to find their fruition, and along the way the compelling I felt deep inside got all mixed up with attempts to flee the pain of my young world. When friends would confide in me or seek me out to talk to me, it gave me that old false sense of control; it provided a false shelter against the buffeting winds of my mom's despair. When I would wander down to the Rio Grande canyon wall and write through my tears on a blustery spring day, it provided me a cherished refuge from reality. After many years of running to people and words, I built a false identity around those very things. I created a false self by being helpful. I built a false refuge out of writing and creativity. That's the difficult thing about our calling. So often the things that genuinely pulse through us with the heartbeat of God's design and intention for us as individuals are the things most vulnerable to attack and wounding and the things most easily manipulated by us into a life where God is not necessary.

The good news for me is that Jesus has been tearing the false things down. Over the years he has been restoring my true identity, and therefore my calling, to my true love for people and words. People aren't so much a burden anymore (with my thinking I have to come through to be helpful), and words are increasingly becoming a cherished avenue to communicate the things in my heart (rather than something I hide inside). Love is faithful to call us from up ahead, helping us to "see ahead, in a kind of way." As we lean in, listen for what he might be calling us into, and step out in faith, the one thing we can know is that he will continue to unveil who we really are along the way.

Not Loving Life

I know a man who, at age forty, has been a corporate CEO, excelling in leadership, finance, and philanthropy. He would tell you he is still bewildered about his calling. He's felt for some time that he has missed it somehow, but he is now giving time and space to cultivate his truest love: fighting for the hidden hearts of other men, especially businessmen. I watched in hushed awe as this man came to spend some time with my brother during Dick's chemotherapy. By the time this man came, my brother had lost forty-five pounds and was despairing that he would ever feel strong again. The man came tentatively because he didn't know Dick well, but he came purposefully because he knew what God had laid on his heart. As a few of us watched, this man knelt before Dick and gave him a symbolic gift, a ring that had been given to him long before as a symbol of how seen and loved he is by God. "I want you to have this," he said, "because God has told me that he sees the fight you are fighting, and he wants you to know you are loved and you are a warrior. Others may never see your fight, but he does. And for today, so do I, and I am fighting with you. There is always hope, and regardless of what happens, victory is certain for you." The room hushed as this man offered himself and his passion and lived out a moment of his calling before my brother. All my brother knew was that he was reminded, for a moment, that he wasn't forgotten by God.

Each of us has a presence that—if we allowed ourselves to fully release it—could cause a room to hush. That's because our *presence* is what Jesus has in mind for us. Mary pondered God's purpose in her heart when she was told she was carrying a holy baby. I imagine that she wasn't sure it was what she wanted, but she knew she had to see it through. As she gave herself to this purpose, she offered a presence in the world that lingers even now. Moses wasn't looking to lead torrents of people out of a land he once loved as his own. But following a voice from a burning flame, he found he offered a presence that was his own, yet far beyond him—a presence that even his shyness or shame could not veil. The woman at the well wasn't looking for her life to change. She wasn't looking to be released from guilt or self-deception, but she walked away from a dusty encounter on a sultry afternoon knowing the conversation, the encounter with Living Water, had restored her presence and would see her through—to what, she wasn't sure.

Our friend John, along with a great little team, has been entrusted with a message that is opening up the gospel for millions of people. John and his team used to gather in the basement of a house, not fully sure of what they were after but wanting to recapture a truer pulse to Christianity than they had known. But now, because the message of living from the heart has struck a chord with so many, it has become a movement of retreats, training, counseling, mentoring, and spiritual battle for people. All of this birthed out of a simple desire in my friend's heart. Each person on the team would say that this "came to them." They didn't go looking to have a huge impact. But now the computers are jammed and the phone lines full of people responding to the message, and they must see it through.

This is the nature of calling. It comes to us, compelling us to let those around us encounter the presence we are meant to offer. It starts out awkward, but its strength grows with each step we take in its direction. *We don't rightly know what we want…but we know we must see it through.* Each step taken in response to this call should rank among the miracles. The result is the same: those who witness it are hushed, and we are changed for having responded. We are changed into our true identity.

Discerning our calling or God's specific intentions for us can seem so unclear. "I want to be obedient and follow your intentions for me, God. But is it okay to follow sometimes what I want? Is it you when I'm asked to forgo my desires, or is it you when it seems as if you are stirring my desires? When is it you, Jesus?"

CAPTURED ENTIRELY

Understanding what we are made for is a lifetime process. I've spoken to folks in their sixties who are still trying to zero in on this "thing that lies ahead" and their place in it. The one thing that is clear about our calling is that we find it as we lean in and listen for it "along the way." What compels us to head out in the general direction of our purpose in the first place makes all the difference. The whole idea of Christianity is to be so captured by God's love that nothing else matters. Second Corinthians 5:14 says that the love of Christ compels us; we become constrained, actually bound, by a love so strong we become willing to lay down our own lives. Remember, this is what will be said of us: "They have defeated him [the Evil One] because of the blood of the Lamb and because of their testimony. And they were not afraid to die" (Revelation 12:11).

This is what compelled a young Albanian woman into the stench of death in the central slums of Calcutta. The world grieved when Mother Teresa died. I didn't grieve so much because she gave herself to India—there have been and will be others worthy of our respect called to those trapped in the lowest tier of caste society—but I grieved *who she was*. When Mother Teresa died, I remember having an immediate, involuntary thought, *One of the lights of love is gone*. I had a sense that the world was darker without her. I scanned my mind's eye for other beacons to the world—lights that have risen up with such purity of abandon and sincere following of Jesus that they cannot be dismissed. I thought of a few people but knew the landscape was more dim for losing her, at least for a while.

What was it about Mother Teresa that caused a hush when she spoke? Though she owned nothing, the word *extravagant* fit her, because she lavished herself on others. She had a simple view of herself (which *was* her glory): "I am God's pencil. A tiny bit of pencil with which he writes what he likes." She did not love her life, even unto death. She relinquished career, esteem, applause, and reputation, knowing her life was judged by only one pair of eyes. She lived what is spoken of in 2 Corinthians 5:13–15:

If it seems that we are crazy, it is to bring glory to God. And if we are in our right minds, it is for your benefit. Whatever we do, it is because Christ's love controls us. Since we believe that Christ died for everyone, we also believe that we have all died to the old life we used to live. He died for everyone so *that those who receive his new life will no longer live to please themselves.* Instead, they will live to please Christ, who died and was raised for them. (emphasis added)

This kind of love controlled the early church. It was pure devotion. As we read the book of Acts, we see something more than a lifestyle choice, definitely something more than an occasional experiential worship service or spiritual gifts test. These people were caught up in the love of Christ. They had lived their calling as they dropped their nets and headed out to follow. They had come face to face with their holy Judge, only to find him weeping over them. He, their Judge, saw right through them, drew them out, looked them in the eye, healed them, and gave them hints but nothing more about this long road ahead. He ate with them, laughed at their ways, got fed up with them at moments, but always patiently showed them he was for them in every way. Their Judge *did* judge them. They knew he must. Their sin *was* cursed and *was brutally punished.* But they didn't understand, even to the end, that the cursing, the guilt, the scourging fell on his—their Judge's—back.

How could they possibly have known? They got a glimpse of his love as he lived with them, and they could "see ahead, in a kind of way," but the route to God's victory was so, well, unrecognizable. As Oswald Chambers says,

Jesus Christ called his disciples to see him put to death; he led every one of them to the place where their hearts were broken. Jesus Christ's life was an absolute failure from every standpoint but God's. But what seemed failure from man's standpoint was a tremendous triumph from God's because God's purpose is never man's purpose.[2]

The disciples didn't understand during the three long days before Jesus's resurrection what was accomplished for them. And they barely recognized it when life and victory brought him back, free of judgment, price fully paid. Even as they strained, staring into the ascension-filled sky, they could not have seen ahead to the fullness of his promise to them: "But when the Holy Spirit has come upon you, you will receive power and will tell people about me everywhere" (Acts 1:8). They heard him say they would tell people close to home and to the ends of the earth, but what could that have meant to them when they heard it? How could they have seen ahead to their own hands healing the sick, their words having full and transforming shape to them? And to share everything they had with each other? How could they have seen ahead to a wave of power and love that would take them away from everything they had ever known or had control of?

This love continued to constrain the "second generation" of Christians (those who followed the disciples) like Polycarp, who followed John. His life was incredibly rough—nothing but opposition for eighty-six years until he was burned at the stake. The victorious Christian life? Well, yes. The power that kept his heart during those dark days compelled him as the Roman authorities *tried* to nail his hands to the stake. Before a huge crowd, he said, with otherworldly, elderly faith, "Let me be as I am. He that granted me to endure the fire will grant me also to remain at the pyre unmoved without being secured by nails." An ancient account states, "All the multitude marveled at the great difference between the unbelievers and the elect."[3]

And so it goes. The love of Christ captured the young German Dietrich Bonhoeffer. In prison, before he was executed by the Nazis in 1945, he wrote of those captured by Love:

> Those they encounter
> they transfigure...
> with strange gravity
> and a spirit of worship.[4]

And today, there are people like my friend Andrew Sanker, the Indian pastor I mentioned who so patiently dealt with the torment of a young girl. Andrew was raised in a South African Hindu family, and when the love of Christ found him, his family disowned him. They let Andrew stay around, but no one was to speak to him. Andrew bought a tent and camped in front of his family's home for nearly two years. Every day his family would walk past his tent, pretending he wasn't there. Andrew never argued or spoke to them; he just smiled at them and prayed fervently in his tent. This really got to his father. Eventually he couldn't stand it anymore; he had to find out how Andrew had the tenacity to put up with the cruelty for so long. So his dad broke the silence and asked what would compel him to be so stubborn. "Love for you," he told them. "I've discovered a True Love, and I can't bear for you to be without it." This is what melted his father's heart, and soon the whole family understood this Love.

What Love Is After

How do we get from here to there—from irritations on the freeway and the frustrations of our calendars not working out to the kind of passion that prayerfully waits in a tent or puts out a for-sale sign for the sake of others in need? How do we get from griping about a family member who embarrasses or disappoints us to living with the quiet courage of one willing to surrender life? Again, Oswald Chambers offers, "If we are in communion with God and recognize that he is taking us into his purposes, we shall no longer try to find out what his purposes are."[5]

Those who love the sea can tell you about this. I have a friend who grew up by the sea, and his countenance when he is on ocean water is inexplicable. When the boat pulls away from shore, his command of it is as natural as breathing, and the light of "home" comes to his eyes. The unpredictable nature of currents, tides, winds, and storms is merely intrigue for him. He respects the water and is sober that it is in charge in all its swelling, shifting power. But he has come to know the water's ways, so he no longer fears what he cannot see.

He knows that the water has its own adventure for him for this day. He wonders what it will be.

What would it be like to respond to God this way—sober, respectful of his power, but loving the pleasure of being carried by him and anticipating the surprises he has in store so that we shove off from shore aware of, but not hindered by, the weather? This is the nature of our calling. When we are at home with the One who is Love, not fear, we can flow with his intentions, knowing it might be a calm day or maybe a squall in which all our navigational instincts will surface. Chambers says,

> There comes the baffling call of God in our lives also. The call of
> God can never be stated explicitly; it is implicit. The call of God
> is like the call of the sea, no one hears it but the one who has the
> nature of the sea in him. It cannot be stated definitely what the call
> of God is to, because his call is to be in comradeship with himself for
> his own purposes, and the test is to believe that God knows what he
> is after.[6]

The Bearable Lightness of Being

Jesus knows what he is after. As I've been loved by him, he has, over time, released the implicit language of my heart. I'm meant to be a threshold, a doorway, for people to be ushered into the love of their God. My Valley of Achor, the valley of suffering spoken of in Hosea 2:15, has become a door of hope, because Jesus has led me into the wilderness of questions, doubt, and unbelief time after time and has spoken his kindness to me there. If Jesus didn't come for me, my life could easily be a barren valley of suffering. I probably would have always kept a religious front, but I would be an embittered, sarcastic, hardhearted, judgmental, insecure woman—smiling a forced smile when I was with people and then hating them for not caring for me.

But Jesus came. Now I know the implicit language of my heart is elegant strength and kindness. It is Jesus's language, placed uniquely inside my heart. Again, I didn't go looking for this; it was placed in me. I don't own it, but I must respond to it. When I do, it naturally invites those in the presence of it to change—the kind of change that comes from being loved by a King. This is a glimpse of what Jesus said when he spoke my name before the foundation of the world, and I'm slowly learning to live into it. What brings a hush to me is the thought that I am being beckoned, given a bond-servant's charge, into deeper levels of love and relationship with people. But now, instead of it being a burdensome, threatening proposition (wondering what they will want from me and if I will have it to give), it is increasingly a pleasure and a delight.

Those who are well loved are more apt to say yes to the bond-servant nature of Love's call. When you can face your own sin and still laugh, you've been well loved. You've known the deepest kind of healing and are the most accessible to God's beckoning. When you can say without shame, "I still hurt people even though I'm alive in Christ," and "Satan, even on my worst days of doubt, even when I rage because I still walk with a limp, you cannot have my heart," then evidence of the truest healing starts to appear, freeing you to follow. You don't have anything to lose, you don't have anything to prove, so you might as well expend your energy on others.

How do we keep that kind of light heart, not being undone by evil's attempts to tell us the things that compel us are selfish, unwise, foolhardy, unreasonable? How do we keep a light heart when we've listened to the wrong voices or made a false shelter of the very thing designed to bring God glory? Our calling has everything to do with what Jesus says about us individually. And our calling has everything to do with *who we are in the kingdom*—an identity bestowed on us. It is not something we create; it is something that we discover and creatively live into.

Dignity or Big Brother?

Sometimes I slog through a day, feeling heavy from the "nipping at my heels" messages that evil throws my way: "You're so selfish, you're so proud, you're so lazy." Then, catching me off guard, Jesus whispers, "I love you, Jan. You are beautiful to me," and I lose what feels like twenty-five pounds.

What Jesus says about us lifts the cloud of evil's voice and frees us to embrace our true calling. There's no better illustration of this than Victor Hugo's *Les Misérables*. Jean Valjean, a released convict, fully expects the bishop (from whom he has sought help) to view him and treat him like a criminal. Instead, the bishop handles Valjean with respect and dignity. The bishop addresses him with the title "monsieur" rather than "criminal," lighting up Valjean's countenance. "*Monsieur* to a convict is a glass of water to a man dying of thirst at sea."[7]

In the "secret things of God," the names given us are just as life-giving. And just as shocking. We expect—and deserve!—names such as Promiscuous, Selfish, Unfaithful, Betrayer, Fearful, Soiled, Jealous One, Proud, Stupid, Hardened, Ugly. Those titles have been, and still are at moments, if we're honest, accurate. We have scenes and memory and evidence for each condemning name. But Jesus again startles us with love. He calls us: Chosen. A People for His Own Possession. Child. Friend. Adopted. Royal Priesthood. Clean and Spotless Bride. Holy. Rebuilt on a Foundation of Sapphires and Jewels. Strong One. Once Not a People, but Now the People of God. Maybe you've had the privilege of hearing him whisper to you an intimate name or a sense about who he knows you to be—just between the two of you. I would tell you mine (I have shared it with a few), but honestly it would feel like sharing bedroom secrets from my honeymoon. That's how priceless what Jesus says about us is. These names are the glass of water for our hearts, parched and dried up by evil's accusation and the condemnation we load onto ourselves. When the Accuser comes, we can turn his attention to the One seated at the Father's right hand, blood stains on his robe as a reminder of what it took for him to offer us this glass of new identity, this freedom of calling.

Imagine a couple who have waited long for a baby. They bring their little boy home, with all the expected grandparent and extended-family fanfare. With a new outfit on him, they bring him to a picnic where a friend says, "What an amazing thing; he's a miracle really" only to have the baby's father reply, "Yes, it is wonderful. We're hopeful that he will be on the television show *Survivor* one day." Nothing like having a "proud" father hoping his son lives out names like *Deceptive, Vindictive, Conniving, Heartless,* and *Mean.*

I realize this is a ludicrous example, but this is precisely what we do with our own hearts when we allow the wrong voice to tell us who we are. Madeleine L'Engle says, "God understands that part of us which is more than we think we are." That's an understatement. Our Perfect Parent sees the splendor intended for us from the beginning. ("Yes, it is a miracle. And no one knows it yet, but this boy is brilliant of mind, pure of heart, and will display his strength in amazing ways.") In Ephesians 2 he calls us his workmanship—his *poema,* his work of art, created for a unique (meaning no one else can fill it) place in this kingdom.[8] You can hear the tragedy of how we diminish the handiwork, especially the redeemed handiwork of God, when we join in a dark chorus about ourselves. Angelus Silesius says, "God, the devil and the world all wish to enter me. Of what great lineage my noble heart must be."[9] Why would the Adversary even bother with you if you were only intended for reality television–level identity? Why, when thinking of yourself, would you join the chorus that names you Average, Selfish, Hopefully Someone Will Notice Me when even the dark ones themselves acknowledge you to be Worth Having, Noble, Royal Lineage, A Threat, Marked for Mind-Blowing Wonderful Things, Belonging to Jesus?

Liberated Convicts

Maybe facing the darkness with a light heart comes from seeing how unimpressed God is by our sin. If we can learn this lesson, we give ourselves a great weapon to mock evil and to discover the doorway into healing. Confounded by the kindness he encounters from the bishop, Jean Valjean hears the bishop ask his sister, Madame Magloire, to set a place at the table for him. Listen to your own struggle with grace as you hear Valjean's retort:

> *"Stop,"* he exclaimed; as if he had not been understood, "not *that,* did you understand me? I am a galley-slave—a convict—I am just from the galleys." He drew from his pocket a large sheet of yellow paper, which he unfolded. "There is my passport, *yellow as you see.* That is enough to

have me kicked out wherever I go…. See, here is what they have put in the passport: 'Jean Valjean, a liberated convict, native of—you don't care for that—has been nineteen years in the galleys; five years for burglary; fourteen years for having attempted four times to escape. *This man is very dangerous.*' *There you have it!* Everybody has thrust me out; will you receive me? Is this an inn? Can you give me something to eat, and a place to sleep? Have you a stable?"[10]

What does it sound like in your heart? What is the piece of evidence you use against yourself—your yellow paper? What do you use to prove to yourself and to others that you should not receive mercy, let alone anything kind? And what is your reaction when, in response to your detailed proclamation of guilt, God, like the bishop, says, "Madame Magloire, put some sheets on the bed in the alcove."[11] After all, those who need healing do well to accept a warm bed with clean sheets. We're usually too busy picking up the rocks of our slavery to accept the offer.

New Life in Our Calling

It is the kindness of God that leads to repentance (Romans 2:4). It is our *drinking* from the glass of his kindness that begins our healing, and it is in pouring out that kindness that we discover our calling.

Jean Valjean cannot bear the balm of homemade soup and a warm bed. His mind and heart race back to the prison quarry, where he was brutalized and treated as a criminal. Wanting so much to flee back into his yellow-paper identity, he beats up the bishop and runs off with the rectory silverware. The police catch him, bring him to the bishop, and wait for the bishop's reply. Of course Jean Valjean (and all of us reading the story) expect a full reprimand and a scornful eye for his betrayal of kindness. But the bishop tells the police that he, in fact, gave the silverware to Valjean and asks that they release him since there was no robbery. Then he adds, to Valjean, "Oh, and by the way, didn't you forget the candlesticks as well?"

This would be enough to astound. Enough to produce indebtedness. But the power of God's kindness is reflected most when the bishop says:

> Jean Valjean, my brother, you belong no longer to evil but to good. It is your soul that I am buying for you. I withdraw it from dark thoughts and from the spirit of perdition, and I give it to God![12]

It is this scandal of kindness, this "foolish thing that confounds the wise" gesture, that gives Jean Valjean a sense of his newness and the power to disarm evil. Evil is mocked through his affection of an unlikely prostitute, Fantine, and in his care of her orphaned daughter, Cosette. And it is mocked as his long-suffering ways unravel the most tightly wound hypocrite in his community of Vigo, Jabert. Valjean takes on an unlikely authority as he begins to live out the truth about himself: I no longer belong to evil. He goes through the doorway to his calling with his head held high, showing his face, because forgiveness and a new identity were bestowed on him. Kindness, healing, and repentance lead him into his calling and true identity.

THE FACE

Part of the pouring out of kindness that we do actually comes from the face we display to the world. Part of living our calling is to allow our true identity, our true face, to be seen and to speak of a kindness greater than the world knows.

There is a whole industry devoted to the altering and preservation of our face. There's something to the energy behind it all. I don't have to tell you of the processes—Botox, lasers, creams—devoted to this mission. What is it about our face that holds such power? Why is the image from *Gladiator* of Maximus's wife waiting for him in the golden fields of wheat so easily remembered? Her face is stunning, yes. But the reason I can recall her so quickly is that it is a true face. She's at rest; she's confident of her groom's return. It's amazing, really. Her face is on the screen only forty-five seconds out of the whole movie. She is remembered because her face is confident in the kindness of love.

Our face tells the world about our calling. No matter how hard we try to cover up, our face still reveals secrets, good and bad. We could spend millions on the preservation of our shoulder, our calf, our elbow. Now, of course that is ridiculous (though I'm sure there is a doctor somewhere in West Hollywood who is financing his son's college education through the preservation of someone's obscure body part). We know it is our eyes, countenance, the radiance of our face—no matter how blemished, freckled, or wrinkled—that captures the attention and reveals both who and how we are. Nicholas of Cusa, a mystic who lived in the fifteenth century, wrote beautifully about his own face:

> O Lord God, who enlightenest men's hearts, my face is a true face
> because Thou, who art truth, has given it to me. My face is also an
> image, since 'tis not the truth itself, but an image of absolute truth.[13]

This man is saying, "God, I like my face. It shows you off but just a little." He understood that his face was meant to radiate the very heat of God, *and* he understood that he could never fully do that. I love that he knew he had a true face. And I love that he knew his face was just a small reflection of the immense glory in his God.

Can you imagine being Moses when his face shone so fully the people couldn't look at him? And this was because he had been in God's presence when given the Law. The apostle Paul is so right to ask, "Shouldn't we expect far greater glory when the Holy Spirit is giving *life?*"

Being able to come directly into God's presence without shame should do mind-blowing things to our face. Moses covered his face with a veil because he was ashamed that the glory was fading; he knew his face wasn't like it was when it was first exposed to God's burning, loving fire. We do the same thing when we avert our gaze, when we pass off compliments with a falsely humble shrug. We veil ourselves and veil God's glory with bravado, mockery, judgment, or distance. We dim our presence by hiding behind religious pressure, by sarcastically bantering or biting rather than relaxing and allowing others to know us. It is important to recognize this, because we can plow through life in the name of our "calling," but if our face is not unveiled along the way, we shroud God's glory.

My true face was unexpectedly unveiled recently when I participated in a conference call that I had been dreading. Eight people from different parts of the country felt prompted to organize a regional seminar centered around the themes of this book. I had been silenced and amazed at the momentum of the whole thing. These folks were taking the ball and running with the event planning. Word was getting out, and registrations were beginning to come in. The call was about finalizing plans.

From the event's inception, my heart had been excited about teaching the material alongside several others whom I trust, and I looked forward the team event. Something of my true face emerged in the delight that the event was God's baby, and all I had to do was show up and teach.

Then my brother's cancer hit, and the landscape of my world changed logistically in ways that couldn't be understood unless you've walked it. Though the seminar was a few months out, I was burdened when I thought of it. I reasoned that the team would carry the load, and I prayed much to give the burden to them. Even so, I awakened in the middle of the night troubled. I wanted to see what God had in mind for the seminar, but I was so tired I could barely think of preparing the material in seminar form. I also didn't want to let these folks down. I found myself in a vulnerable place of longing, wishing I had a husband to lean into, to think it all through with, and perhaps for him to step in on my behalf. As I was barely aware of this longing, Jesus rushed in. "Here I am," he said. "This is too much, isn't it? You don't have to do this if you don't want to." Relief filled my lungs; the love of Jesus came to release me, again, from the old message, "You must be enough."

I dreaded the conference call because I knew I needed to collapse in front of these people, showing them where I was and telling them what I was hearing from God. It was counterintuitive and went against my pride, but I told them I thought the event would be too much. One by one their responses came back, filled with grace, echoing God's care for my heart above any ministry. I said no to an event that, on the surface, seems to be my calling. I was released instead into the fullness of my true calling—to lean in, to listen, and to respond. My face filled with glory—the glory of being loved.

We try so hard to keep that veil in place, but the Holy Spirit is out to reveal us to the world, and he will change our face as he's changing us. As Paul reminds us,

> But whenever anyone turns to the Lord, then the veil is taken away.
> Now, the Lord is the Spirit, and wherever the Spirit of the Lord is, he
> gives freedom. And all of us have had that veil removed so that we can
> be mirrors that brightly reflect the glory of the Lord. And as the Spirit
> of the Lord works within us, we become more and more like him and
> reflect his glory even more. (2 Corinthians 3:16–18)

I remember the little crowd of faces surrounding me the night I found out my friend Brent had been killed (when I was out of town and couldn't fly back until the next day). They were living out their callings and were literally faces of God to me. C. S. Lewis says, "Next to the Blessed Sacrament itself, your neighbor is the holiest object presented to your senses. If he is your Christian neighbor, he is holy in almost the same way, for in him also *Christ vere latitat*—the glorifier and the glorified, God himself, is truly hidden."[14] Hidden? Maybe sometimes. But in these moments I had no trouble recognizing it was Jesus.

Some friends of mine wanted to look through old photos recently. It had been a long time since I wiped the dust off the albums, but I'm so glad I did. I was amazed to see how much my face has changed through the years. Oh, there was a more healthy glow, a more natural physical beauty to me when I was in my twenties and early thirties, but I liked the transformation that I saw in my countenance, my eyes, my face in the photos from recent years. It's a transformation that I know comes from a deeper sense of rest with God. One of my friends said of the recent photos, "You look really well loved." Now, tell *that* to the Botox manufacturers.

IT'S NOT ABOUT YOU, AND OF COURSE IT IS ABOUT YOU

Lately—and this is most likely a gross overgeneralization, but it sure seems true—I hear Christians talking in two ways. The first is an adamant "It is *not* about me; it is about Jesus." And the second is talk about our own individual glory, sounding like this: "I want *my glory* to be restored." Which of these is closer to the heart of Love? The answer, I believe, is both.

The concept of glory has been reintroduced to Christianity of late, and I'm so grateful, because it has everything to do with our calling and living into our new identity. Having a face that reveals God is the most humbling thing in the world. Presenting our face to the world as we live out our unique calling is even more humbling. Sounds contradictory, doesn't it? Not when we realize that the glory on our face has shown up there as a gift; we don't deserve it.

The devastation of the Fall brought death to all that we were meant to be. Because of our rebellion, the Fall brought destruction to our most central identity. The restoration of this identity is the restoration of our true nature, the redemption of who we were meant to be, and this is what is restored when we are made alive in Christ. All that was dead is made alive in him. He breathes life into the corpse of our identity. We slough off the old nature until the day we die, but our most central identity is made alive because of his grace. This new life, over time, finds its way into our eyes, our countenance, and the fulfillment of our calling.

The reason it's important to view it this way is because when I talk about forgiveness in a corporate, blanket way, rather than talking about how Jesus has forgiven me in order to restore my identity, my true heart (my ability to reason, respond emotionally, how I handle my affections), I tend not to clue in to how devastating my sin has been, the extent of what has been lost. When I grasp the severity of how my identity has become skewed, warped, bent because of the deadness of my heart, then I can stand in awe of how beautiful it is that my personal identity is made new in Christ. This is not boasting; it is gratitude. To think that God wants to be reflected in a myriad individual unveiled faces, including mine, is humbling, to say the least. He put the judgment for my sin on Jesus in order to restore my face, to give me my calling. He is jealous to be seen, and he is merciful beyond words.

When I'm told I look well loved, my first thought is, *Wow! Isn't that amazing.* I know how unresponsive to Love I can be. The glory others see in us should bring us to our knees in gratitude, because what they are seeing surely tells us that Jesus is more than who we think he is. It is Jesus who does this, not ourselves, and he does it to show *his* face so we can enjoy him. Yes, he glorifies himself through our face—which is mind-blowing in and of itself—but he then makes us bond servants to this Love. We are not to be enamored with the glory we reflect; we are to present it as a humble offering to the one we're now indentured to, in Love.

THE FORWARD MOMENTUM OF IT ALL

Please hear the simultaneous nature of your own healing, repentance, deliverance, and *calling.* They are woven together in a tapestry of responsiveness and surprise. The freedom to respond to and follow what compels us comes as we turn in the direction of Love, and God reveals the face we were meant to have.

Our calling has a forward-motion momentum, even in the darkest times of grieving. Love is at work at all times, behind the scenes, under the surface, propelling, carrying our hearts forward despite our unbelief, our bitterness, our jealousy of others' lives or our betrayal of him. Second Timothy 2:13 says, "If we are unfaithful, he remains faithful, for he cannot deny himself." In other words, if you don't even have the strength or heart to say, "Lord, I believe, but help my unbelief," have no fear. Jesus will believe in you, for you. He is bound to you in blood. When we experience the withdrawal of the presence of God, there is something more primary carrying us through the dark miles on this road; the faithfulness of Love is there when we cannot see. Our calling is to listen to and respond to Jesus's love while we're looking for the bigger picture to unfold. It's such a relief to admit this. "Faith…is the confidence and assurance that what we hope for is going to happen. It is the evidence of things we cannot yet see" (Hebrews 11:1).

It is so important that we understand this. Otherwise we are *driven* by our wounds instead of *responding* to them with the love and power of Jesus, allowing them to transform us, reveal us. Isn't it a huge weight off to think that rather than having to eradicate the things that pierce the heart, we're asked to lean in, listen, and learn from them—even live from them?

When we see another's face, we can humbly be about the business of loving them into their true face. Like artists in partnership with God, we can recognize the masterpiece covered with grime. When we allow others to see our face, we open the door for Love to come, confirming our true identities, showing us how to be poured out in kindness, showing us how to see ahead and follow into our calling—something that unfolds each day into the mystery of his intentions.

Ten

LISTENING TO BEAUTY

The Sensual Side of Obedience

Beauty captivates the flesh in order to obtain permission
to pass right to the soul.
—SIMONE WEIL

The ministers of the soul are the five senses.
—LEONARDO DA VINCI

W hen I was a teenager, you couldn't keep me indoors. I don't know if
I needed to get away from home or had an inbred need for fresh air,
but my spare time was spent hiking, running under stars that hung low over
the high desert of New Mexico, skiing, or riding my bike around town. And
in the summer, I couldn't wait to go to Lake Vallecito. There I rode horses. My
friend Lisa and I loved taking this trip together. She was a horse fanatic; I
caught her enthusiasm. There was a small outfitter set up on an obscure spot
on the lake. We learned that if we hung around the stable, helping out and getting to know the owner, he would allow us to take some horses out by ourselves with no trail guide. One evening we took the horses up a fairly steep trail
that was used for weekend pack trips…into the backcountry. The shadows
were long across the meadows and the field grasses luminescent as we wound
our way up, up through aspen groves and across streams, through clearings
that told us dusk was near. The trail leveled out, and we found ourselves

trotting, then galloping, through the trees. The wind whipped my face, and an occasional aspen branch would graze my leg. We knew we should turn around, but freedom compelled us…just a little farther. As darkness fell, sparks flew as the horses hoofs hit the granite in the trail. The faintest hint of pink on the horizon through the trees, sparks, the sound of thundering hooves, and the silence of the forest—heaven had shown up, and I was awake to welcome it. I tasted the goodness of God.

We descended eventually, of course. But I carried with me the smell of wet pine and horse, the touch of mist and leaves, the taste of magic. That moment, like so many that become frozen in time for us, was a moment my friend Brent referred to as "a haunting of eternity." When we are haunted, we are haunted through the senses.

What if Lisa and I had mounted those horses in fear, anticipating dark things on the unknown trail? What if all we had thought about was the time? What if we had anticipated a boring ride? What if we had felt the chill of mountain evening and decided it would be better to crawl into a safe sleeping bag in warm pajamas?

Our approach to obedience usually sounds like, "Yeah, yeah, yeah, I'm listening…just a minute, I'm coming…give me a second…" as we reluctantly open a package we assume will be burdensome and heavy. When responding to the God of our Worst Fear, we don't risk—we calculate. We are lulled to sleep under a voice that promises a safer, more definitive path. No dark trail, no threatening unknown. But also no thrill, no beauty of sparks and hoofs.

When we're listening to the God of our Worst Fear, we can't hear Love, even when its call is clear. The prophet cries, "Awake, awake, O you sleeper, get up! Arise from the dead and let the light shine." These are the words which call us to plunge in, bathe in, and splash around in the third posture of our hearts: "Oh good, it really is you, Jesus!" Jesus is for us and active in the affairs of our lives for good. We remember this only when we are present in life—awake.

SLUMBER ABOUNDS

As Annie Dillard writes, "We wake, if ever we wake at all, to mystery."[1] I don't know about you, but I don't readily stay in mystery without trying either to fix it or run from it.

On September 11, 2001, we did wake. We'll never forget the faces of thousands of New Yorkers who stood in stunned silence as their world, our world, was jolted by those airliners. Slumber ceased for a moment. All that was predictable exploded into a momentary awareness. And then they ran, just ahead of the billowing cloud of dust.

As the international fight against terrorism began, Bruce Cockburn's words came to mind: "We are lovers in a dangerous time.... We have to kick at darkness until it bleeds daylight."[2] From conversations in coffee shops to the expressions of families as they watch their loved ones deployed into a "new kind of war," the momentary awakening is felt. Oh, but we underestimate the extent of our love of sleep.

Immediately after September 11 we wanted answers. We wanted clarity on how this could happen. But clear answers didn't come. We relished the heroes, all those who kicked at darkness, bleeding the daylight of a resurrected community spirit and patriotism. But as our questions came, showing us how asleep to evil we had been, we awoke only to more mystery. We swore it would change things forever, but within weeks we were heading back to the malls, driving to overcrowded sports schedules, scrambling to protect our assets. Missing our lives. It takes more than terrorist blasts to get our attention.

So what does get our attention? What wakes us up? The slight touch from a lover. The jolt of adrenaline from a whitewater rapids ride. The ache of loneliness. The shock of grief. Hearing the voice of a child who has moved away from home. An unhurried stroll through the Metropolitan Museum of Art. Our sight, smell, touch, hearing, and taste rouse us from our slumber and nudge us to face the day. When the Colorado horizon effortlessly moves from gray to pink to crimson to gold, something nudges my heart to engage in the day. When I'm skiing and feel my heart pound as I navigate a field of moguls, I feel the rush that skiers feel when I "find my line." But even more, when I catch a peripheral glimpse of snow glistening as it clings to the pine, or hear a snow bird in the trees, something quiets my heart, and I commune with Jesus, not just my skis.

Leonardo da Vinci says the ministers of the soul are the five senses. They are the doors to our heart and the invitation to hear Jesus. The problem is, our senses are often ministered to, but we still sleep. I did it this morning. My dog came in my bedroom and gave me a sweet nudge on the face with her nose—something you'd think would wake me up. An hour later I was still sleeping until she moaned to be let out. Sometimes it takes the smell of bacon (don't you love those mornings?) or two rounds of alarm clocks. You get it—our slumber is a stubborn thing. Persistent even when our senses are roused. Tony Campolo's words capture this:

> We are caught up at a particular stage in our national ethos in which we're not only materialistic, but worse than that; we're becoming emo-tionally dead as people. We don't sing, we don't dance, we don't even commit sin with much enthusiasm. Kierkegaard once said that this age will die, not from sin, but from lack of passion. There is a deadness everywhere. High schools are apathetic. Colleges are apathetic. I mean, everybody's gone to sleep.[3]

Maybe Love wants us to wake up in the course of "normal" life, as we stop deadening our senses in all forms. Even my best routines can become lifeless, lulling me into autopilot deadness. I can put a weekly event on my calendar because I look forward to it, and then two months later I'm dragging myself out of bed and showing up at the event because I, or someone else, expects it of me. I need structure in my life, and there's certainly nothing wrong with a routine or commitments, but I must listen carefully to what is happening to my *presence* as I live out my routine, or I can easily fade, showing up in body only, not in spirit and heart.

We've all experienced arriving at church seven minutes late, coffee stains on our buttons, slightly disheveled. We make our way upstream through the folks still mingling in the entryway, hoping not to catch the eye of anyone, because we're not in the mood for interacting. We drop the kids off at their classes and make our way into the sanctuary, where we're relieved to see some teenagers enacting a drama. We think, *Oh good, I haven't missed much.* We land in one of the back pews, glad to be sitting down, when the worship leader says, "I'd like you to take a minute to stand and greet your neighbor..."

Our presence ebbs away subtly, without our realizing it. Rarely do we ask the question, "Why are we doing this? What are we after?" My friend Gayle, a bright and very alive woman, worked in a position for over three years before she was able to admit to herself that she was miserable, before she realized it was possible to make a change in employment. What kept her from waking up sooner? I know a man who boards United on Monday and American on Thursday, regularly shutting out the flight attendants' safety spiel as he prepares for his next meeting. Just last week he allowed himself to wake for a moment as he asked, *When was the last time I enjoyed this?* One Sunday morning in the midst of the most stressful part of my brother's battle with cancer, I woke up and heard Jesus say to me, *Stay put today. Rest.* I rolled over, grateful and present to this loving admonition. So why was it that two hours later I had to call a friend to ask her to tell me it was okay not to go to church? How is it that a counselor I know schedules a constant flow of people through his office, rattling off familiar advice and communication suggestions without ever asking, "Do I believe someone can change?" As I figure someone else will check in on my shut-in, elderly neighbor, I sleep. You get the point. When we do finally stumble out of bed into the alertness of being present in our own lives, that's when the adventure begins, because that is when we hear Love speak, and change can come.

How Love Speaks

What is the message woven into the vibrant trembling of aspen leaves aflame in gold and auburn—their brilliance coming in the cycle of decay and death?

What is being said to me as I encounter a whole new world of medicinal smells—the sterile environs of chemotherapy, the putrid odor that accompanies a body's fight against itself? What is being spoken as a woman I know softly weeps in a dark and empty nursery, as she smells the talc she'll no longer rub on the baby she lost. As we chart through an unstable world, how can we stay awake, not missing our lives, with faces that reveal our trust in Love?

If you are like me, you think that more involvement in spiritual things will somehow help you to stay awake. I envision myself praying more, reading poetry, studying more. Joining a group maybe. All those things are great, but on this road of "lean in and listen" obedience, sometime we miss the most obvious ways Jesus is speaking to us. And on this journey where Jesus whispers our name, the only reason we would ever go along for the ride is Love.

Ever fall in love? Love itself is somehow the benefit for all its unbridled consequences. John Donne wrote, "Take me to you, imprison me, for I, except you enthrall me, never shall be free, nor ever chaste, except you ravish me." And this from a poem that begins, "Batter my heart, three-personed God."[4] As opposed to the pressured face we so often associate with Christian obedience, true obedience forgets the cost or disruption that obedience can bring, because it is compelled into something it can't live without. It is willing to pay a price. It knows that Love is worth the hassle.

Love beckons us to strip off layer after layer of protective sleeping clothes. Our pride, religion, autonomy, reputation, denial, even our vocations can become coverings under which we don't have to respond. Under these coverings we sleep—constricted, but safe. When we give ourselves to love, we're giddy at the prospect of leaving home, driving all night through storms to get to the one we love. The thought of nakedness is a joy as the desire for intimacy outweighs any fear.

The way we either ignore or pay attention to the natural world around us tells us a lot about how responsive we are to being led into the unbridled, risky path of Love. A breeze across the cheek or sometimes a thunderous, frightening lightning storm may have something specific to communicate to us. The jolt of the elements is a great mercy, waking us long enough to hear.

THE QUESTIONS AND LESSONS OF NATURE

The sea, wind, owl, mist. The sandstorm, hurricane, petal, tornado. The fox, the eagle. All these draw us to our place in the whole and to the power and authority of Love. Even in Central Park something tells us, "This is not all there is," and reminds us of the eternal. The admonition of naturalist John Muir says it well: "Let children walk with nature, let them see the beautiful blending and communions of death and life, their joyous inseparable unity, as taught in woods and meadows, plain and mountains and streams…and they will learn that death is stingless indeed."[5]

Northern New Mexico is home for me, and as you know, a forest fire ripped through the mountains surrounding my hometown a few years ago. But what comes to mind now at the thought of "blending and communions of death and life" are the effects of the fire and a multiyear drought that have impacted that once-indomitable place. I had never, not once, thought of the terrain around Los Alamos, my hometown, as fragile. But I do now. I recently visited this mountain community that is located more than seven thousand feet above sea level and is surrounded by charred ponderosa on the mountain hillsides. Although I knew the fire's sad impact, I anticipated still seeing the green blanket of piñon and juniper that grow on the hills and canyons around town. They had not been touched by the fire, so the thought of them was welcome. Rounding the rambling highway curves into town, my heart sank. The drought and a bark-beetle infestation had turned the expected green into a blanket of brown. The piñons were dead. There was little life in the hillsides. I was aware, as I drove, of a deep sagging inside my heart. But I was also aware of something that transcended that grief. Jesus whispered, *This does not have the final say.* Death is stingless indeed. Then I remembered Isaiah 42:14–16:

> I have long been silent;
>> yes, I have restrained myself.
> But now I will give full vent to my fury;
>> I will gasp and pant like a woman giving birth.

I will level the mountains and hills
    and bring a blight on all their greenery.
I will turn the rivers into dry land
    and will dry up all the pools.
I will lead blind Israel down a new path,
    guiding them along an unfamiliar way.
I will make the darkness bright before them
    and smooth out the road ahead of them.
Yes, I will indeed do these things;
    I will not forsake them.

God speaking in the blight. Strangely, this thought was comforting to me. I wondered what he was trying to say. I heard many in that mountain community, a town known for its intellectual and spiritual pride, ask, "I wonder what God is doing here?" I doubt anything but fire could have brought that question to that sleeping town.

How does nature do it? How does it provoke the heart's truest inquiries? I've observed the rancor of trash dwellings around Manila and have walked in the squalor of African townships. But I've also lived in Colorado. You'd think living here would "work" to keep my soul awake. Nope. I was driving home last night through one of the prettiest mountain passes in North America after having visited some friends. I had much on my mind, so I was driving, as we do, a bit mindlessly and very unaware. Suddenly a buck bounded from the dark woods, causing me to slam on my brakes. *Now* I was awake. The buck kept going, oblivious to what had just occurred, but I sat there for the first time that night seeing the white mist hanging over the mountains in the wet moonlight. And through the breaking clouds, there were those stars. I've seen them hundreds of times, but only now did they make me gasp, prompting me to ask myself, *Where were you?*

The German poet Rainer Rilke asked a similar question:

Unknowing before the heavens of my life
I stand in wonder, O the great stars.

...How quiet.

As if I didn't exist. *Am I part?*[6]

The stars speak for themselves, or better said, they speak of Jesus without trying. I was at a winter mountain retreat where several of us decided to take a hike under the night sky up a lengthy hill in significant snow. We worked hard to keep our balance in the snow and rock as we ascended. We were working so hard that we were laughing. When we reached the top, we stopped to catch our breath and finally had a chance to look up. Corporate gasp. The stars took our breath away, knocking us to our knees in the snow. We got down, snow-angel position, in the snow and quietly took it in. There was an occasional shooting star, prompting a murmur, but for the longest time there was silence. Our small eyes taking in vast space. Quietly one friend said to herself (and we overheard), "And we're so big, huh?"

This is what nature is meant to do: confront us and rouse us from our faulty interpretations of things, from our routine living, from our little dens of self-protected sleep. Nature is his embossed invitation to the feast he's preparing for us. Jesus wants us to feel not small but a part of the bigger whole. My friends Brent and John, in their teachings on the Sacred Romance, addressed the real reason for our losing heart in the Christian faith: the gospel no longer takes our breath away. We have to be knocked to our knees. We have to slam on our brakes for the beauty of a holy overture to remind us that we cannot hide from such advances.

Whirling Dervish of Love

Fyodor Dostoevsky said, "Love all God's creation, the whole and every grain of sand in it. Love every leaf, every ray of God's light."[7] I've slept through countless beautiful sunrises, so I'm already behind! When we are asleep, we don't have eyes for the obvious ways God pursues us, let alone the smaller, detailed, and intimate ways.

When I lived in southwestern Colorado, I had a little porch that looked across a high desert plateau toward the San Juan range of the Rockies. It backed up to the lush greenery of spruce and pine but was arid—a haven for rock squirrels, lizards, chamiso, yucca, and an occasional black bear (such as the one that decimated my garbage on a consistent basis).

The other inhabitants of this terrain were the hummingbirds. When sugar nectar was put out for them, word spread like wildfire among this littlest bird's kingdom, and they'd come in ones and twos to check out the new source. Red, yellow, green, and brown, they would come—a whirling dervish of delight and sound.

One morning I rose earlier than I had hoped and stumbled to the porch to take in the sweet air of summer morning. Coffee was perking but hadn't yet begun to assist me in joining the living. I sat on my porch swing, half-asleep, when the most violent and wonderful sound came. The hummingbirds, drawn to the color of my pajamas, decided to have a closer look. One by one, they hovered and whirled and zipped and lingered just near my neck. Each invisible flap of their powerful, tiny wings exploded in my eardrum. The torrential sound came and went in an instant. A fluttering, furious force, then silence. Their abrupt return like a meteorite piercing a calm sky. This playground of quiet and force went on for twenty minutes until they decided I had nothing more to offer them than the shirt on my back. So they perched, one by one—momentarily—on a little ledge just near me. I watched these creatures no more than an inch tall, with fragile, spindly beaks, and marveled that they could raise such a commotion. They had awakened me. Love had spoken through the comic onslaught of these little birds.

The hummingbirds were unexpected, but their message was obvious. God wanted me to delight; he simply wanted me to remember him. God seems to think it is always obvious:

> For the truth about God is known to them instinctively. God has put this
> knowledge in their hearts. From the time the world was created, people
> have seen the earth and sky and all that God made. They can clearly see
> his invisible qualities—his eternal power and divine nature. So they have
> no excuse whatsoever for not knowing God. (Romans 1:19–20)

And as God says through Isaiah:

Come closer and listen. I have always told you *plainly* what would
happen so you would have no trouble understanding. And now the
Sovereign LORD and his Spirit have sent me with this message: "The
LORD, your Redeemer, the Holy One of Israel, says: I am the LORD
your God, who teaches you what is good and leads you along the paths
you should follow. Oh that you had listened to my commands! Then
you would have had peace flowing like a gentle river and righteousness
rolling like waves." (Isaiah 48:16–18, emphasis added)

If we think about it, he is quite clear: the stillness of dusk, a warm Pacific
breeze through our hair, the creativity of Orion and Pleiades, summer grass,
the tenaciousness of a columbine. These reminders leave our hearts with "no
excuse;" we have reminders of his voice. We have hummingbirds.

THE SENSES AND THE SPIRIT

When I think about my life following Jesus, I realize I've had times when my
intellect was fully engaged, but my soul was tied up in pleasing people. In
other seasons my emotions were engaged, but I stopped reasoning with God
and became dismissible and overdramatic. It is a rare thing to find our heart,
mind, strength, and soul engaged all at once. It takes courage.

Jesus said:

Everything that is now hidden or secret will eventually be brought to
light. Anyone who is willing to hear should listen and understand! And
be sure to pay attention to what you hear. The more you do this, the
more you will understand—and even more, besides. To those who are
open to my teaching, more understanding will be given. But to those
who are not listening, even what they have will be taken away from
them. (Mark 4:22–25)

More understanding will not be given to me unless I am paying attention, unless my senses are awake and receptive. If the gospel message is to be realized, it must be received viscerally—with and through the senses. A child receives a Christmas gift with shivers and shrieks. Lovers receive affection with sighs and trembles. God speaks of his relationship with us in more sensual terms than we might think, inviting us to actually listen to Love through our senses. He asks us to taste and see his goodness. A lifeless, sensually devoid gospel is a dead gospel. A gospel that is alive is more than a proclamation; it is a touch, an aroma, an unexpected word rousing us to leave everything behind and follow because we don't want to do anything else but be with the One we love. As Os Guinness says, "Disciples are not so much those who follow as those who *must* follow."[8] Our truest hearts want to follow this One who rouses us into the unthinkable.

To listen to the voice of God with our senses is to entrust our whole being and our future into his hands. The result is a full life, an abundant life. A life the thief cannot (though he may try) steal, kill, or destroy. And neither can we, though we try.

The mystics were awake to this. They knew the senses take us into the more mysterious realms of God. St. John of the Cross wrote in the sixteenth century that there is "a supernatural knowledge that reaches the intellect by way of external bodily senses (sight, hearing, smell, taste and touch). Through these senses, spiritual persons can, and usually do, perceive supernatural representations and objects."[9] This Spanish Carmelite priest spoke of visions, images, good and bad angels, lights, splendors, fragrances—all of which come to us individually from the other world in order to stir our hearts and whet our appetites. St. John of the Cross, through his own despair (the dark night of the soul), had reason to be attuned to how personally God meets us. You can hear the natural weaving of spirit and body in his thinking—something our Western worldview is just now regarding as important. He adds:

> Concerning touch they feel extreme delight, at times so intense that all
> the bones and marrow rejoice, flourish, and bathe in it. This delight is

usually termed spiritual unction because in pure souls it passes from the spirit to the senses. And it is common with spiritual persons. It is an overflow from the affection and devotion of the sensible spirit, which individuals receive in their own way.[10]

Common? I personally know only a few folks who have experienced God this way. Only a few times in my own life has God come so tangibly. Once during a lonely weekend as a freshman in college, I decided to visit the local charismatic gathering place—a huge church known for its freedom of expression in worship and miracles. It was not my usual scene, so I went, skeptical but curious. During that service, in a sincere moment of opening my heart to God, I was transported into a blinding bright light. Inexplicably, within that light I was taken on a tour of the world—continent to continent. I had not traveled at that point in my life, so the peace I felt as I was "shown" the faces of foreign individuals and the suffering of the masses was disarming. I believe I was given the gift of knowing, just for a moment, the sorrow in God's heart over this world. I also believe I got a taste of his delight in us. All of this within a moment or two—a timeless, eternal, weighty moment that I'm sure has shaped my life in ways I can't see. It is what Jesus said: "Love the Lord your God with all your heart, all your soul, all your mind, and all your strength" (Mark 12:30). In that moment, my intellect understood the burden of his heart.

Listen to the words of John: "The one who existed from the beginning is the one we have heard and seen. We saw him with our own eyes and touched him with our own hands. He is Jesus Christ, the Word of life" (1 John 1:1). Jesus is not abstract, isolated to paper and print, but the Word to be heard, the Light to be seen. He's to be encountered along a dusty road to a city called Emmaus or embraced at a wet, misty breakfast by the sea. Note John's urgency: "I touched him! I saw both his kindness and his fierce ways! I smelled him as he came out of the crowds, soaked in sweat, yet we were compelled to leave our businesses for him! We heard him scream; we saw him cry; we drank, and we ate with him!" John is spilling over from having been with Jesus and longing for us to understand.

The Sensual Presence

What do those of us do who cannot feel his skin or see the glint in his eye? We turn to the Comforter, Guide, the Companion who was promised to reveal who Jesus is. The Holy Spirit is a more sensual presence than we might want to admit. The Spirit allows us to encounter Jesus's power the way John did, his tenderness the way Mary Magdalene felt it, the sadness and belief that Peter experienced. Jesus as a companion is just a philosophy or theory without the Spirit's bringing him right to our side. Our senses, saturated by the Spirit of God, allow us to know he's with us—hearing him in prayer or in a child's laughter, tasting him in moments of communion, feeling him nudge us in the middle of the night when we know we must pray for a friend. His companionship comes as we see him washed across the sky in the morning or see him in our mind's eye as we picture his patient eyes toward us when we struggle.

Think for a minute what you know about the Holy Spirit. He came to point to the Son, the way Jesus pointed to his Father. Now think about how Jesus pointed us to God: he was constantly catching people off guard, teaching them that they didn't know God the way they thought they did. Through his touch or his parables or his miracles, he said, "Let me reveal, by touching you and changing you, how amazing my Father is." The Spirit does the same thing, showing us at every turn that we don't know Jesus the way we think we do, that there is so much more Jesus. And the Spirit came to guide you into all Truth. This is more than being guided into correct doctrinal training. The Spirit takes us deeper into the One who calls himself the Way, the Truth, and the Life. The Spirit came to comfort you, to be the Paraclete, the One who walks alongside you, covering your back, through this life. He came to convict with regard to sin so nothing would be in the way of his touch. He came to remind us of his holiness and the coming judgment so we'd remember our need. We're sleeping and blinded by the god of this world, but the Spirit reveals the light of the glory of God in the face of Christ.

Jesus got my attention through nature but has been my transforming companion by his Spirit. The other day when I was questioning again what he is doing with my life, this Companion came and whispered, *You may not*

remember, but in the desperate times of your life as a little girl, you gave me every-
thing. You told me, "Jesus, take all of me. Do what you wish." That is what I'm
doing, Jan. And I'm doing it because I love you.

C. S. Lewis said:

> Nature is mortal; we shall outlive her. When all the suns and nebulae
> have passed away, each one of you will still be alive. Nature is only the
> image, the symbol; but it is the symbol scripture invites me to use.
> There, beyond Nature, we shall eat of the Tree of Life. At present, if we
> are reborn in Christ, the spirit in us lives directly on God; but the
> mind and, still more, the body receives life from Him.[11]

Nature—with her streams and food and trees—beckons to us, but we are
dependent on the Spirit for life. He is the Vine from which our branch's sap
flows. The Spirit feeds us the Bread of Heaven; he pours the New Wine into
the new wineskin he put within us. He is the daily Water of Life that saturates
what would otherwise be dry, cracked earth.

Responsiveness Opposed

No wonder the enemy of God tries hardest to keep us from being responsive
through our senses. At every turn, responsive, awakened living is opposed.

One of the most difficult examples is sexual abuse, where the Enemy's
scheme reaches to the very core of a heart's responsiveness. It is fair to say that
most abuse would not occur if it weren't for the free and naturally responsive
hearts of little girls and boys, making it easy for an abuser to gain trust. When
a little girl is abused, her ability to trust her own responses—to attention, to
bonding, to enjoyment of others, and to pleasure—is called into question. Evil
takes a receptive little heart—one that leans in freely to affection and attention—and turns the responsiveness upside down in a shattering violation that
introduces suspicion into the young heart about her own responsiveness: "I
was the one who brought this on myself. I liked the attention. I liked the care."

My responsiveness was called into question in a different way when, as a child, I became furious over all that was happening outside of my control. Anger is a legitimate response for a child when she is confused, as long as she is tended to and instructed how best to direct the anger. That shepherding and instruction didn't happen for me. Instead, I was ridiculed and shamed for being overemotional, for making too much of things. I ingested those words, and over time I came to view my anger as suspect, something to hide. Only as the Spirit has worked in me for over thirty years have I begun to glimpse how important and redemptive my anger can be—when it rages against evil and when it is fighting for true things in myself and in others.

Ready to Wake Up

Love is calling. All the time. Only if we are listening to love are we stopped short, savoring the opportunity to be awake, loving God in return through our responsiveness. Love calls through creation; we either choose to drive mindlessly or to be stopped. Nature indicts us, and we either stand in awe of its convicting power, or we continue to ruminate. Our senses tell us, all the time, that there is more. Our battle is to allow the love of Christ to keep our senses alive, without suspicion or shadow.

When is the last time you thought about a good friend and said, "Ah, I can't wait for her fragrance"? When is the last time you thought of Christianity and said, "Tastes wonderful"? When is the last time you took a hard look at a face that you love, allowing it to trouble you for what is hidden and delight you for what shines? It's a tragedy, really. We've so tamed our Christian existence, calling our senses into question and labeling them illicit and impure. What gets lost in the translation are open hearts—responsive, awakened hearts willing to lose all—that love life and embrace suffering, that laugh with a laughter undaunted by evil. Sensual Christians. Christians who drink in all God has for us.

Eleven

Listening to Love Despite Our Fear

Don't you want to be where there's strength and love
in the place of fear?
—Jackson Browne

There is no fear in love.
—the apostle Paul

W ho is this Love? We open the door; he quietly enters and then asks all. Who is this who uproots our tent pegs, rocks our boats with his waves, quiets the same waves, wrestles with us about our blessings, argues with us about our self-righteousness, then surprises us with music and feasting? This God refuses to be pinned down. Just when we think we "know" him, when we see a certain aspect of his personality, he flashes a corner of another side to who he is. Just when we glimpse him as Father, he flashes images of his nurturing, maternal ways. Just when we see that he is the silent Lamb before his shearers, he roars with the vengeance of the Lion of the tribe of Judah. Just when he heals and restores, he is the God who allows life to tear at our hearts for purposes only he understands. The minute we presume to know him, he reveals more—not to taunt us or trick us, but to remind us of our finite need and his infinite nature of Love. As George MacDonald states, "Oh the folly of any mind that would explain God before obeying Him! That would map out the character of God instead of crying, Lord, what wouldst thou have me do?"[1] I hope it is clear at this point: to obey God is to lean in, wrestle with what he says, and then respond from the heart *because of who he is.* And I hope it is clear that our biggest challenge is to let go of our control and to face our fear, as Love breaks through.

BREAKTHROUGH

It's been about a year since Jake and I hung out. I haven't forgotten him, poor guy. If that sounds like pity, it is because living in my world was hard for him. But Jake came, and he tried. I don't think we'll ever fully know how hard he tried.

The minute Jake's eyes met mine, I knew we had a future together. He was handsome, but desperate (trying to hide it, but failing miserably). Perhaps he saw the same desperation in my eyes. I had, come to think of it, wandered off to the Humane Society on a whim. My friends have come to worry about my whims.

Did I mention Jake is a dog?

Jake was in the corner kennel—cowering, matted, and rocking, autistic-style. I knew I was crazy. I didn't need another dog. Cito had been my trusted friend for years, and she more than brought life to my world (like bringing home a mountain lion head and a Canada goose in her jowls). But here was Jake—the mirror image of Cito. They could be siblings. Well, siblings like the ugly duckling and the White Swan. Through Jake's tremors I saw his tail wag and his eyes connect with mine. I'm such a sucker.

I will never try to make a case for loading that dog in my backseat with a somewhat put out Cito pushed against the window for fear of touching this new, maniacal beast. Jake had reason to be a bit off; he had been abandoned in a trailer with over thirty other animals. He had no concept of training of any kind. The language Jake knew was survival of the fittest, and he had been harmed in perhaps the most insidious way any of us can ever be: he had been abandoned. With a dog like that, most dog professionals would tell you to beware of latent rage and arbitrary attack. For some reason I just didn't suspect

Jake of that. Neither did the dog professionals at the Humane Society. They said I'd just have to handle him with great care.

Jake became, for me, a picture of my own fear. When I unloaded Jake into my backyard in Charlotte (and *unload* is a literal term—clutching and hoisting all sixty pounds of him and depositing him behind the fence), he was the picture of how fear becomes our prison. He didn't know what to do. There was green grass, and food and water on the porch, but Jake stayed in a mud puddle in the corner of the yard, looking around as if for an enemy. He seemed to think he belonged in that mud and protected his little corner as if it were all that was left in the world.

It took five weeks to get Jake to darken the archway to the door of my house. The ritual that ensued at this point became a graphic picture of the love we keep ourselves from because of fear. Over these five weeks, Jake had mustered up the courage to come to the porch at night to eat. *Scarf* is more like it. It was as if there was no muscle control over his jowls. He hovered over the bowl, inhaled, and licked his chops. And then he darted like a rocket back to his corner or under the garage. But I had seen him eat, so I knew he like the food. It did my heart good to see him eat.

Over time, I left the back door open. Trembling, Jake would creep up and peek in the house from about ten feet away. I would praise him effusively every time he made any movement toward me. It was a painstaking and patience-producing process, sometimes taking an hour to coax him forward. He would whimper and moan; you could literally see how the idea of love thrilled him. It felt so good to be praised. And so exciting to be so close to touch and warmth!

And then, like a thud he would hit an invisible barrier. If it had been material, he would have hit concrete. Jake would look at me, yearning, longing to get to me and the little piece of food on the floor near my feet. He would walk straight toward me and suddenly stop. There on the threshold of his fear, he would whimper and whine and jump straight up and sometimes turn 360 degrees around, as if to say, "I want it, please know I want it. I want your love! I want to be a dog! I want to be free!" But the invisible barrier of fear kept him outside.

Then one day Jake crossed the threshold, ate the food, and let me pet him. Yes, just like that. I could not believe my eyes. When Jake broke through that barrier, a dignity came to him, downright nobility in his gate. He strutted around my home with his head held high, and even though in his excitement he left behind a stream on the carpet, it didn't matter, because Jake had let himself be loved. He responded to training after that; it was rudimentary, but it was progress.

And through it all, that dog impacted the way I think about the fear in my life.

WHAT WE FEAR MOST

When it comes to our fear, it's judgment—or better said, condemnation—that we fear from God. We all know the words "There is no fear in love. But perfect love drives out fear" (1 John 4:18, NIV). But we forget what comes before and after these words:

> God is love, and all who live in love live in God, and God lives in them. And as we live in God, our love grows more perfect. So we will not be afraid on the day of judgment, but we can face him with confidence because we are like Christ here in this world.
>
> Such love has no fear because perfect love expels all fear. *If we are afraid, it is for fear of judgment,* and this shows that his love has not been perfected in us. We love each other as a result of his loving us first. (1 John 4 16–19, emphasis added)

Some might think me cavalier, but I don't fear seeing Jesus on Judgment Day. I'm awed by, but confident of, the new nature given to me when Jesus breathed life into my dead soul, making me like him here in this world. I believe Jesus did this when I trusted him for salvation. He sees the perfection that comes from shed blood so there will be no condemnation on that terrible, wonderful day.

Yet, and I know it sounds crazy in light of such confidence, I also believe he is waiting for me to mess up. Scripture says, "We are like Christ here in this world.… If we are afraid, it is for fear of judgment." These words help me know I'm not alone in this struggle. I'm really good at assuming I'll be judged around every corner, in interactions with people, especially with God.

I don't live as though I know my love is growing more perfect or as though I know he first loved me. I live as though I have to love him first and have to prove it to him with aplomb before he'll be satisfied. It is crazy, but I know you understand. You assume, as I do, that if Jesus were on the beach preparing breakfast for you, he would, as you both sat down around the coals, only be interested in hearing about how well you performed, how well you served him while he was gone for three days. We've not been perfected in Love, because we still fear judgment.

But that is not who Jesus is. If Jesus sat down to breakfast with me, he would be interested in the hidden places of my life and would draw them out so naturally I would hardly notice. By the time I clued in to the fact that he was really there, truly back with me, that he hadn't left me the way I thought he had, he would have already engaged my heart and handed me my eggs and toast. This is how it will be for all of us. We won't be able to figure out how he got us across that old concrete threshold of fear, but somehow we will be there with him.

Just by being with Jesus, we are exposed. He wants to be with us, and if you haven't noticed, he gets what he wants. When we are with him (not just thinking about him and musing and wriggling about him behind our barrier of fear, but *with* him), we cannot hide. We assume our exposure will mean automatic reprimand or, worse, automatic rolling of the eyes. We never knew we'd receive a kiss and a meal. We never knew he would chase away fear with one glance in our direction. We never knew he'd love us first.

FACING WHAT WE'RE MOST AFRAID OF

Jesus addressed our fear more often than anything else, and he did it directly: "Fear not." That always seemed cold and abrupt to me. ("Oh, okay, Jesus. Yes, sir. No more fearing.") Then I started to recognize his voice as Love. Sometimes we don't know what we really believe about Love until we face the very thing we're most afraid of.

That's true for Madison, the five-year-old daughter of my friends Christy and Scott. Christy took Madison to get her last round of immunizations. Knowing her daughter's fear of needles, she realized reinforcements might be necessary, so Scott came along to assist in damage control. Christy and Scott had prepared Madison well for the necessity of the shots, the procedure, the fear she might feel. Madison seemed okay with the process and was cooperative. Until the needle came. As soon as Madison saw the nurse wielding this instrument of pain, she became terrified and cried out. But it was *how* she cried out that can instruct us.

"Daddy, please help me!"

Scott responded immediately and went to her side. Madison wasn't comforted; she squirmed and yelled too much for the nurse to do the procedure safely. Finally Scott had to wrap himself around little Madison, holding her down against her will. The nurse gave the shots. Tears were dried, Scott drove away, and Christy loaded the kids in the car, wondering how Madison was feeling, whether she felt betrayed or angry. The car was quiet for a while, and then Madison said, "Mom?"

"Yes, Madison?"

"Daddy *sure* loves me, doesn't he?"

Christy was shocked. She had wondered how long it would take Madison to get over being held down against her will. Where did this come from? "You have no idea how much your daddy loves you, sweetheart," she replied.

More quiet. Christy marveled at the tenderness of her little girl's heart, knowing her mind was racing.

"Would Daddy kill a bear for me?"

"Absolutely."

More silence.

"Daddy would climb a mountain for me, wouldn't he, Mama? Daddy would do *anything* for me."

At that moment, Christy realized that her daughter knew more of God than she realized. Madison understood Love.

Madison already had enough trust in her daddy to cry for help. But the help she received was not exactly what she had bargained for. She was forced; she was held down. This does not look, sound, or feel like love. Even in the terror of this terrible beauty, her heart knew the truth: her daddy loved her and would move the world for her if he needed to. Somehow knowing this helped her surrender to the very thing she feared. Somewhere in her little heart, she heard, "Fear not, Madison."

I can't thank Madison enough, because hearing Love in the midst of my fears doesn't come so naturally to me. I've been held down the past few years, and I've reacted by kicking and screaming, telling God that he got it all wrong. Slowly I'm learning that the One who has held me down, taking away precious people and dreams, is the One who would, yes, kill for me. He would kill his Son for me. Gently he reassures me that I cannot see the whole picture, that I can rest, rather than wriggle, in his arms.

THE PRIMARY THING

I'm comforted by the fact that Jake was not rejecting the food, water, warmth. No, he was going nuts for it, longing for it as we long for the streams of life in our hollow place. His thirst and need were not the problems; it was that he allowed something else to be primary. It is amazing how we allow fear to become the primary thing, keeping us from receiving even the most basic gifts from God's hands. When we see it in Jake, we feel bad for him, but of course we think, *Well, he's* just *a dog.* Sure. And we're *God's chosen beloved.* That's the point. Fear kept Jake from being who he was to me, from receiving my good gifts for him. Fear keeps us from being well-tended sheep, away from lush green grass. Fear keeps us from being children, unabashed about questions. Fear keeps us from being beloved warriors and artists. It keeps us from living into our calling.

The invisible barrier shows its power in our life when we assume someone has an opinion about us and we fear his judgment, so we avoid the phone when we see his name on our caller ID. A husband might make assumptions about how his wife would react if he talked to her about her distance, so he gets distant as well. We may fear rejection in talking to our kids about their computer use at a neighbor's home or in stating our convictions in a small-group study. I've been confronted with this when teaching retreats and seminars. The invisible barrier for me is the familiar fear of not being enough—not being substantial enough, spiritual enough, bright enough, or lovely enough to capture the attention of the audience. Sometimes it is so powerful it takes oxygen away from me, leaving me lightheaded and dizzy. Some would say I've been attacked by a spirit of fear, and there's no question this is true at times. But by now I think you can recognize that just like any battle against our hearts, the Enemy's tactics are predictable. Attack where she is weakest (her fear that she must come through), and hope the barrier of fear keeps her from knowing the love of her God in the moment. The only answer in those moments is to call to mind the fact that I answer to no one but Jesus. No one's opinion or judgment matters but his. When I call this to mind, perfect love casts out all fear.

It turns out that, just like Jake, I've been weakest in the area of fearing punishment. As 1 John puts it, I've not been perfected in love. I've allowed the opinions of others and my assessment of myself to be primary over God's love for me. Jesus's touch is finding me in everyday encounters with my fear and in Kauai-like encounters with his kindness. The invisible barrier is evaporating. The message "you must come through" is becoming a faint echo, trailing off into the distance like Tom Bombadil's wights. In its place is growing a sensual but childlike delight in the privilege of getting to talk about the Love that saved my life. And saves it still.

Courage from Love, Not Power

I love the fact that we live in a kingdom of Love, not power. The picture of the prophesied Messiah in Zechariah 9:9 says, "Shout in triumph, O people of Jerusalem! Look, your king is coming to you. He is righteous and victorious, yet he is humble, riding on a donkey—even on a donkey's colt." I love this picture, because it shows that even before he arrived, we were told Jesus would not try to conquer fear with power (though he could) but with the courage that comes from humility and love.

Think of the people who catch your eye and keep your attention—people you respect and want to emulate. I'm guessing they have said yes to Love, sometimes over and over and over for months or years on the threshold to the door of kindness before they waltzed through the invisible barrier. I'm guessing they are thirsty people; they don't want to miss out, don't want their fear to keep them from their particular calling, but even more, they don't want fear to keep them from Jesus. They want to bring him pleasure, they want to make him proud. It is not bravado that compels them but the fearlessness of wanting God.

I think of little Agnes in *The Lost Princess,* who lived with a fearlessness that was only bravado because she had not yet suffered; she had not yet been humbled. A very wise counselor told her this:

> Whether it be a good thing or a bad thing not to be afraid depends on what the fearlessness is founded upon. Some have no fear because they have no knowledge of the danger; there is nothing fine in that. Some are too stupid to be afraid; there is nothing fine in that. Some who are not easily frightened would yet turn their backs and run the moment they were frightened; such never had more courage than fear. *But the person who will do his or her work in spite of his or her fear is a person of real courage.*[2]

I see the faces of so many people who are willing to work in spite of fear. I see Suraya Sadeed, an Iraqi woman who established a group called Help the Afghan Children. She let her rage over the Taliban take her into areas of Iraq where she might certainly die. "I am so angry I forget all about fear."

I see our friend Leigh, who has fought the message "everything you say is stupid" all her life, yet she gets up to address large gatherings of women. At a recent conference, the crowd was moved to silence and tears as she spoke of the passion of current-day martyrs.

I think of Tamara, who has all the typical inner-city reasons to fear but began a small coffeehouse for street children, which has now evolved into a housing project and a job-placement, training, and mentoring program.

I think of a friend who lives each day knowing he will break into cold sweats in even a small group of people. But he gets up and goes out the door. He couldn't, were it not for Love.

I think of Lori, who wonders constantly if she is a good mother yet allows Jesus to lift her head and her countenance as she pours her lifeblood into her two little girls while her husband has to fly away on business.

I think of my brother, who faces his day's work, which lately is defined as sleeping most of the time and allowing the wretched chemotherapy to do its job. He does this despite a hundred hidden fears that you and I could never be privy to in the process of dying.

Recently I was silenced by two women. Lisa has a degenerative muscular and autoimmune disease but has faced this, plus the legion fears associated with becoming an author. Her writings captured the eye and heart of Kathleen, who is in publishing, but Lisa's life captured her even more. Kathleen determined to assist Lisa in moving across the country to a climate more conducive to her health. She made arrangements, drove with Lisa across country, and has helped to settle her in to life in a new community. I don't need to put words to the fear that would keep most of us from drawing near to such a situation, for either of them. But as I listened to these two women, I realized they are both doing their work, without bravado, in spite of fear.

FEAR OF CHANGE

If we live like the people I've just mentioned, our lives will change. Love has a way of messing up our lives, remember? Change is the nature of life. It is going to come, whether it comes from engaging ourselves in the kingdom or from just being on earth. But for followers of Christ, change is a guarantee. A guarantee as Love desires more and more of our hearts.

The past twenty years have brought constant change for me—cross-cultural challenges, life-threatening illness, loss, job transition. As you've noticed, I like to find things that bring me joy, and I hang on tight, so each change has been rough. But I'm also coming to see change as a beautiful gift if I can receive it with open hands. If I can receive instead of fighting change (and this is surely a process), it can give me the gift of knowing, even more, who this Love is.

I'm imagining that you have some kind of change happening even now— a shift in your children's needs (a new soccer coach, a new teacher, a new friendship drama), a relocation, a transition in career or your way of thinking. Maybe you're just heading into a new venture or a new relationship. Maybe you've been in the same home for fifty-three years, but you're looking ahead to the phase of life we misname retirement, with the uncertainties of healthcare and pension security. Change is the hardest when we've put down roots—in a neighborhood, in a professional setting, or with friends. I've had enough conversations with military families to know that no matter how brave we have to be, good-byes and change are killers on the heart. Just below the surface of the "it's no big deal; that's just the way it is" attitude they have to adopt in order to survive the constant relocations, there are tears over childhood friends, adolescent loves, and those with whom you share the first milestones of life.

Some of the most difficult changes to navigate are in our circles of friendship or our communities. My community is spread out all over the place— people who love the world and different cultures, good food and music. Most are influenced by or involved in two different movements or schools of thought: the message of true change from deep repentance and the message of the heart, emphasizing Jesus's restoration of us rather than external religion. Both communities have experienced growing pains, as beliefs and views and opinions and convictions have been challenged. This is a really good thing. The message of deep repentance left us wanting more of the Spirit. The message of the heart is fluid and dynamic and full of the life of the Spirit, and because the message itself is that we cannot make God into a small story (though we try), the message is no longer big enough to hold the hearts of those who have articulated it for years. Isn't that beautiful? That is a sign of true life, if we'll respond to it. Two messages have changed our lives, and now neither is big enough. Only Jesus is big enough.

"The Christian community is not a closed circle of people embracing each other, but a forward-moving group of companions bound together by the same voice asking for their attention," writes Henri Nouwen.[3] I don't know what your community looks like, or even if you have one. But I love this definition of community, because it reflects the kind of "hang on to each other as we're compelled by the gospel" attitude seen in the New Testament. Change is implicit in an attitude like that.

Change is the nature of the new life Jesus gives us. Remember, this life of Christ has a forward motion to it; it was *given* so we would change. We are living into what has already happened (we live from glory to glory). Change is precisely why it is hard to open the door to Love. I love how Macrina Wiederkehr says it:

> Yearning for God is not safe if you want to stay as you are. If you yearn
> for God, a sacred presence will begin to fill you. It will hover over you,
> nudging you to a new and eternal life. It will mean, of course, a radical
> change from your old lifestyle, for God will come and upset your entire
> life with a haunting presence, a presence that is both terrible and beau-
> tiful. It will be a terrible beauty.[4]

It is still too early to truly say, but I think a terrible beauty descended on those of us who love my brother when the words "incurable cancer" were first uttered. It has been a severe and unwanted change, so much so that the worst in all of us has shown up in the terrible. The other night Dick and I argued so harshly that I ended up screaming, "If you weren't dying, I would kill you!" Thankfully, the comment stopped us long enough to bust up laughing at our foolishness. The reality of this terrible, beautiful change also showed up as Dick waited for his first intensive chemotherapy. He was alone as the waiting room music started playing. Dick sat stunned and then started to grin as the Bee Gees started serenading him with, "Staying alive, staying alive. Ay, ay ay ay staying alive…I've been kicked around since I was born…staying alive." Three weeks prior to this ironic display of Muzak, Dick would have never even heard the lyrics in a waiting room. But that day he was poised and ready because he has been made aware of life on every level. This moment made him aware of the hovering, nudging presence that had propelled him forward into a terrible future he isn't sure he wants and a beauty—being made to laugh at the oddest times—he could never obtain on his own.

NO FEAR OF DEATH

No force prompts fear more than death. Our government's entire Department of Homeland Security bears witness to this. We're meant to hate it; death is, after all, the enemy. But it is remarkable how much energy we expend trying to steer clear of this thing that will happen to us all, this thing that will be obliterated at the coming of Jesus as he rides in with the keys of sin and death in his hands. Do we steer clear of death so we can *really live*, or do we steer clear of death because we are scared?

Nicholas Wolterstorff, who lost his son suddenly in a climbing accident in Europe, gives us the privilege of reading his journal—his wrestling with the reality of death—in his book *Lament for a Son*. He writes of his struggle not to allow his son's death to take his own life—his will and spirit. He says that if death takes both his son and his own heart as well, "then death, be proud." He wants to steer clear of death so he can really live. "So I shall struggle to live the reality of Christ's rising and death's dying. In my living, my son's dying will not be the last word. But as I rise up, I bear the wounds of his death. My rising does not remove them. They mark me. If you want to know who I am, put your hand in."[5] This is a man who has looked death in the eye and has acknowledged that it does, indeed, win for a while. But death has no sting for this man. It marks him, like all suffering, but he wants to keep living, even if it is with the scars of death's victories along the way.

My mom is facing death. The doctor gave the orders for hospice care, so we wait with the woman who despaired of living at times and tenaciously held on at other times, as she surrenders to death. If you've encountered it, you know that hospice is beautiful, allowing people to give themselves to the process of dying with dignity rather than trying so hard to stay alive. There is great relief in this, and it's common for new hospice patients to experience a "hospice euphoria."

The threshold between here and heaven is so very slight. If you grasp at the air in front of you, you can realize for a moment that the threshold to heaven is "right here." Our lives are but a vapor, and even while we live, it is closer than we know. During these days, it is so clear that Mom is right on the edge of her eternal life. She is on the threshold to heaven. As a family we always joked with Mom that she would get to heaven and wouldn't have anything to do, because there wouldn't be anything to worry about. She's always been like C. S. Lewis in saying, "We are not necessarily doubting that God will do the best for us, we are wondering how painful the best will turn out to be."[6] She's thought, *Oh no, it is you, Jesus* more than the rest of us combined. I think we've all been afraid that she wouldn't be able to say, "Yes, it's you, Jesus!" until she saw him face to face.

I'm glad we were wrong. She is experiencing a release from what gave her the reputation as a professional worrier. "I'm not worried about anything," she has said. "I'm not bitter. It's amazing." She isn't holding on to grudges she's nursed against people who have harmed her or her kids. She has more important things on her mind now; she's seeing true life, so she doesn't see much reason for hardheartedness. She told me that the first person she'll find when she gets to heaven is her brother, Jack. She wants to sneak up behind him and say, "Hello, big boy. Mary Louise is here," and then she wants to find her father and tell him, "I'm home!"

What about Jesus? When asked if she wants to see Jesus when she gets to heaven, my mom said, "Well, yes, of course, of course." It's not that Jesus is an afterthought so much as he is implicit in it all; all the other reunions will be about him. She's glimpsing what Lucy and Caspian saw in The *Voyage of the Dawn Treader* when they turned eastward into the Silver Sea.

> Whiteness, shot with faintest color of gold, spread around them on
> every side...there seemed no end to the lilies. Day after day from all
> those miles and leagues of flowers there rose a smell which Lucy found
> it very hard to describe; sweet...a fresh wild, lonely smell that seemed
> to get into your brain and make you feel that you could go up moun-
> tains at a run or wrestle with an elephant. She and Caspian said to one
> another, "I feel that I can't stand much more of this, yet I don't want it
> to stop."[7]

I can't tell you when this transformation began in my once-burdened mom. But I'm pretty sure she can also relate to C. S. Lewis when he says,

> There have been times when I think we do not desire heaven; but more
> often I find myself wondering whether, in our heart of hearts, we have
> ever desired anything else.... Beneath the flux of other desires and in all
> the momentary silences between the louder passions, night and day,
> year by year, from childhood to old age, (is it not what) you are look-
> ing for, watching for, listening for?"[8]

THE SENSUAL WORLD TO COME

I heard a reporter covering Julia Roberts's wedding in Taos, New Mexico. What caught my attention was the description of her dress and her groom's attire. The reporter was detailed and passionate as he described the red silk threads in the groom's suit and the princess tiara in Julia's swept-up, glorious hairdo. What is it about us that longs to look on such a sight? Is it just a worldly desire, or is there something set in our hearts that longs to be noble, romantic, clothed in finery? (I *know* I have a longing, set from eternity, to look like Julia Roberts.) No matter how jaded you might be about marriage, you've felt this at the wedding of friends when you really believe they grasp the covenant and commitment they are making to one another. A friend of mine attended a lavish Italian wedding recently where the bride's best friend sang an original composition that prompted the bride to weep. My friend said the whole crowd was captivated by the way the groom was gazing at his bride's tears and smiling. To be adorned as ones prepared for betrothal, to adore one another so deeply that tears and laughter freely flow—this *must* be set in our hearts. Listen to what stirs when you hear what is coming for you:

> Then I saw a new heaven and a new earth, for the old heaven and the old earth had disappeared. And the sea was also gone. And I saw the holy city, the new Jerusalem, coming down from God out of heaven like a beautiful bride prepared for her husband.
>
> I heard a loud shout from the throne, saying, "Look, the home of God is now among his people! He will live with them, and they will be his people. God himself will be with them. He will remove all of their sorrows, and there will be no more death or sorrow or crying or pain. For the old world and its evils are gone forever. (Revelation 21:1–4)

This is what is coming, and every detail matters to us. There is a noble wedding, yes. But even more, each area of life that we have sought to relinquish into Jesus's hands—death, sorrow, pain, loneliness—will be handed over. No more struggle to let go. No more fear.

> Blessed are those who wash their robes so they can enter through the gates of the city and eat from the tree of life. Outside the city are the

dogs—the sorcerers, the sexually immoral, the murderers, the idol worshipers, and all who love to live a lie. (Revelation 22:14–15)

I should be outside the city, outside the lilies and gold and light. I should not even be invited to the wedding, let alone be presented as the beloved. I've betrayed him in my adultery; I've murdered in my thoughts; my idolatry has shown on my face; and no question, I love to live lies. I think you can be honest to say this is true for you, too. This is the stunning glory of Love: instead of remaining outcast in our rebellion, our robe has been washed in blood, so the Tree of Life is ours, so we can run up mountains. We can smell the feast and see the beckoning of the One we're coming to trust. "Yes, it is you, Jesus."

"I, Jesus, have sent my angel to give you this message for the churches. I am both the source of David and the heir to his throne. I am the bright morning star."
    The Spirit and the bride say, "Come." Let each one who hears them say, "Come." Let the thirsty ones come—anyone who wants to. Let them come and drink the water of life without charge. (Revelation 22:16–17)

Dream with me for a minute about the coming kingdom. What will it be like? Will it have the elegance of Great Britain without its stuffy protocol, the spice and sensuality of Brazil without the perversion, the mystery and intrigue of India without the futility of caste and reincarnation, the deference of Asia without the falsehood of losing face and shame? What will it be, this blending of the glorious from all cultures, with shadow, filth, and perversion not even a memory? Will we find faithful friends from childhood romping in the fields with canine companions? Will we see our old pet rabbit, happy and plump? Will we stumble into our old towns and neighborhoods, now restored and vibrant and think, *I never knew*, or will we be shocked at a landscape that transcends every beautiful place we've ever been? Will there be a perfect autumn, a perfect spring, or will there be one eternal season to blow the mind? I'm reminded of Lewis's words:

> You have never had it.
>
> All the things that have ever deeply possessed your soul have been but hints of it—tantalizing glimpses, promises never quite fulfilled, echoes that died away just as they caught your ear. But if it should really become manifest—if there ever came an echo that did not die away but swelled into the sound itself—you would know it. Beyond all possibility of doubt you would say, "Here at last is the thing I was made for."[9]

I *need* it to be a place where the food is laced with unearthly green chilies and sopaipillas are puffy and light. I *need* it to be a place where the music always changes, where words form perfect images, light casts the loveliest shadows, long walks are uninterrupted by worry. And I need the seasons—I need falling leaves, cool winds, and bundling up. I need skiing and snorkeling and the true face of every friend I love. I need it be to be a place where I finally know—all the time—that I'm deeply and passionately enjoyed, a place of gardens and puppies and wine and laughter and the best kind of tears. Now, I know some of you are thinking, *But what about Jesus?* I wish you could see my eyes. All I've just described are the things through which he found me, and I want that Love echoing into eternity. I can't know fully the thing I'm truly made for, but I can't wait to eat salsa on the beach with my God.

> We cannot tell each other about it. It is the secret signature of each soul, the incommunicable and unappeasable want, the thing we desired before we met our spouses or made our friends or chose our work, and which we shall still desire on our deathbeds, when the mind no longer knows spouse or friend or work. While we are, this is. If we lose this, we lose all.[10]

We can't lose it. It is too imperative for our lives. It is imperative for us who, like Caspian, cannot yet go on into Aslan's country. Lucy, Edumund, Eustace, and Reepicheep can go. Mom can go. Dick is going. Brent has gone. Mark, Jim, Jack, Gloria, Jennifer, Ken, and Paul are there. But we have to stay.

When we break through the invisible barrier of fear, we encounter a Love more brilliant than all our dreams of heaven combined. We finally see each other—with dignity—restored. In rare moments of caught-off-guard worship, when we catch a stunning sunset or hear a laugh we thought had been left back in our younger days—it is then we glimpse what we were made for and are taken to the threshold of heaven, for a moment.

But then we have to sail back to our earthly homes, always sooner than we wish. The same Love that called us up is the same Love set in our hearts from eternity that compels us back, away from the threshold of heaven and into this life. We go back to reveal our face, to engage in the restoration already taking place, awaiting the day to come.

Not As It Appears

Once I was with a small group who gathered on Baldhead Island off the coast of North Carolina. I came prepared to teach. I was not prepared for how Love would come to me through the natural forces around me.

Baldhead is a lazy, remote, relaxing island with only bicycles and small motorized carts. But it is surrounded by the waters of Cape Fear. In fact, you ferry through those waters to get to the island, so during our gathering this became a picture for some—a reminder that we must often chart through fear, leaving all that is familiar behind, to get to a place of rest and hope.

One morning we went out individually to simply listen to what might be said to us through the beauty there. It was a dark, blustery morning, causing the ominous waters of Cape Fear to be stirred up and threatening. As I looked out on the water, it was filled with agitation, cold, and fright. I found my mind reeling, thinking of many heavy and unmanageable things in my life.

As I walked along the shore, I bundled up in my jacket in retaliation to the wind, but after about an eighth of a mile I realized the wind was exhilarating and fresh.

Then I looked up. Above and in the churning waters was a gleeful flock of pelicans flying upwind, downwind, diving, coasting, having an absolutely glorious time as they feasted on a large school of fish. Cold, dark Cape Fear was tending to them quite nicely. This thought made me smile and took my heavy thoughts and lightened them a bit.

As I continued to walk on the sand, I started to experience the fatigue you feel when you are on the deep, dry sand. I altered my course and walked onto the wet sand that had been nursed by waves. This sand was solid, steady, and a welcome foundation on which to walk…I was steadied by the waters of Cape Fear.

I found myself asking, "How can these fearful waters feed these quirky pelicans? How can water saturate the sand and make it sturdy for my feet? How can the wind blowing off these dark waters be refreshing and cleansing?"

Suddenly I heard: *There is no fear in love.*

These words made me remember that the dark, churning waters I was looking across were the waters of a harbor. Her appearance was dark, but hidden in her waters was life-giving sustenance. Her surface was threatening, but she is a safe haven for the North Carolina coast against the brutal force of the sea. As I looked at the waters through this different lens, my troubled mind was suddenly still. I felt loved, not threatened.

There is no fear in love, but perfect Love casts out all fear.

This is the Love that gets our attention. This is the Love that messes up our lives. This is the honored guest that quietly enters and then asks, and gives, all. Yes, it is Jesus. Thank you, Perfect Love.

Notes

Chapter One: The Voice of Love

1. James Strong, *Strong's Exhaustive Concordance* (Nashville: Nelson, 1990), 26.

2. Mark Buchanan, *Your God Is Too Safe: Rediscovering the Wonder of a God You Can't Control* (Sisters, OR: Multnomah, 2001), 32.

3. Brent Curtis and John Eldredge, *The Sacred Romance: Drawing Closer to the Heart of God* (Nashville: Nelson, 1997), 54.

4. Brennan Manning, *Ruthless Trust: The Ragamuffin's Path to God* (San Francisco: HarperSanFrancisco, 2000), 37.

Chapter Two: Listening to Sorrow

1. Blaise Pascal, *The Mind on Fire,* ed. James Houston (Minneapolis: Bethany, 1997), 287.

2. Bianco de Siena, "Come Down, O Love Divine," trans. Richard F. Littledale.

3. Simone Weil, quoted in *Spiritual Classics,* ed. Paul Ofstedal (Minneapolis: Augsburg Fortress, 1990), 344.

4. Loreena McKennitt, "Dante's Prayer," on *The Book of Secrets,* Quinlan Road Music, 1997.

5. George MacDonald, *The Heart of George MacDonald: A One-Volume Collection of His Most Important Fiction, Essays, Sermons, Drama and Poetry, Letters,* ed. Rolland Hein (Wheaton, IL: Shaw, 1994), 15.

6. C. S. Lewis, *The Problem of Pain* (New York: Touchstone, 1962), 43–44.

7. See Malachi 3:2.

Chapter Three: Listening to Our Need

1. Canon Barnett, quoted in Steve Brinn, *The BootJack Ranch Devotional* (Pagosa Springs, CO: privately printed, 2001), 4.

2. Frederick Buechner, *Telling the Truth: The Gospel as Tragedy, Comedy, and Fairy Tale* (San Francisco: Harper & Row, 1977), 53.

3. Barnett, quoted in Steve Brinn, *The BootJack Ranch Devotional,* 4.

4. George MacDonald, *The Heart of George MacDonald: A One-Volume Collection of His Most Important Fiction, Essays, Sermons, Drama, Poetry, Letters,* ed. Rolland Hein (Wheaton, IL: Shaw, 1994), 14.

5. M. Craig Barnes, *When God Interrupts: Finding New Life Through Unwanted Change* (Downers Grove, IL: InterVarsity, 1996), 69.

6. MacDonald, *The Heart of George MacDonald,* 14.

7. Larry Crabb, *Shattered Dreams: God's Unexpected Pathway to Joy* (Colorado Springs: WaterBrook, 2001), 17.

8. Thomas R. Kelly, *A Testament of Devotion* (New York: Walker and Company, 1941), 26.

9. Ignatius, quoted in Richard Foster, *Prayer: Finding the Heart's True Home* (San Francisco: HarperSanFrancisco, 1992), 174.

10. Howard R. Macy, *Rhythms of the Inner Life* (Old Tappan, NJ: Revell, 1988).

Chapter Four: Listening to Each Other

1. Henri J. M. Nouwen, *The Path of Waiting* (New York: Crossroad, 1995), 26.

2. George MacDonald, *The Heart of George MacDonald: A One-Volume Collection of His Most Important Fiction, Essays, Sermons, Drama and Poetry, Letters,* ed. Rolland Hein (Wheaton, IL: Shaw, 1994), 15.

3. MacDonald, *The Heart of George MacDonald,* 15.

4. C. S. Lewis, *The Weight of Glory* (New York: Collier, 1980), 93.

5. Carol Davis (Leadership Network Conference, Glorieta, New Mexico, October 1998).

6. Aleksandr Solzhenitsyn, quoted in David Aikman, *Great Souls* (Lanham, MD: Rowman and Littlefield, 2003), 153.

7. G. K. Chesterton, *Orthodoxy* (Wheaton, IL: Shaw, 1994), 100.

Chapter Five: Listening to Reality

1. Brent Curtis, "The Wildness of God" (lecture, Sacred Romance lecture series, Glen Eyrie, CO, fall 1997).

2. C. S. Lewis, *The Horse and His Boy* (New York: Macmillan, 1952), 139.

3. George MacDonald, *George MacDonald: An Anthology*, ed. C. S. Lewis (New York: Touchstone, 1947), 127.

4. G. K. Chesterton, *Orthodoxy* (Wheaton, IL: Shaw, 1994), 104.

5. Chesterton, *Orthodoxy*, 105–6.

6. Chesterton, *Orthodoxy*, 106.

Chapter Six: Listening for the Threat of Love

1. Brother Tom Wolf (Leadership Network Conference, Glorieta, New Mexico, October 1998).

2. Kathleen Norris, *Amazing Grace: A Vocabulary of Faith* (New York: Riverhead, 1998), 45.

3. Norris, *Amazing Grace*, 48.

4. My thanks to Dan Allender for this thought during his teaching at Mars Hill Seminary, Bothel, Washington, June 25, 2003.

5. Ted Loder, *The Haunt of Grace: Responses to the Mystery of God's Presence* (Philadelphia: Innisfree Press, 2002), 32.

6. J. R. R. Tolkien, *The Fellowship of the Ring* (New York: Ballantine, 1965), 180.

7. Tolkien, *The Fellowship of the Ring*, 180.

8. Tolkien, *The Fellowship of the Ring,* 181.

9. Norris, *Amazing Grace,* 47.

10. C. S. Lewis, *Screwtape Letters,* quoted in Frederick J. Schumacher with Dorothy A. Zelenko, eds., *For All the Saints: A Prayer Book for and by the Church* (Delhi, NY: American Lutheran Publicity Bureau, 1994), 1042.

Chapter Seven: Listening to Our Exhaustion

1. Oswald Chambers, *My Utmost for His Highest,* special updated ed. (Grand Rapids: Discovery House, 1995), August 5 reading.

2. Howard Stringer, quoted in *The BootJack Ranch Devotional* (Pagosa Springs, CO: privately printed, 2001), 3.

3. Richard A. Swenson, *The Overload Syndrome: Learning to Live Within Your Limits* (Colorado Springs: NavPress, 1998), 67.

4. Thomas Kelly, quoted in Swenson, *The Overload Syndrome,* 65.

5. Swenson, *The Overload Syndrome,* 192.

6. Sally Breedlove, *Choosing Rest: Cultivating a Sunday Heart in a Monday World* (Colorado Springs: NavPress, 2002), 26.

Chapter Eight: Recognizing His Touch

1. Eivind Josef Berggrav, quoted in Frederick J. Schumacher with Dorothy A. Zelenko, eds., *For All the Saints: A Prayer Book for and by the Church* (Delhi, NY: American Lutheran Publicity Bureau, 1994), 436.

2. Bryce Courtenay, *The Power of One* (New York: Random House, 1989), 52.

3. David Wilcox, *Big Horizon,* compact disc, A&M records, 1994.

4. Berggrav, quoted in Schumacher with Zelenko, *For All the Saints,* 436.

5. Dallas Willard, *Renovation of the Heart: Putting on the Character of Christ* (Colorado Springs: NavPress, 2002), 209.

6. J. I. Packer, *Rediscovering Holiness* (Ann Arbor, MI: Vine Books, 1992), 68.

7. Courtenay, *The Power of One*, 7.

8. Willard, *Renovation of the Heart*, 209.

9. Robert Coles, *The Spiritual Life of Children* (Boston: Houghton Mifflin, 1990), 104.

Chapter Nine: Listening to the Call

1. J. R. R. Tolkien, *The Fellowship of the Ring* (New York: Ballantine, 1965), 118.

2. Oswald Chambers, *My Utmost for His Highest*, special updated ed. (Grand Rapids: Discovery House, 1995), August 5 reading.

3. John Piper, *Desiring God: Meditations of a Christian Hedonist* (Sisters, OR: Multnomah, 2003), 271.

4. Dietrich Bonhoeffer, *Letters from Prison* (New York: Touchstone, 1997), 334.

5. Chambers, *My Utmost for His Highest*, August 5 reading.

6. Chambers, *My Utmost for His Highest*, August 5 reading.

7. Victor Hugo, *Les Misérables* (New York: Fawcett Premier, 1982), 19.

8. In Ephesians 2:10, the Greek word for *workmanship* (NIV) is *poema*, which means *poem*.

9. Angelus Silesius, quoted in Macrina Wiederkehr, *A Tree Full of Angels: Seeing the Holy in the Ordinary* (San Francisco: Harper and Row, 1988), 90.

10. Hugo, *Les Misérables*, 17, emphasis added.

11. Hugo, *Les Misérables*, 17.

12. Hugo, *Les Misérables*, 33.

13. Nicholas of Cusa, *The Vision of God*, trans. Emma Gurney Salter (Escondido, CA: Book Tree, 1999), 73.

14. C. S. Lewis, *The Weight of Glory* (New York: Collier, 1980), 19.

Chapter Ten: Listening to Beauty

1. Annie Dillard, quoted in Brent Curtis and John Eldredge, *The Sacred Romance* (Nashville: Nelson, 1997), 13.

2. Bruce Cockburn, "Lovers in a Dangerous Time," *Stealing Fire,* disc, Rounder Records, 1993.

3. Tony Campolo, *Publishers Weekly,* September 6, 1991.

4. John Donne, "Batter My Heart," quoted in Curtis and Eldredge, *The Sacred Romance,* 141.

5. John Muir, quoted in Kathleen Norris Cook, *Spirit of the San Juans: Photography* (Ouray, CO: Western Reflections, 2003), 41.

6. Rainer Rilke, *Uncollected Poems* (New York: North Point Press, 1996), 55.

7. Fyodor Dostoevsky, quoted in Cook, *Spirit of the San Juans,* 22.

8. Os Guinness, *The Call: Finding and Fulfilling the Central Purpose of Your Life* (Nashville: Word, 1998), 67.

9. John of the Cross, *John of the Cross,* in *The Classics of Western Spirituality* (New York: Paulist Press, 1987), 104.

10. John of the Cross, *John of the Cross,* 105.

11. C. S. Lewis, *The Weight of Glory* (New York: Collier, 1980), 19.

Chapter Eleven: Listening to Love Despite Our Fear

1. George MacDonald, *George MacDonald: An Anthology*, ed. C. S. Lewis (New York: Touchstone, 1947), 89.

2. George MacDonald, *The Lost Princess* (Elgin, IL: Chariot Family Publishing, 1984), 57, emphasis added.

3. Henri J. M. Nouwen, *Reaching Out: The Three Movements of the Spiritual Life* (Garden City, NY: Doubleday, 1975), 154.

4. Macrina Wiederkehr, *Tree Full of Angels: Seeing the Holy in the Ordinary* (San Francisco: Harper and Row, 1988), 90.

5. Nicholas Wolterstorff, *Lament for a Son* (Grand Rapids: Eerdmans, 1987), 92.

6. C. S. Lewis, *The Problem of Pain* (New York: Touchstone, 1962).

7. C. S. Lewis, *The Voyage of the Dawn Treader* (New York: Macmillan, 1952), 201.

8. Lewis, *The Problem of Pain,* 130.

9. Lewis, *The Problem of Pain,* 131.

10. Lewis, *The Problem of Pain,* 131.

About the Author

Jan Meyers is an author, speaker, and counselor who lives in Colorado Springs, Colorado. Jan is the author of *The Allure of Hope* (NavPress, 2000) and *Hope and Joy Will Find You* (with Karen Lee-Thorpe, NavPress, 2002). She conducts seminars nationally, does counseling for Wounded Heart Ministries (Bainbridge Island, Washington), and is a close ally of Ransomed Heart Ministries (Colorado Springs). She is happiest when she is gardening, creating something in the kitchen, singing, or exploring the trails of Colorado.